POPULAR ERRORS
EXPLAINED

POPULAR ERRORS EXPLAINED

Stewart McCartney

preface
publishing

Published by Preface Publishing 2010

10 9 8 7 6 5 4 3 2 1

First published in Great Britain in 2010 by Preface Publishing
20 Vauxhall Bridge Road
London SW1V 2SA

An imprint of The Random House Group Limited

www.rbooks.co.uk
www.prefacepublishing.co.uk

Addresses for companies within The Random House Group Limited
can be found at www.randomhouse.co.uk

The Random House Group Limited Reg. No. 954009

A CIP catalogue record for this book is available from the British Library

Hardback ISBN 978 1 84809 269 3

The Random House Group Limited supports The Forest Stewardship Council (FSC),
the leading international forest certification organisation. All our titles that are printed on
Greenpeace approved FSC certified paper carry the FSC logo. Our paper procurement
policy can be found at www.rbooks.co.uk/environment

Mixed Sources
Product group from well-managed
forests and other controlled sources
www.fsc.org Cert no. TT-COC-2139
© 1996 Forest Stewardship Council
FSC

Design by Peter Ward

Printed and bound in Great Britain by MPG Books Ltd, Bodmin, Cornwall

For the three reasons I do what I do – Emily, Molly and Daisy

ACKNOWLEDGEMENTS

Where to start? I think it best to follow a mostly chronological order. Firstly I'd like to thank Raymond Spencer, 'The Maester', for letting me be his quizzing apprentice. Also thank you, Ebb Saxton, Worthy (Ian Sutton) and Pete Foster for being the rest of the dream team, be you Babes or Cellar Men. Thanks to Caroline Stewart for persuading Celina Parker that I might have some use working for her in television. Thanks to Simon Magson for inviting me down to London. A huge thank you to radio's finest Paul Bajoria and Jon Naismith, the conduits by which I was introduced to my publishers Trevor and Nicola, who I'd also like to thank for giving me the opportunity to write this book in the first place. On a personal note, I'd like to thank Ang, without whose patient level-headedness I would never have done anything, and thank you, Lisa, for supporting me with grace, tolerance and wonderful humour (for that read 'putting up with me') through the long hours of the process of writing this book.

CONTENTS

—⁂—

Introduction   xv

Can you be in Cambridgeshire and the middle
of London at the same time?   1

Rutland v. the Isle of Wight   3

There is no proof Dr Johnson patronised Ye
Olde Cheshire Cheese   5

'Wich' salt mine?   6

Who gave us the grin of the Cheshire Cat?   8

Which cheese causes the most intense and
vivid nightmares?   9

Why can't you go to Stilton to see the cheese
being made?   11

Is gout a rich man's disease brought on by
eating pheasant and drinking port?   16

Stomach ulcers are not caused by stress   17

Is it dangerous to presume all animal fats are
saturated and all vegetable oils are not?   18

The solitary artichoke   19

Mrs Beeton's cookbook   20

All carrots aren't orange   21

Cholesterol isn't bad for you   21

Braces for teeth are cosmetic   22

Mars, Milky Way and Galaxy   24

Jacuzzi   25

Why do adverts tell you your pores need to
breathe?   26

Lewis Armstrong   26

EON only makes James Bond films   28

Bob Holness played saxophone on 'Baker
Street'   29

Troublemaker Mandela   29

Cirrhosis isn't caused by booze   30

What is the world's oldest continuously
active distillery?   30

St Bernard dogs and brandy barrels   32

Dogs do not sweat through their tongues   33

Every human year is seven dog years   34

A nip of whisky keeps out the cold   35

Coffee helps you sober up   35

Guess what the Romans used a vomitorium
for?   36

Macaroni   37

Betty's posh cafés   38

A bistro is a chic French place to eat   39

A restaurant is run by a restauranteur   40

France was ruled by eighteen kings called
Louis   40

The Bastille was stormed to release
prisoners   41

Lucifer   42

Devil's Island is a penal colony off the coast
of colonial French Guiana   43

The daiquiri   44

The tango is a sexy dance   45

The tango is a Latin dance   46

Cha cha . . . cha   47

Foxtrot   47

Bela Lugosi wanted to be buried in his
Dracula outfit   48

The elephant's the only animal that can't
jump   49

Fray Bentos on the Plate   49

Humble(d) pie   50

Ships sail through the Panama Canal from east to west from the Atlantic to the Pacific   51

Surely the Panama hat originated in Panama?   51

Where is the dead centre of England?   52

The Aztecs didn't have the wheel   53

Moth-eaten   53

The Scots historically wore different tartans to show to which clan they belonged   54

Queen Victoria – born to rule a great British empire   56

'She keeps-a Mow-way and Shan-don in a pretty cabinet . . .'   58

Alexander the Great and Eric Bristow   59

Kangaroo? I don't understand . . .   60

Mrs Wettin? Or is that Vicky Brown?   60

'Stop all the clocks' isn't a poem   63

Manchester University is not a red-brick university   64

Yorkshire wasn't historically divided into just three ridings   66

Is the 'Four Yorkshiremen' the funniest *Monty Python* sketch?   67

Whip-Ma-Whop-Ma-Gate and the pillory   68

Dick Turpin was not such a brilliant horseman   69

Having a nightmare   71

Ye Olde Trip to Jerusalem   72

Robin Hood – Hallamshire man!   73

Chester Racecourse   75

I'll swing for you . . .   76

Dick Whittington   77

The not-so Right Honourable Lord Mayor of Bristol   77

Order in court!   79

Why going to the Small Claims Court is a bad idea   80

. . . Allegedly   80

Can the police travel in first class for free?   81

Is Britain's busiest railway station in Clapham?   82

Lloyd's of London is the world's biggest insurance company   82

There isn't a Nobel Prize for economics   83

Why do some towns call themselves cities when they don't have a cathedral?   83

London and New York are on the same latitude   85

The shortest distance between two points isn't always a straight line   86

The Tower of London and Rudolph Hess, and Ronnie and Reggie   87

Get Carter is a story set in and around Newcastle   88

St Trinian's . . . and those girls' pinafores   89

Nylon = N(ew) Y(ork) + Lon(don)   89

Diamond isn't the hardest natural substance   90

Compasses do not point to the magnetic North Pole   91

What's the news?   92

Posh   93

Before Columbus, everyone thought the world was flat   95

Charles Lindbergh was the first person to fly the Atlantic non-stop   96

Air pockets don't exist   96

Air pollution isn't such a bad thing   97

The Wright Brothers achieved the first powered flight   98

Fax machines need a telephone line connection   99

CONTENTS

Henry Ford – inventor of the production
line 100

Pocahontas was a beautiful young woman
and was married to John Smith 101

When is a Mohican haircut not a Mohican
haircut? 102

The Girl Guides were founded by Agnes
Baden-Powell 103

William Wallace wasn't a national hero 104

Boris Johnson – a true Englishman 105

Guy Fawkes was not hung, drawn and
quartered 105

Pirates always speaks like this . . . 106

Red Indians scalped their victims 107

The Battle of the Greasy Grass River 108

Battles are always named by the victors 109

FDR never walked after 1921 110

The Ashes is the oldest international rivalry
in cricket 111

Pearl Harbor wasn't an American disaster 112

Stalin, Genghis Khan and Attila were good
leaders 113

Mussolini made the trains run on time 114

Talking of time . . . 115

The League of Nations was succeeded by
the United Nations 116

The British empire and the Commonwealth
of Nations 117

Saladin wasn't an Arab, or even Turkish 119

Did Washington confess to cutting down
the cherry tree? 120

Beech trees don't get hit by lightning 121

Lightning never strikes twice in the same
place 122

Sheet lightning 122

Tornadoes – UK v. USA 123

A suntan is healthy??? 124

The standard for UK mains electricity is set
at 230 volts 124

People who wear sunglasses are posers 125

Monsoon weather can be dry 125

'White Christmas' isn't about being in the
snow . . . 126

. . . and 'Jingle Bells' wasn't originally about
Christmas 126

Antifreeze 127

Where's the driest place on earth? 128

Iceland 129

Solstices and equinoxes 129

Cats hate water 130

Snowflakes 130

A google 131

All polar bears are left-handed 131

Polar bears have white fur 132

Bears don't hibernate 133

Paddington Bear 133

Whalebone is the bone of a whale 133

There are more animals away from human
habitation than close to it 134

Darwin never used the term 'evolution' 135

Moles are good for the plants 136

A coot is bald 136

Tu-whit, tu-what? 137

Nothing on earth has ever seen a
brontosaurus 138

Giving Cleopatra the needles 139

Gypsies originated in Egypt 139

Aryans were pure-blooded, blue-eyed and
blond 140

Stonehenge 140

Hitler never had a hideaway called the
Eagle's Nest 142

Who do you think you are kidding, Mr
Flanagan? 143

Arthur Lowe and John Le Mesurier 143

Hitler was a vegetarian 144

Luther pinned the 'Ninety-Five Theses' to the door of Wittenberg Cathedral to start the Protestant Reformation 145

Minster means big church 146

Catholic priests can't be married 146

It's heresy to call your baby son Jesus 147

St Patrick cleared Ireland of snakes 148

U2 are not an Irish band 148

'When Irish Eyes Are Smiling' 149

Scotland's official national anthem is still 'God save the Queen' 150

De Valera also wasn't Irish 151

Britannia was created in the eighteenth century 151

Bagpipes are Scottish 152

Cool Britannia 152

Britain has not been invaded since 1066 153

Cabal 154

Doomsday and Dread 155

The French King of England 157

Culloden was not the last battle on British soil 158

At Culloden the English defeated the Scots 160

The biggest volunteer army 160

The marathon 161

Three hundred Spartans – and then there were the others 163

Sparta was not a state of ancient Greece 164

Metaphysics 165

The ancient Greek world was full of statues of pure white marble 166

A belfry is a place to keep bells 166

Bell weather 167

Bats have radar 167

St Thomas à Becket 167

Two small fs 169

'Stewart' is Scottish, 'Stuart' is English 170

'Disnumerate' is a dyslexic spelling 171

Robert the Bruce was not King of Scotland 172

The Shetlands and the Orkneys 173

Pontius Pilate's Bodyguard 173

Singing meatloaf 175

The bagel was not named to honour a Polish king 175

Coffee is not a bean . . . 176

. . . but a black-eyed pea is! 176

There are no mandarins in China 177

That's just not pizza 177

Riviera is a French word 178

Venetians don't speak Italian 178

Is 'Volare' a traditional Italian song? 179

The Eurovision theme was written for the TV network 180

'La Marseillaise' was sung during the French Revolution 180

Red Square was named by the communists 181

Kennedy didn't say, 'I am a doughnut' 182

Latte 182

Modern archers are far better than medieval ones 183

If you hit someone it's assault 184

'The Assyrian came down like the wolf on the fold' 184

'A poor thing but mine own' 185

Thirty-nine commandments? 185

Fornication 186

The Romans invented the crucifix 187

Julius Caesar's dying words 188

A painful elbow is tennis elbow 188

Playing at St Andrew's 189

Was golf invented in Scotland? 190

Medal play 191

Contents

OBE means Order of the British Empire 191
The Viking blood eagle 192
Pride goes before a fall 193
Meeting your Waterloo 193
O' Wesley – the victor of Waterloo 194
The last British monarch in battle 195
The madness of King George (III) 196
Nelson's last words 197
On which eye is Nelson's eyepatch? 198
To the bitter end . . . 199
Heir tomorrow, not heir today 199
The English Civil War – civil but not English 199
Franco was fighting revolutionaries 200
The English gave tea drinking to the world 201
Cortez was the first European to see the Pacific 202
The Mosquito Coast is named after an insect 202
An autogiro is not a type of helicopter 203
A butterfly flutters by 203
Nice! 204
Divas v. prima donnas 204
Music, both classical and romantic? 205
'Trumpet Voluntary' 206
Pink Floyd are not friends of Dorothy 207
'You Do Something to Me' and 'There She Goes' – heroines not lovers 208
Far from the maddening crowd 208
Samuel Richardson and Pamela, J M Barrie and Wendy . . . and Peter Pan 209
J K Rowling and Hogwarts 210
Spike Milligan wrote 'The Goons' 211
The Lord of the Rings is a trilogy 212
Clay-clanger 214
'Alice in Wonderland' 214

The Human League 215
Fitz 216
Ménage à trois 217
French fries are not French 218
America's Sweetheart and the Brazilian Bombshell 219
Which Richard was the best king of England? 220
Are the current royal family Windsors, Mountbattens or Mountbatten-Windsors? 223
Mrs is not an abbreviation of Missus 227
Nets are not compulsory in football 227
The letters on Russian football shirts 227
Czech is actually Polish 228
QVC 229
Acronyms 229
The yogh and Sir Menzies Campbell 229
Harlequins and Grasshoppers 231
The lowest rank in the army is private 231
Baseball is 'all American' 232
When is an island not an island? 233
Rabbiting about Coney Island, Coneythorpe and Coney Street 234
'I Love Rock and Roll' 236
The Windy City 238
The US Constitution is not the Bill of Rights 239
The World Series 240
Miniature paintings 241
Not very 'original' sin 242
The immaculate misconception 243
First fruits 244
Spanish fly 246
The Nazis invented the swastika 247
Concentration camps 251
Grew like Topsy 252

The Law of averages 252

Cross-county arrests 253

Double negative 258

Prerogative, pejorative and schedule 258

He's not *the* Messiah . . . 259

Pouring oil on troubled waters 259

Lough Neagh 260

The largest freshwater lake in the world 261

India ink 262

Pittsburg 262

The Rat Pack 263

INTRODUCTION

'A little knowledge is a dangerous thing,' wrote Alexander Pope. Well, that's the popular error. He actually wrote the following in his *An Essay on Criticism* in 1709, a work that was published two years later:

> A little learning is a dangerous thing;
> Drink deep, or taste not the Pierian Spring:
> There shallow draughts intoxicate the brain,
> And drinking largely sobers us again.

For those who do not know, in Greek mythology the Pierian Spring was near Mount Olympus in northern Thessaly (now a Greek 'periphery' or region to south of Makedonia), Pieria being the seat of worship of Orpheus and the Muses. The spring can be regarded as the original fountain of knowledge, as drinking from it inspired the individual to artistic greatness. As to the misquote's origin, I know not from where it sprung, but it seems its continued use lies in a general misrepresentation of Pope's original phrase. Pope seems to be saying that one should not try and produce great art without first seeking inspiration from those things that one can learn from, the great artworks of the past. Only when you have 'drunk deep' of what has gone before, will the muse truly visit your endeavours. Indeed, if you do not take the time to study and draw inspiration from the great works of the past, you will be incapable of adding to art's future value. You will be deluded into thinking your work is marvellous when it patently isn't. As to the misquote, by substituting 'knowledge' for 'learning' the meaning changes: guidance to an artist becomes a catch-all statement that a basic understanding of something does not make one an expert in the field. A person might endanger themselves socially, physically or by reputation if they act as if they are. The misquote can thus be used widely as a put-down in our cynical times, whereas a reference to learning now seems to limit any meaning to a reference to our now widespread and formalised educational system. To criticise any sort of learning, be it a little or a lot, seems perverse to the modern mind, and the original quote without the following three lines appears to be a strange thing to say.

Pope's essay also provides us with another aphorism now in common use in English: 'Fools rush in where angels fear to tread'. Interestingly, the song inspired by this phrase, often associated with either the man who had a huge 1963 hit with it, Ricky Nelson, or Elvis Presley, who didn't record it until 1970, was actually written as long ago as 1940. Although often thought of as a pop or rhythm and blues song, the first to have a hit with Johnny Mercer and Rube Bloom's work were bandleaders Glenn Miller (vocals by Ray Eberle), and Tommy Dorsey, who had a young Frank Sinatra doing the warbling. I'll come back to Sinatra later on in this book to explain a different generally held misconception.

That aside, I hope that the way I have constructed the opening paragraph of this introduction encapsulates the purpose of the book as a whole. It is not my aim to flatly correct a series of generally held beliefs that hold a degree of misinformation in their details and then leave the process there. I see no value in that. Rather, I hope that following the exposure of the popular error I can provide some information as to the original truth from which the error has digressed. Then to a greater or lesser degree I will explain the reasons why the error has become widely and popularly accepted. Sometimes I will be armed with a factually proven and definitive explanation, while at other times I will have to speculate. I see knowledge as a wonder in itself; I love knowledge for knowledge's sake, and I love information. This volume is not, however, intended to be an encyclopedia; I hope that it will be an engagement between you and me. What you will read is not an attempt to give you a neat, definitive package of bare facts in which I move quickly and mechanically from one to the next; the pieces vary in the amount of chiaroscuro they hold, and in their depth and breadth. Most are by no means fully comprehensive as it is also not my aim to provide every morsel of information that I can. Each is as long or as short as I want it to be. Sometimes I will pepper the articles with supporting facts that in themselves do not add to the debunking of the myth. I will sometimes digress to provide additional related information that is, although not specifically related to the core of the subject in question, an eye-opener in itself. I take this approach because I draw my inspiration from the man who wrote a book with the title I have borrowed for the one in your hands – or in these modern times possibly on your screens.

In his preface to the original *Popular Errors Explained*, Victorian antiquarian John Timbs started with an explanation of the purpose of his work. Seeing a possible fault in the other 'plans . . . devised for the spread of knowledge' around at the time, he outlined his aim by quoting from Laurence Sterne's *Sermon XX* – 'The Prodigal Son'. He hoped 'to take us from the track of our nursery mistakes, and, by showing us new objects, or old ones in new lights, to reform our judgements'. This might seem a little paternalistic to a twenty-first-century ear, and to be truthful I think if I took that approach I would quickly alienate my readers. It's from what he says a little later in the preface that I drew my inspiration. Referring to himself in the third person, he says, 'He does not instruct the reader how "to tell the clock by algebra," nor "to drink tea by stratagem," though he aims at being accurate and agreeable, by way of abstract and anecdote, so as to become an advantageous and amusing guest at any intellectual fireside.'

This I feel is much more on the money. One has to remember that Timbs lived in an era when good works and helpful instruction bestowed by the haves on the have-nots were all the rage and not seen as patronising. He saw his books as part of the process of improvement. Books, newspapers and similar media were far less accessible to the general population, and information was almost infinitely less available and immediate than it is today. The only quizzing that went on down at the local hostelry was as to your ability to pay for your drink, and a 'man of knowledge' wasn't seen as someone who might be able to win vast amounts of money on a television game show. Rather, his knowledge was a passport to friendship and fine discourse in a convivial setting. While not denigrating the quizzers of the world – heaven knows I stand firmly in their ranks – this is not a work to fill heads with facts to win anything from a gallon of ale to a million pounds. Use it in a different way – perhaps to start or to contribute to a conversation by introducing matters of interest to your companions, not to be either a sophist (in the modern sense) or a know-it-all who always gets the last word. Treat what I outline as just a beginning, and use the strings of information I provide as bases for your own future enquiries.

Some of the subjects covered you will know, some you will have a passing acquaintance with, and others you will never have given a thought to. Some discussions will be of more interest than others. You might even fundamentally question some of the things I say, and to that I respond,

'Hurrah! The day is saved.' Good conversation is based as much on belief and faith as on proof. To me, an opinion counts as much in a conversation as bare knowledge. I defer to that great historian Asa Briggs, who advised me via the medium of television that history is about interpretation of the facts. Rather than merely placing cold bricks of fact on other cold bricks, only by taking this approach can mankind hope to enrich its collective knowledge.

I hope that you will be intrigued by the nuggets of knowledge scattered throughout this book, and that they encourage you to investigate further yourself. As a coda, I return to my reference to Makedonia, the most northerly area of Greece. Why do we call the country Greece when it is known to the Greeks as the Hellenic Republic? Why is there a province in Greece called Makedonia when there is also a newly independent former part of Yugoslavia with the same name? Actually, why is it referred to as the Former Yugoslav Republic of Macedonia? Why is it Makedonia in Greek when we call it Macedonia? Well, go and find out. Please believe me when I say: if you are a fan of knowledge the answers to all these related questions are intriguing. Then the real challenge will come, in the way that you impart what you discover to others.

POPULAR ERRORS
EXPLAINED

CAN YOU BE IN CAMBRIDGESHIRE
AND THE MIDDLE OF LONDON
AT THE SAME TIME?

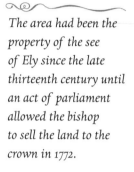

A lot of people believe this, but it just ain't so. In Ye Old Mitre near Holborn Circus is a glass case holding the stump of a tree around which Elizabeth I reputedly danced when she was a girl. This is not beyond the bounds of possibility because the pub was built at the edge of what were once the grounds of Ely Palace, that bishop's London residence until the eighteenth century. She could have easily tagged along on a visit by the grown-ups while still a little princess. On the other hand, the location of the former palace, now replaced by a fine cul-de-sac called Ely Place, has led to the unsustainable legend that the bishopric's lands in London were, and remain, technically in Cambridgeshire. As late as 2005 the *Independent* newspaper even claimed this to be so in a perhaps tongue-in-cheek article. It just isn't the case; nor is it also required that the Metropolitan Police stop pursuing a suspect at the ornate gates to the street and call in the boys from Cambridgeshire. (This idea, that officers of the various police forces in the UK only have powers of arrest in their own area, is another common misconception that I will cover later.)

The area had been the property of the see of Ely since the late thirteenth century until an act of parliament allowed the bishop to sell the land to the crown in 1772.

There are a number of arguments that undermine the popular legend. First, let's consider one of the most powerful landowners in history, the Catholic Church. Like many religious foundations throughout England in the Middle Ages, Fountains Abbey in Yorkshire owned vast stretches of countryside. Many of these parcels of land were outside the boundaries of the county in which the abbey was located, but this did not make those far-flung properties part of Yorkshire.

Second, let's look at the important dates relating to the development of the land in question. The area had been the property of the see of Ely since the late thirteenth century until an act of parliament allowed the bishop to sell the land to the crown in 1772, which in turn, three years later, sold the area to a private developer. The dilapidated medieval buildings were flattened, with the exception of St Etheldreda's Chapel, and replaced by those that stand to this day. The clergy of Ely in the meantime lifted the hems of their collective cassocks and tripped over to Dover Street near Piccadilly, where we now find Ely House. This is still the house of the current bishop when in the capital. So if the legend is based on the idea that land owned by the see is not in London but in the home county, it is Dover Street that should lay claim to being in the Fens.

If the legend is based on the idea that land owned by the see is not in London but in the home county, it is Dover Street that should lay claim to being in the Fens.

However, the clincher is that even if the bishop owned the land until 1772, at that time the Isle of Ely wasn't even in Cambridgeshire! Since the Dark Ages it had been the Liberty of Ely, a county palatine in its own right ruled by the Church on behalf of the monarch. It was not until the Liberty of Ely Act in 1837 that the direct rule of the bishop was taken away, and although designated at that time as a division of Cambridgeshire, the Isle regained its independence in the 1880s. It was not until 1965 that the majority of this historic area was merged with Cambridgeshire, nearly 200 years after the bishop had upped sticks from Holborn.

The belief that Ely Place is in Cambridgeshire may also have arisen from an 1842 act of parliament that established a body of commissioners for paving, lighting, watching, cleansing and improving Ely Place and Ely Mews, thus creating a sort of self-government. Unfortunately for believers, the locations were described in the act as being located in Holborn, 'in the County of Middlesex'. The area is now part of the London Borough of Camden, and that, as they say, is that.

Oh, and sending a letter to the pub marked 'Cambridgeshire' and then claiming its prompt delivery is proof just highlights the tolerance of the Post Office – they deliver to Father Christmas, do they not?

RUTLAND V. THE ISLE OF WIGHT

R utland has long been recognised as the smallest county in England. If one supports this theory and one goes back before the 1880s, then one might have an historical point. The claim is generally accompanied by the proviso that Rutland holds the status of being the smallest 'traditional' county. However, due to the developing legality of what constitutes a county, Rutland has not held the title since at least the 1880s, apart from a brief period in the late 1960s and early 70s, and that was only on a day-by-day or even hour-by-hour basis because the claim was seemingly dependent on the phases of the moon. Confused? Let me explain.

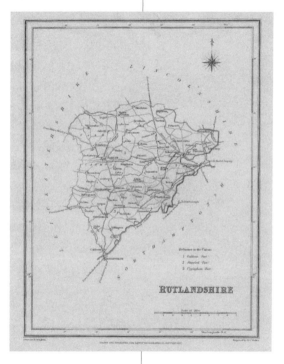

RUTLANDSHIRE

The county system and local government in the United Kingdom in general is very complex and far more changeable in recent times than we might at first think. For many years Rutland sat to the north-east of Leicestershire, safe in the knowledge that its eighteen miles length by seventeen miles width gave it a certain prominence in the analysis of county statistics. Sadly for Rutland, in 1889 the County of London, which now approximates to what a modern man would call inner London, was created and in being created robbed Rutland of its smallest county status.

This affront to the East Midlanders was soon to be compounded in the battle for the honour of being the smallest county authority. For years there has been a separate popular error that the Isle of Wight was for a long period an integral part of Hampshire. Before the rapid increase in the importance of local government in the nineteenth century it might have been convenient to lump it in with its mainland neighbour to the north,

It was only with the creation of county councils in 1888 that the Isle of Wight began to be controlled from the mainland.

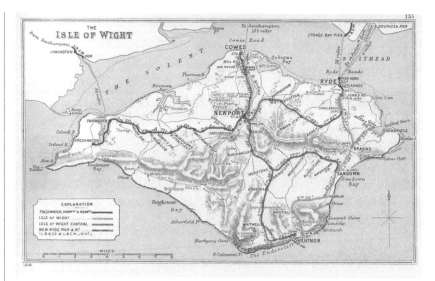

even if the reality was that the island effectively looked after itself. It was only with the creation of county councils in 1888 that the Isle of Wight began to be controlled from the mainland. However, the independently minded islanders didn't think much of this imposition and within two years were looking after their own affairs again.

So within two years Rutland found itself officially falling to third place in the smallest county stakes – at least when the tide was in. This is because Rutland and the Isle of Wight are so similar in size that the evidence points to the Isle of Wight being bigger than Rutland at low tide, and smaller at high tide![1] All at sixes and sevens you might say, or in this case, at twos and threes.

And so the capital was the smallest county for many years until, with the need this time to reorganise London into the larger Greater London Council in 1965, Rutland stepped up one place in the league table. So for nearly a decade it regained its up-and-down on-and-off pre-eminence. This was not to last. A huge national overhaul and reorganisation in 1974 found Rutland being lumped in with Leicestershire as a district council. For over twenty years it lost its self-determination, and it stayed in that position until under a further reorganisation in 1997 Rutland achieved 'unitary authority' status and thus regained self-government at a local level. To

---

1   Investigation of the figures puts the maximum difference in area at around two square kilometres.

add a little lustre, the reinstatement of its lord lieutenancy allowed the citizens of Oakham and Uppingham to feel secure in the knowledge that they lived in a separate county once again. Then again, to take off a bit of the shine for those citizens who feel a competitive edge in the matter, the same reorganisation that robbed Rutland of county status in 1974 had, despite another brief flirtation with Hampshire, confirmed the Isle of Wight's status as a county authority. So the island found itself for a period England's solitary smallest county while Rutland groaned under the occupation of its bigger neighbour.

Since then, in what seems to be a national government mindset of feeling the need to tinker continually with local governance, both the Isle of Wight and Rutland have probably lost any chance of reclaiming smallest county status. In the last reorganisation to date, in the 1990s, the cities of Bristol and London, both smaller in area than Rutland, became ceremonial counties in their own rights. Sadly for the traditionalists and romantics the chances of Rutland regaining its long held status now look very slim, with the Bristol conurbation being a third of its size, and the City of London being over a hundred times smaller!

Still, there is a way for Rutlanders to feel some sort of succour in the political tides that have washed over them in the last two centuries. In terms of population, they still have the edge.

THERE IS NO PROOF DR JOHNSON PATRONISED YE OLDE CHESHIRE CHEESE

— ✂✁ —

Along with many little knots of appreciative tourists from across the Atlantic, I found myself in this world-famous Fleet Street pub[1] the other day, and a pretty fine pub it is. I am, however, intrigued that despite its many more substantial claims of connections with men of letters such as Oliver Goldsmith, Tennyson and Arthur Conan Doyle – the pub is even alluded to in Dickens's *A Tale of Two Cities* – it's the associations with Dr Johnson that are given pride of place. I'm intrigued because there's no proof that he ever called in for a snifter.

---

1 It actually sits astride Wine Office Court at 145 Fleet Street.

If you go into the Chop Room across the corridor from the main body of the pub, you find a portrait of the good doctor, and his supposed 'pub chair' is also on display. One naturally drinks in the ambience of the place along with the beer, and so one is easily led to accept the presumption that he held court over his literary-minded friends here. We are even told that there is another painting of Johnson and his biographer Boswell, apparently found in the cellar relatively recently, which has been restored.

Now Boswell mentioned many taverns that benefited from his subject's patronage in his *Life of Samuel Johnson* but never this one, despite the closeness of Dr Johnson's house, which is just to the north of Fleet Street. This proximity and the sharpness of a previous landlord with an eye for an opportunity are, I think, the foundations on which the widely held belief about Johnson calling in, when the Cheshire Cheese was not so 'Olde', have been built. One Boswell does mention however is 'The Mitre', and we've already mentioned that there just happens to be a pub down the nearby narrow alley that is Ely Court called Ye Old Mitre. It is as equally fine as a hostelry and just as historic. Perhaps this was the good doctor's watering hole.

'WICH' SALT MINE?

This is not a new consumer magazine for those involved in the extractive industries. Rather, there is a widely held belief that the suffix -wich in a place name denotes the site of a briny spring and by derivation the existence of a salt mine. The great salt-mining towns of Cheshire, Nantwich, Middlewich, Northwich and Leftwich, and the equally salty town of Droitwich in the Midlands seem to add credence to this idea.

This would confuse an Anglo-Saxon, however. Like the suffix -thorpe, indicating a town's origins as a farm in the old Danelaw, such as in the Lincolnshire towns of Scunthorpe or Mablethorpe, -wich, -wic or -wick in the names of places in the old Anglo-Saxon kingdom meant a farm. Such place names could however also derive from the Scandinavian *vik* meaning inlet, creek or bay, especially if on the coast of the Danelaw. A similar derivation is possible from the Anglo-Saxon for port or – and this is the important bit – it can denote any place with a specific manufacturing or trading purpose. Farms would have fallen into this category, but so would many other places known for particular products and commodities.

So it would seem it was the importance of salt as a commodity and the development of communities based on and around salt mines that have cemented the association of -wich with this particular product. If this is not the case, speculators should immediately head for Woolwich, Sandwich and Greenwich and stake their claims to the mining rights there.

WHO GAVE US THE GRIN OF THE CHESHIRE CAT?

The Cheshire Cat is one of the many wonderful characters that Lewis Carroll gave Alice the opportunity to meet during her adventures in Wonderland. Actually, although Carroll (real name Charles Dodgson, a mathematics don at Oxford and, with the benefit of hindsight, a controversial figure[1]) did create some of his characters from scratch, others were derived from common knowledge. The Mad Hatter comes from the association of madness with the workers in Luton's hat industry, a symptom later found to be the result of poisoning from the mercury used in the manufacturing process. The lachrymose Mock Turtle was an idea developed from mock turtle soup, a cheap copy of the real delicacy made with a calf's head instead of a green turtle.

So it was with the Cheshire Cat. *Brewer's Dictionary of Phrase and Fable* advises us that 'grinning like a Cheshire cat' was already an old simile in Dodgson's time and he merely, or perhaps hugely, popularised it. The phrase had previously appeared in print in Peter Pindar's 1792 *Pair of Lyric Epistles* – in line with the subject of this article, Peter Pindar actually being a pseudonym for writer John Walcott. Earlier than that, *A Classical Dictionary of the Vulgar Tongue* by Francis Grose included the entry 'CHESHIRE CAT. He grins like a Cheshire cat; said of any one who shows his teeth and gums in laughing.'

With the phrase in question already being common coinage by the time Dodgson wrote his classic tale, we can look for three possible

1 It seems that, like L S Lowry, Dodgson had a private penchant for creating portraits of young girls that might be regarded as beyond the pale by the modern mind. Lowry painted them, whereas Dodgson was an early pioneer of photography, executing many portraits in this medium.

contenders as to the reason why he felt inspired to feature a Cheshire cat in his book. Intriguingly all are pieces of church decoration. The strongest claimant can be viewed close to his birthplace, Daresbury in Cheshire, where there is a famous carving of a grinning cat on the nearby parish church at Grappenhall. Another contender is a carving on the church at Croft-on-Tees in the north-east of England, where his father had been the rector. The last is a gargoyle on St Nicolas, Cranleigh in Surrey. This claim is pretty tenuous, however, as Dodgson only visited this village on a regular basis when he lived in Guildford, and he moved there after *Alice's Adventures in Wonderland* had been published.

The best explanation I can find for how the phrase came into being in the first place takes us back to Cheshire cheese. Of separate interest here is the fact that this type of cheese is so ancient that it is actually mentioned in the Domesday Book, but I digress. In Dodgson's tale, the way the Cheshire Cat slowly disappears until only the grin remains seems to reflect the way the cheese was shaped and then eaten. A full round of cheese supposedly looked like a grinning cat, and traditionally it was cut from the tail end, the last part eaten being the head of the smiling cat.

WHICH CHEESE CAUSES THE MOST INTENSE AND VIVID NIGHTMARES?

Not one of the kinds of cheese known so far to man has had a scientific link established between its consumption before bedtime and a disturbed night's sleep. However, cheese being the cause of bizarre dreams might be another matter. The British Cheese Board (what a wonderful

name) claimed in the results of a 2005 survey using 200 volunteers that eating cheese before bedtime could actually aid a good night's sleep, and that different cheeses caused people to have dreams about different subjects and of different vividness – but no nightmares were recorded.

An amino acid in cheese called tryptophan is supposed to reduce stress and induce sleep, and dreams are part of a good deep night's sleep. Some of the results about the dreams experienced in the survey are quite appealing:

- 85 per cent of women who ate Stilton had 'unusual' dreams.
- 65 per cent of people eating Cheddar apparently dreamt about celebrities.
- 65 per cent eating Red Leicester went back to school in their dreams.
- All the women who ate British Brie had 'relaxing' dreams – in contrast to the men, who had 'cryptic' dreams.
- Two thirds of those who ate Lancashire had work on their minds.
- But it's Cheshire for those who don't like dreaming – over 50 per cent of those who ate this cheese enjoyed dreamless sleep.

So why do we think eating cheese late at night is such a bad idea? There was a bit of a health scare in the 1950s about cheese not being good for people on antidepressants, but I hold Dickens responsible. It seems he started the whole idea when Ebenezer Scrooge blamed the apparition of Jacob Marley on 'an undigested bit of beef, a blot of mustard, a crumb of cheese, a fragment of an underdone potato'. He thus suggested that any food could cause a disturbed night, and I agree with him, but it is the connection between cheese and nightmares that seems to have stuck in our collective nocturnal minds.

WHY CAN'T YOU GO TO STILTON TO SEE THE CHEESE BEING MADE?

All foodstuffs named after a place originated there, did they not? A bottle of champagne, a York ham and even a cantaloupe melon all sit firmly within this rule. However, don't take a trip to the Cambridgeshire village of Stilton to buy a locally produced cheese of that name – you can't, and you won't be able to in the foreseeable future. So why is the name of a small settlement on the Great North Road near Peterborough synonymous with the 'king of cheeses' if it was originally made elsewhere? Even Cheddar, now the generic name for products that are by turn good, bad or just downright indifferent from all across the world, at least originated in the parish that has lent the cheese its name. This was never the case with Stilton. Let me share with you now the compelling and competing stories relating to the chain of contacts and arrangements by which Stilton became Stilton.

Let's start with a clue as to this curiosity of nomenclature from Daniel Defoe, who in 1722 passed through Stilton, perhaps we might fancy on his way north to York, the home city of his creation Robinson Crusoe. He stopped there, 'partook' of some cheese, and was impressed enough to mention later in passing that the fame of the place for its cheeses was already well established. As it was an important coaching stop, Stilton was indeed a place in which many individuals from across the kingdom could partake of the pleasures of 'local produce'. But although they believed the food to be local, they were mistaken. Cooper Thornhill, owner of the Bell Inn, an unmissable gastronomic stop for those travellers heading about their business both northwardly and southwardly, is known to have sourced his vittles from a wide area.

Don't take a trip to the Cambridgeshire village of Stilton to buy a locally produced cheese of that name – you can't, and you won't be able to in the foreseeable future.

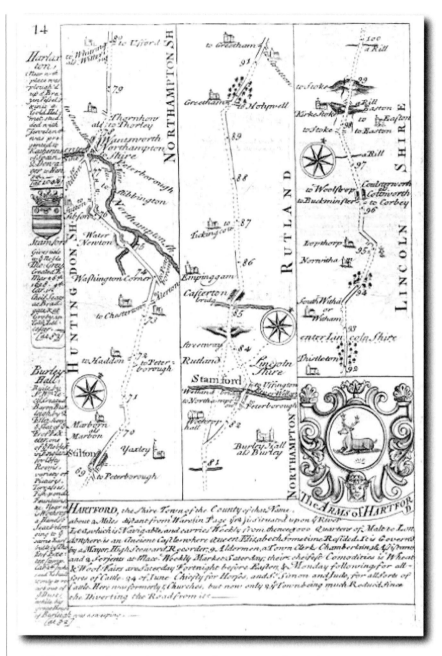

The particular vittle we now know as Stilton cheese was actually sourced from the housekeeper at Quenby Hall in Hungarton, quite some distance away to the north-west, across Rutland and close to Melton Mowbray. The story is Thornhill discovered and 'fell in love' with a cheese the housekeeper had found at a small local farm. Indicative of his sense of

Fred Roe

entrepreneurship is that he swiftly gained exclusive marketing rights for this delicious blue cheese for the Bell – although in 2006 the *Daily Telegraph* reported that it was only in 1730 that Thornhill ventured from the Bell on his search for delights. Whatever the date, soon after the discovery the first of many wagonloads of cheese arrived, and, sitting astride the country's main artery, the Bell was instrumental in the rapid spread of the legend of blue Stilton. As far as Thornhill was concerned, what problem was there in a little misunderstanding among his customers about origins?

It is of some note that to a lesser degree it is thought his counterpart at Stilton's other coaching stop the Angel also sold the cheese, but it is Thornhill's name that comes down to us across the centuries as the mover and shaker in the spread of the fame of Stilton cheese. If Thornhill wasn't going to let a little misunderstanding about where he got his cheese from get in the way of a marketing coup for his coaching inn, then he was equally unconcerned about his competitor's activities.

A variation on the story has it that it was the brother-in-law of the housekeeper at Quenby Hall who sold her wares to the numerous travellers moving up and down the great road, because that was where the market for these goods was most lucrative. She in turn sourced her goods from her locale, and among these was a blue cheese, probably from the Rutland village of Wymondham. Although the story of Cooper Thornhill is more attractive, research leads me to credit one Frances Pawlett, a skilled cheese maker from those parts, for giving Stilton its first standards of quality and shape. Her skills and her husband's business acumen made her the leading light in the cooperative that began marketing what is now known as Stilton. She was so influential that, even in those unregulated times, if other manufacturers didn't meet her standards then, all apologies made, it just wasn't Stilton.

The first written reference to Stilton cheese is from the eighteenth century, actually in the same year as Defoe's journey, and we find it in William Stukeley's *Itinerarium Curiosum* letter number five, written in the October of 1722. The *Oxford English Dictionary* is slightly tardy, giving the accolade for the first use of the term Stilton for this specific type of cheese instead to Bailey's 1736 *Household Dictionary* – but enough of all that. In all these early instances the village, actually then in Huntingdonshire, and the Bell in particular get the credit for the delicious cheese.

Two hundred years later, in 1936 to be precise, so widespread was the fame of the cheese that the Stilton Cheesemakers' Association was formed as a lobby group to protect the quality and provenance of the cheese. They demanded, and got, the requirement to use only pasteurised milk and stainless-steel needles to allow air into the cheese's core, which over the nine-week ripening process gives Stilton its distinctive blue veins. Other characteristics that are now required include the traditional cylindrical shape, the self-development of a crust and for the cheese to remain unpressed during its production. In 1966 Stilton's status was enhanced when the only legal protection in English law granted to a cheese via a certificated trademark came into being. However, this did not stop pirating, and it took another three decades for full protection to be achieved, finally and thankfully, at the hands of the European Union.

Melton Mowbray now sits at the centre of the manufacture of Stilton, a product that since 1996 (strangely, the recent history of the cheese seems to be tied up in periods of thirty years), very much like champagne in France, Jamón Dehesa de Extramadura (ham) in Spain and a little closer to home the Arbroath smokie (among many, many other delicacies), has been designated as having 'protected geographical status', a means by which the ever-increasingly invasive EU protects local produce and the livelihoods of those families that have through the generations created the good names which those products carry. So a good thing perhaps.

However, unlike these other products, when you now search for locally produced Stilton, for there now can't be any other type by law, you do not go to the village in Cambridgeshire but to one of three other counties, namely Leicestershire, Derbyshire and Nottinghamshire. (At this stage could you please spare a thought for poor Rutland, the probable county of origin, now excluded like the village of Stilton for ever from the right to make the famous cheese.)

Currently, you can visit one of eight licensed dairies. All but two of these are in the Vale of Belvoir, an area of outstanding beauty on the Nottinghamshire–Leicestershire border. Melton Mowbray, Colston Bassett, Long Clawson and Saxelby are all represented on this list of dairies and the village of Cropwell Bishop boasts two producers. The previously mentioned Quenby Hall in Hungarton is the site of the other Leicestershire dairy outside the Vale, and as a native of the Vale of Belvoir bought a farm at Hartington over a century ago Derbyshire has gained the right to be included in the designated counties in the PGS. Sadly, this outpost is due to close, and so all production will be restricted to just the two counties.

It might be of interest to note that recent research by BBC Radio's *Food Programme* into food myths in 2008 uncovered a recipe for a cream cheese made in Stilton from the early part of the eighteenth century. This generated discussion to the effect that as most manufacturers of cheese make two or more varieties of their produce, it's not beyond the bounds of possibility that a blue cheese was also made in the area. Sadly for the romantics among us, what is in the past must remain in the past. At the time of the application for PGS status in 1996 no evidence was forwarded that the current recipe for Stilton cheese had ever been used in the village, and in consequence it has, as mentioned, been banished from the list of approved locations of manufacture for ever.

Which brings us to the present, where for those of us who love the 'king of cheeses' and eschew such varieties as Blacksticks Blue, Garstang Blue and Lincoln Blue, we can only agree with a piece of graffiti that I read on the chalkboard of a fellow student's house in Manchester in the late 1970s: 'Port and Stilton is better than sex'.

In another modern reference, you could enjoy your Stilton while reading one of the two essays G K Chesterton wrote on the subject of cheese, especially considering the absence of cheese in art. (This must be a future study in itself!)

In one he recalls a time when, like his literary predecessor Daniel

Melton Mowbray now sits at the centre of the manufacture of Stilton, a product that since 1996 has been designated as having 'protected geographical status'.

Defoe, he visited a small town in the Fenlands of England, which turned
out to be Stilton. This left a deep impression on him, which he expressed
through poetry in his 'Sonnet to a Stilton Cheese'.

> Stilton, thou shouldst be living at this hour
> And so thou art. Nor losest grace thereby;
> England has need of thee, and so have I --
> She is a Fen. Far as the eye can scour,
> League after grassy league from Lincoln tower
> To Stilton in the fields, she is a Fen.
> Yet this high cheese, by choice of fenland men,
> Like a tall green volcano rose in power.
> Plain living and long drinking are no more,
> And pure religion reading 'Household Words',
> And sturdy manhood sitting still all day
> Shrink, like this cheese that crumbles to its core;
> While my digestion, like the House of Lords,
> The heaviest burdens on herself doth lay.

This is in part a parody of Wordsworth's 1802 sonnet 'London', of which
the opening line is 'Milton! Thou shouldst be living at this hour.' I find it
interesting that the belief persisted even among educated men that Stilton
was from the Fenlands not the Vale of Belvoir.

IS GOUT A RICH MAN'S DISEASE
BROUGHT ON BY EATING PHEASANT
AND DRINKING PORT?

Can any rich food or drink, especially these rare items once only to
be found on the tables of the wealthy, be blamed for this painful
condition? It was once thought to be so, but the answer is that gout is never
necessarily the result of an unhealthy diet. Fit young men and women of
small financial means have been known to develop gout, so this association
is unfounded. Gout is caused by elevated levels of uric acid in the blood,
and this in turn can be caused by all sorts of things medical. A propensity
to gout may also be hereditary.

About one in ten cases of gout can be attributed to eating and drinking habits, mainly when they involve high consumption of meat, alcohol, seafood and sugar. A sedentary lifestyle, which may of course be related to eating and drinking too much, can be as much to blame, as can complications following other medical conditions.

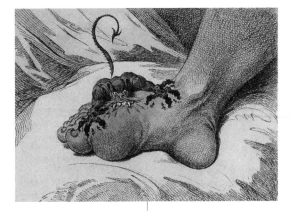

STOMACH ULCERS ARE NOT CAUSED BY STRESS

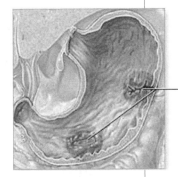

Stomach ulcers

Not one of them, even though this has long been believed. Nor are they caused by spicy food. I don't deny that in this modern world many people who exhibit signs of stress also have stomach ulcers; however they are not linked.

And before you pooh-pooh this assertion, I would refer you to no less a body than the Nobel Assembly at the Karolinska Institute, who in 2005 awarded the Nobel Prize in Physiology or Medicine (please note, reader, Physiology *or* Medicine, not just Medicine) to Barry J Marshall and J Robin Warren for discovering this fact. They taught us that the culprit is a bacterium called *Helicobactor pylori*, which causes infection and leads to over 80 per cent of stomach ulcers and to 90 per cent of ulcers in the duodenum. The majority of the rest are caused by the widespread, perhaps often unnecessary, use of pain relievers or nonsteroidal anti-inflammatory drugs (NSAIDs).

IS IT DANGEROUS TO PRESUME
ALL ANIMAL FATS ARE SATURATED AND
ALL VEGETABLE OILS ARE NOT?

If you are having trouble with your cholesterol levels, one thing you can do is avoid cooking with animal fats like lard, butter and dripping, and switch to natural vegetable-based oils. On the whole this is a very good idea. Only be very wary of coconut oil. This natural oil is actually very highly saturated, and you really would find no benefit in swapping from using animal fats to using coconut oil.

THE SOLITARY ARTICHOKE

The artichoke has a number of varieties, and it is thought that it originated around the Mediterranean. A member of the thistle family, it's attractive used in a floral arrangement, never mind being rather nice to eat. One of the more well-known varieties is the Jerusalem artichoke, which differs from all the others in as much as they are all varieties of globe artichoke. There is also a thing called the Chinese artichoke, which is unrelated to the globe artichoke as it is a member of the mint family. It is known in the West as an artichoke as it has an edible tuber, but what's in a name?

Actually, quite a lot. The Jerusalem artichoke is about as related to the globe varieties as the Chinese artichoke. It's a sunflower. It hasn't got anything to do with Jerusalem. It's North American. The current thinking is that when Italian settlers came across it in North America they named it *girasole*, the Italian for sunflower. 'Jerusalem' is in this case probably a modern anglicised corruption of this word.

So, all varieties of real artichoke are of the globe variety.

The Jerusalem artichoke is about as related to the globe varieties as the Chinese artichoke. It's a sunflower.

MRS BEETON'S COOKBOOK

Often thought of as the original cookbook, over 900 of its original thousand pages are dedicated to 'general observations' and 'recipes', broken down into various areas of produce and with a specialist section on 'invalid cookery'. Actually, this particular section includes one recipe that caused me much amusement, a 'toast sandwich', made from a slice of toast between two slices of bread.

But the book is so much more than a source of recipes. This wonderful publication's full title is *Mrs Beeton's Book of Household Management*, and as well as the fulsome general observations and recipes there is advice on fashion, religion, the care of children, the management of servants, science, industrialism, the law, perhaps surprisingly the husbandry of animals and, perhaps unnervingly, advice on poisons.

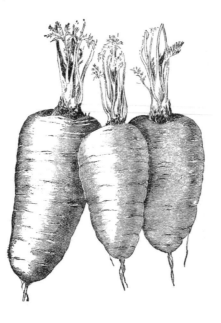

Eastern carrots can be yellow or more commonly purple. In fact, so can Western ones, and also reddish or white.

ALL CARROTS AREN'T ORANGE

All carrots are orange, are they not? Well, all those in my local supermarket are. However, Eastern carrots can be yellow or more commonly purple. In fact, so can Western ones, and also reddish or white.

The orange colour comes from carotenes in the vegetable, and whether by accident or design the popularity of orange carrots in Europe seems to have started in the Netherlands in the seventeenth century. I have even heard that patriotic Dutch farmers showed their support for independence under the house of Orange-Nassau by creating a hybrid.

CHOLESTEROL ISN'T BAD FOR YOU

In the usual advice that high levels of cholesterol are bad for your heart a certain truth lies hidden. It was only when my cholesterol levels were tested did I realise this. In general terms, the body needs to maintain at least some cholesterol and at levels that add to the health of the body. Cholesterol is a waxy steroid metabolic found in the membranes of cells

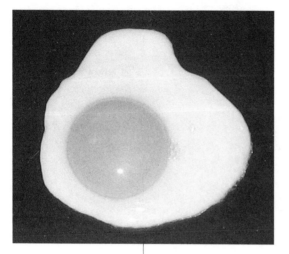

and is transported in blood plasma. It is actually an essential component of cell membranes in mammals, where it is needed to guarantee fluidity and permeability in those membranes. It's also an important component in the body's manufacture of steroid hormones, bile acid and several fat-soluble vitamins.

There are certain types of cholesterol that can be called good and certain types that can be called bad. In simple terms HDL (high-density lipoprotein) is mostly protein and not much fat, and prevents cholesterol build-up in your blood vessels. A high level of this type of cholesterol actually lessens the risk of heart disease. This is the good stuff. Women tend to have higher HDL levels than men, but don't despair, boys. The good news is it can be increased. The bad news is that this involves physical exercise. On the other hand, LDL (low-density lipoprotein) accounts for 70 per cent of your cholesterol. This type consists mainly of fat, and does not have much protein within it. LDLs mainly transport cholesterol from the liver to the cells. A high level of LDL is associated with deposits in your blood vessels, and is the bad type of cholesterol.

As with most things to do with science, it's a little bit more complicated than what I've outlined here, but the basic rule is aim for a high level of HDL and a low level of LDL.

BRACES FOR TEETH ARE COSMETIC

The usual belief in the UK (and probably in the rest of Europe for that matter) is that Americans are so obsessed with their looks that they put their kids through years of torture by making them wear braces on their teeth. In retaliation, any representation of Brits in the funnier and more cutting-edge animations from the USA usually involves them talking in a cockney accent worse than that of Dick Van Dyke in *Mary Poppins* through a set of teeth that look like headstones lying around in a long-disused graveyard.

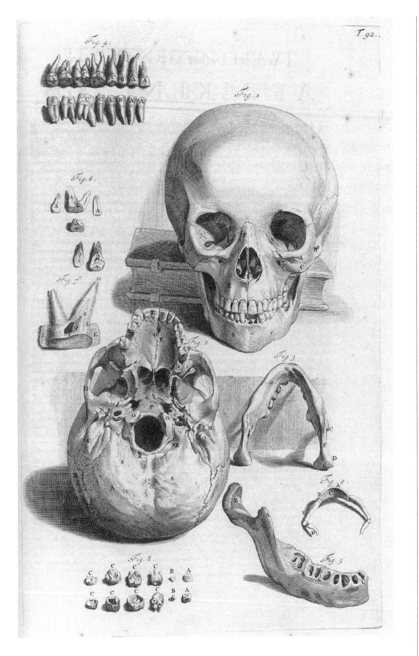

In fact, the attractiveness of a set of neatly aligned teeth is a beneficial by-product of using braces during childhood. Dentists will tell you that most orthodontic treatment is done for functional purposes, to ensure proper occlusion, which in turn helps in the avoidance of 'periodontal breakdown' later in life.

MARS, MILKY WAY AND GALAXY

Spot the odd one out of these astronomically named confectionery products. I undertook a quick survey among friends recently and they of course all went for the first one. On asking their reasons for choosing this option, all but one proudly advised me that Mars is a planet, while Milky Way and Galaxy are named after, well, galaxies.

The singular friend who did not give this as her reason was already in on a little-known fact, which is that the Mars family is one of the richest in the USA and still owns the candy company that bears its name. It is Forrest Edward Mars, Sr. we have to thank for inventing the eponymous Mars Bar, something he did while in Britain during a period of estrangement from his father, the founder of the empire, Frank C. Mars, in the 1930s.

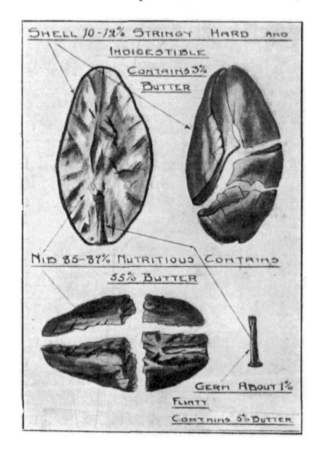

JACUZZI

It was a burning curiosity as to what this word meant that had me reaching for my Italian–English dictionary. Bubbles perhaps? Or does it mean whirlpool? Or maybe it is something like health-giving? Alas, I was undertaking a futile task, it seems, as not only have I been pronouncing the word incorrectly (using JAKOOZEE instead of the more proper YAKOOTZEE), but I was not aware that, like Hoover or Biro, it is a proprietary name that has by development become a generic term for such products.

The original company was founded by seven Italian brothers who had immigrated to California, namely Frank, Rachele, Valeriano, Galindo, Candido, Giocondo and Joseph. After various manufacturing initiatives, it was Candido Jacuzzi, looking for a means of relieving the pain of his son's rheumatoid arthritis between hydrotherapy treatments at hospital, who twigged that agricultural pumps could be adapted. The rest, as they say, is history.

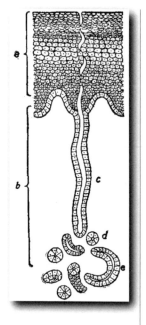

WHY DO ADVERTS TELL YOU
YOUR PORES NEED TO BREATHE?

For those of us (mostly males) of a certain age, it is a fondly remembered iconic film scene. Jill Masterson, played by Shirley Eaton, is lying face down on a bed, dead from suffocation, murdered in a most inventive way by the eponymous villain in James Bond's latest caper *Goldfinger*. He had covered her entire body, hair an' all, in gold paint. Only we were reassured that the actress didn't have to risk death, as the film-makers cleverly left a patch of skin on her stomach unpainted, thus allowing her to breathe and get enough oxygen to keep her alive – although an urban myth grew up that Shirley Eaton actually did die for her art. When she later appeared in other TV and film roles, the myth-makers simply killed off a body double. All this added credence to a parallel myth, and since 1964, when *Goldfinger* first appeared on our screens, millions of dollars, pounds and various other currencies have been spent persuading consumers that there are cosmetics, soaps and cleansers that help to keep the pores open and allow them to breathe.

Poppycock. I can't imagine that it is pleasant to be covered in any sort of paint for any length of time, but pores don't breathe. As long the flow of oxygen to the lungs is maintained, being painted won't kill anyone. Frogs can absorb water through their skin, but humans do not have a similar and equivalent ability with oxygen. In extreme circumstances toxic reactions to the paint, or perhaps overheating through not being able to perspire enough if the air temperature is high might contribute to death. However, death in such circumstances cannot be attributed to the pores not being allowed to breathe.

LEWIS ARMSTRONG

A man with good breath control was the great jazz musician Louis Armstrong. That's Louis pronounced in the French style: LOOEE. He was, despite claiming to be born on Independence Day 1900, born in

New Orleans (pronounced locally NOO ORLANS, not NEW ORLEEANS) on 4 August 1901. That city's in Louisiana, which is historically very French, so the pronunciation of his name makes sense.

The problem is there is a bit of debate as to whether this is actually correct. There is a faction that says that this was how he preferred to be known, which I am not contradicting, and they go so far as to point out in the US census of 1920, he is registered with the interesting spelling 'Lewie'. I'd like to check the handwriting on that one if it's not typed. Someone at one of the major genealogy sites interpreted my grandfather's name, Charles Rooke, as Chester Roole on the 1901 census for Hammersmith. I mention this because of the issue of how individuals like to be addressed. He liked people to call him Charlie even though his proper name was Charles. It's because he was a friendly fellow, and liked to be addressed familiarly. So it was with Louis Armstrong. If he preferred others to use the friendly LOOEE, he referred to himself using the pronunciation that Americans see as the correct one: LOOIS.

What the LOOEE side's arguments fail to take into account is the variety of local and common practices across the rest of the USA. Louisville in Kentucky is referred to as both LOOEEVILLE and LOOISVILLE. St Louis in Missouri is seemingly always pronounced in its anglicised form of Saint LOOIS in the USA, if not by the British. This specific inclusion of the pronounced final 's' is the current form in the majority of the non-French-influenced regions in America, and was also the case back then. It is especially prevalent among the better (if I may use this word in this objectionable sense) classes and more wealthy families. Here I draw the reader's attention to Dan Ackroyd's character Louis Winthorpe III in the 1983 hit film *Trading Places*.

So, as he travelled the States, and jazz became more and more popular with the white middle classes, the majority of Louis Armstrong's fans would have followed their usual practice and anglicised the pronunciation of his forename. At the height of his fame the evidence is that, even if he had once had a preference the other way, Armstrong had accepted this inevitability, and in public at least went with the flow. There might also have been an element of him deciding, having left behind his poor Southern African-American roots and now socialising with people from Washington and Beverly Hills, that to have his name pronounced LOOIS added a bit of class.

I will support this view with two examples. In the 1956 film *High Society* Bing Crosby clearly calls his fellow performer LOOIS. It would have been strange if Armstrong had allowed this to happen if he objected to it. Further, in the greatest version of the song 'Hello Dolly', which Armstrong recorded in 1964, he delivers the line 'This is LOOIS, Dolly.'

EON ONLY MAKES JAMES BOND FILMS

Although other companies have tried to get on the bandwagon, the 'official' James Bond films are made by EON, the production company started in 1961 by Albert R 'Cubby' Broccoli and Harry Saltzman. Since then they have made nothing but films based on Fleming's hero.

There is, surprisingly, one exception. It's probably the poor regard with which the exception is remembered that persuaded them to concentrate on the spy films. Despite having Bob Hope starring opposite Anita Ekberg and a cameo appearance by Arnold Palmer, the 1963 Comedy *Call Me Bwana* wasn't successful enough to premiere a new genre for EON. Just as a point of interest, I invite readers to spot a prominent poster for the comedy, and Connery's related witty comment, in *From Russia with Love*, made by EON the same year.

BOB HOLNESS PLAYED SAXOPHONE ON 'BAKER STREET'

No, I haven't gone mad. Everyone knows that this urban myth was started by Stuart Maconie while working as a music journalist – the naughty pup. I've even heard a denial from the non-saxophone-blowing lips of the man himself, just prior to him being a wonderful host for a major quiz final I attended somewhere in my distant past.

Why I mention this is that, other than his long TV and acting career in the UK, Bob Holness does have a generally accepted and interesting claim to fame. He is widely regarded as the first man to play James Bond, which he did in a South African radio production of *Moonraker* in 1956, more than half a decade before *Dr No*. However, I'm sorry to be the bearer of bad news, as in 1954 CBS in the USA adapted *Casino Royale* into a one-hour TV special as part of a series called *Climax!* They had bought the rights to the story from the author, Ian Fleming. Although working for the CIA, Jimmy Bond appeared in this production played by Barry Nelson. Of note is that Hollywood veteran Peter Lorre also appeared, as the character Le Chiffre.

TROUBLEMAKER MANDELA

Not a personal political opinion, nor support for the attitude of many Western governments towards the great statesman while he was still in jail. I'm just telling you the truth. Mandela's actual birth name is now usually taken to be his middle name, that being Rolihlahla, meaning to pull the branch of a tree, which is a euphemism for troublemaker in his local language.

So why is he known as Nelson Mandela? In his own words,

No one in my family had ever attended school [before] . . . On the first day of school my teacher, Miss Mdingane, gave each of us an English name. This was the custom among Africans in those days and was undoubtedly due to the British bias of our education. That day Miss Mdingane told me that my new name was Nelson. Why this particular name, I have no idea.

CIRRHOSIS ISN'T CAUSED BY BOOZE

Healthy

Cirrhosis

Not every time. Alcohol is probably the biggest self-inflicted cause of this disease at the moment, but there are about fifteen different potential causes in total. Cirrhosis develops in around 10–20 per cent of those who drink heavily (in relation to their comparative capacity to consume alcohol safely) over a long period, so we can't just blame the demon drink for the disease. It's just that with all the other problems that accompany heavy drinking, along with high-profile cases such as that of George Best, it's what we see and remember.

In fact in 2008 obesity overtook booze as the major cause of liver diseases in the UK, and according to experts in the know at King's College Hospital in London it's going to get worse. They predict if we continue to follow the American pattern, in a few decades fat will become the major cause of cirrhosis in the UK. However, please don't take this information as an attempt by me to advocate a drinking free-for-all; everything in moderation, as the wise man surely said.

WHAT IS THE WORLD'S OLDEST CONTINUOUSLY ACTIVE DISTILLERY?

I read many articles that seem to support the generally held belief that the Old Bushmill's Distillery in Antrim, Northern Ireland is the world's oldest continuously active distillery. There is also another Irish distillery, Kilbeggan, which claims the title in the face of the overwhelming vote for Bushmill's, which receives over 100,000 visitors a year and appears on Bank of Ireland sterling banknotes; but can either lay claim to be the world's oldest, given the criteria? I see here an opportunity to fudge the boundaries between the initial granting of a licence and the reality

of continuous production on the
same site since the granting of that
licence.

The backers of Old Bushmill's
quickly refer to the licence granted
in 1608 by King James I to Sir Thomas
Phillips. Although a major prop for
their claims, this is not a licence
to make whiskey[1] at the current
distillery, which dates from the
1880s. Indeed, experts have pointed
out that the Bushmill's Old Distillery
Company was not founded until the
1780s, and that there is little or no

evidence of distilling on the site until 1833. If Sir Thomas Phillips actually
distilled whiskey, and there is no evidence that he utilised his licence, and the
distillery of the 1608 licence was indeed nearby, it was not on the modern
site and nothing to do with the modern brand. The other Irish claimant,
the Kilbeggan distillery, was founded in the 1750s and in production for two
centuries, but according to the modern owners' own website it closed in
1953, only for distilling to recommence in 2007. I fear this is too big a gap
for a claim of continuous production to be made.

One competitor to the Irish was the Littlemill distillery near Glasgow,
which was quite possibly the oldest malt whisky distillery in Scotland with
roots going as far back as 1750. Despite the vagueness of the documentation
around this potential claim – as in the majority of claims as to the world's
oldest distillery – I feel Littlemill could have been given the worldwide
accolade until recently, but as it was closed and demolished a few years
ago, no more I fear. There is also little chance of Littlemill rising again,
despite the hopes and aspirations of its many fans, as the remnants of the
distillery were destroyed by fire in 2004.

So as the debate ranges among whisky/whiskey lovers, I for one seek
for the site that has been associated continuously with the production of
the 'water of life' for the longest. It is a difficult place to find, and at times
feels almost mythical. So, although I will make a commitment as to my

1   As the Irish and Americans spell the word.

current individual belief, I reserve the right to change my opinions in the face of future evidence.

I would like to propose the Bowmore distillery on the Isle of Islay, which claims to have been licensed and established in 1779. Do not, however, take this as the definitive answer as to the question set at the beginning of this article. The right to claim continuous licensed production might be over a much shorter period than we would assume. Bowmore, as with most Scottish distilleries, was taken over by the military during the Second World War, so can there be anywhere in the UK a claim to continuous production stretching beyond 1945? I will investigate further, perhaps even outside the British Isles, and return with my findings some time in the future.

ST BERNARD DOGS AND BRANDY BARRELS

Ask anyone what they associate with these wonderful oversized beasts and they always come back with the same reply. When they rescue stranded mountaineers in the Alps, they sit patiently so that the weakened victim can warm and revive themself by taking a good nip of brandy,

conveniently contained in a small barrel slung around the faithful dog's neck.

This is nonsense. Apart from the stupidity of giving alcohol to a person suffering from hypothermia (see the next-but-two piece), a quick call to the monks at the St Bernard Hospice, where these rescue dogs were first bred, will disabuse anyone of this belief. The Victorian artist John Emms probably started the idea, as one of his paintings has a monk with two dogs about to set out on a rescue, and at least one of the dogs has a barrel around its neck. That isn't to say the monks are not beyond having a few dogs with barrels around for publicity purposes when the tourist coaches arrive, but this came after Emms, and then when Hollywood had persuaded the rest of the world that their interpretation was the truth.

The Victorian artist John Emms probably started the idea, as one of his paintings has a monk with two dogs about to set out on a rescue, and at least one of the dogs has a barrel around its neck.

DOGS DO NOT SWEAT THROUGH THEIR TONGUES

Sometimes linked in with this idea is that dogs do not sweat at all. These are both misconceptions. Dogs do regulate their body temperature by panting, but as this does not involve sweat glands it must be regarded as an alternative means of keeping cool to perspiration. Then again, a bit of panting does help us to cool down too, I suppose.

On a hot day, after exercising a dog will open its mouth wide and allow its tongue to hang out. This way of cooling down is actually very efficient as it maximises heat loss while conserving moisture, mainly due to it conveying heat from the hottest part of the body, the interior part of the thorax. Sweating, on the

First dog team Nome to Seward
S. Sexton

other hand, cools the body by the evaporation of moisture from the skin. This is much less efficient as the skin is already the coolest part of the body. The science behind this is that greater efficiency of thermal loss is achieved by dogs than humans relative to moisture conservation, as heat flow is proportional to temperature gradient.

Dogs actually can sweat, but through the pads of their feet, which unlike the majority of the rest of their skin doesn't have a covering of fur. This can be seen when a dog walks a cross a wooden or tiled floor on a hot day, especially after exercise: the dog will leave a trail of wet footprints.

EVERY HUMAN YEAR IS SEVEN DOG YEARS

A dog ages at the equivalent of ten and a half human years for the first two years, then this reduces to about four for all the years after that.

Another way we compare ourselves with dogs is through the concept that every human year is equivalent to seven dog years. It might average out in some species I suppose, but as different breeds of dog have different life expectancies this doesn't hold water. The rule of thumb, to which of course there are exceptions, is that smaller breeds last longer than bigger breeds. So if aesthetics don't matter to you, and length of canine companionship is what counts, you should get a Jack Russell rather than a Great Dane.

In addition, if the ratio was actually seven to one, we wouldn't see dogs becoming sexually mature as quickly as they do, often well before their second birthday. So after exploring different theories I think the ratio below seems more or less on the money. A dog ages at the equivalent of ten and a half human years for the first two years, then this reduces to about four for all the years after that. I can accept this. One of my pets, which lived to the grand old age of seventeen human years, could be said to have achieved an equivalent age of 81, rather than 119.

A NIP OF WHISKY KEEPS OUT THE COLD

—⁂—

Another favourite fallacy spread by film, TV, books and the like. I suppose that if you have enough whisky (remember that's whiskey if you're Irish or American) you just might forget you're cold, but you forget most things by that stage anyway. Alcohol is a vasodilator, so causes blood vessels to expand and thus lowers body temperature. You might 'glow' and feel warm, but that's the heat leaving, not coming in. It seems that all those creative minds have been taken in by those people living in cold climes who have used this notion as an excuse for a drink.

COFFEE HELPS YOU SOBER UP

—⁂—

Ditto the above in laying the blame for this belief on its constant promotion in visual and written media. The only thing that aids sobering up is time. Humans 'use up' alcohol at the rate of about half an ounce an hour, with the rate varying between individuals. It is only the body processing any alcohol present in the bloodstream that causes increased sobriety. Caffeine has no known effect on this function, either in speeding it up or slowing it down. In fact, it is a sobering thought to

contemplate how many people have been plied with coffee after a drinking session, only to be put behind the wheel of a car by their friends and waved off to their deaths.

GUESS WHAT THE ROMANS USED A VOMITORIUM FOR?

As the idea behind a good Roman nosh-up was to eat so much that the only way to get through all the courses was to – how to put this delicately – 'make room', and as they liked to have a different room for almost everything they did, why not have one to vomit in, away from the dinner party?

Sadly a vomitorium is merely a passage below or under the seats in an auditorium by which the crowd can quickly enter and leave. The Colosseum was full of them. The name is related to the Latin for being physically sick, and seems to derive from the way a crowd would have 'spewed out' onto the streets.

MACARONI

———❧✦❧———

Macaroni is a long, hollow and fairly thick type of pasta, oft served up in a cheese sauce as comfort food. It is very different to the thinner sorts of pasta such as vermicelli or the ubiquitous spaghetti. But to the people who invented the stuff, spaghetti and vermicelli are types of macaroni. *Maccheroni*, as they spell it, is a generic term for a group of comestibles that includes eight types of pasta, including the two mentioned here.

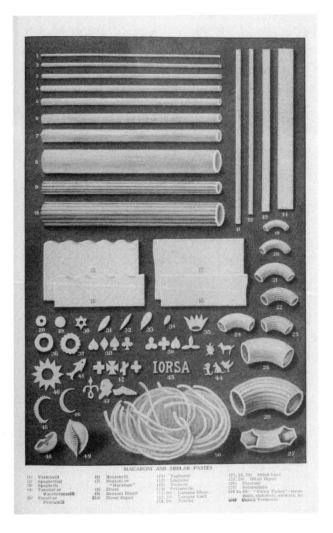

MACARONI AND SIMILAR PASTES

Just as an aside, in the song 'Yankee Doodle Dandy' the lines 'Stuck a feather in his cap / And called it Macaroni' have more to do with the fact that macaroni is an archaic term for a dandy or fop known for excessive finery, big wigs and flamboyant clothing. This sense has nothing to do with pasta but comes from the medieval Italian *mackarone*, which meant a foolish person. The intriguing thing is how this term also ended up being applied to types of pasta. Perhaps that's an investigation for another time.

BETTY'S POSH CAFÉS

This chain of six cafés in the more genteel parts of northern England, namely Harrogate, Ilkley, York and Northallerton (there are two in each of Harrogate and York), are tourist magnets. In addition to the American lady who vociferously misnamed one of the specialities of the house, proclaiming her desire to try a 'fat bastard' instead of a 'fat rascal', many visitors waste the time of the staff by asking who Betty is or was, interested in the lady who created such a pleasant environment for, to quote T S Eliot, 'the taking of a toast and tea'.

It's a waste of time because even if she did exist, she had nothing to do with the business. The company's own website offers four potential explanations as to who she was.

- The late Queen Mother, born Elizabeth Bowes-Lyon in 1900.
- A former manageress of Harrogate Spa, Betty Lupton, known as 'Queen of the Harrogate Wells'.
- A doctor's daughter who died of tuberculosis and whose father's practice on Cambridge Crescent, Harrogate later became the first Bettys Café Tea Rooms.
- A small girl called Betty who interrupted the first board meeting when the issue of what to call the tea rooms was being discussed.

There is no clincher here, I fear, so perhaps another reason exists. I have a friend who noticed that there is no possessive apostrophe – it's Bettys not Betty's. His theory is that the company was founded by a Swiss confectioner with the surname Bettys (pronounced BETTIS). Well he got the Swiss part right, but as the company was started by a confectioner from Switzerland called Frederick Belmont who accidentally found himself in Yorkshire in the early twentieth century, this is not worth pursuing. It seems the missing apostrophe is down to nothing more than Belmont's poor grasp of English.

A BISTRO IS A CHIC FRENCH PLACE TO EAT

In the UK restaurateurs add 'bistro' (or 'bistrot') to the names of their establishments to make them sound a bit Gallic and a little sophisticated. Not in France. The term indicates a small eatery with moderately priced and simple food in a modest environment. The French don't expect professional service or even a menu in a bistro; the main idea is the food is delivered to the table quickly and with little fuss. Not my idea of a place trying to be a cut above.

As the word didn't become common coinage until the end of the 1800s, the French are probably correct in insisting the name developed from *bistrouille* (brandy mixed with coffee). However, a popular theory is that Cossacks occupying Paris after the fall of Napoleon in 1814 would shout *'Bistro!'* at café owners and their staff – it's Russian for 'Quickly!' If this is true, it's not even a French word.

A RESTAURANT IS RUN BY
A RESTAURANTEUR

————— ❧❦ —————

Not in my book. I might be a little pedantic but it's an issue of pronounciation – sorry, pronunciation. A restaurateur runs a restaurant.

FRANCE WAS RULED BY
EIGHTEEN KINGS CALLED LOUIS

————— ❧❦ —————

The last king of France called Louis was the eighteenth of that title, taking the throne around the time the Cossacks were shouting 'Bistro!' at the waiters of Paris and reigning until 1824, when his brother Charles X succeeded him. This is true. However, only sixteen reigning monarchs called Louis reigned: Louis I and Louis XVII never ruled France.

The Frankish empire forged by Charlemagne at the end of the eighth century had split by 843, following the reign of a monarch known as Louis the Pious – also called Louis I. It was only after a series of civil wars and three years after his death in 840 that France emerged as a separate entity from Germany, Burgundy and the Low Countries at the Treaty of Verdun. Louis the Stammerer was the first Louis to rule a distinctively French country – and he was Louis II.

Around a thousand years later Louis XVII died as a child in prison a few years after his father was guillotined in 1793. At this time France was a republic. His uncle only succeeded him nearly twenty years later after the monarchy was restored, making only sixteen kings, not eighteen.

THE BASTILLE WAS STORMED
TO RELEASE PRISONERS

July 14 is celebrated across France (and beyond) as the day the citizens of Paris struck a huge blow for liberty by emptying the old Bastille prison of its political prisoners. I don't see any reason to stop a national party, but this does seem something of an exaggeration. They released exactly seven people: four counterfeiters, a young aristo there because his family didn't want him at large, and two madmen, one of whom was English. Of note is that if it had been stormed in June, they could have released the Marquis de Sade, but as he had been abusing people in the street from his window in a tower, he had recently been moved to an asylum. The Bastille was simply too old to be an efficient prison, so had effectively fallen into disuse.

Don't come away with the idea that the *sans-culottes* were rather dim, as they did have a good reason to attack the old prison. They wanted its store of gunpowder, which they would have preferred to get their hands on without a fight. History tells us there was quite a battle.

The storming of the fortress resulted in a massive boost to the

revolutionaries' morale and produced the amusing irony that on 14 July 1789 the king, happily a good distance away at Versailles, wrote in his diary, '*Rien.*' Sadly, when he wrote 'Nothing' he was actually referring to what had been caught on that day's hunt.

LUCIFER

Lucifer is applied to the planet Venus in the early morning, and is also an early name for a match, the type you'd light your pipe with if you were so disposed to smoke one. The matches were so named from a biblical reference to the devil, only it's all a big mistake.

The original meaning of the name Lucifer is bright morning star. The biblical Lucifer is an allegorical reference to the king of Babylon, not Satan. The passage of scripture that caused this misunderstanding is in St Jerome's Vulgate Bible – '*Quomodo cecidisti de cælo, Lucifer, qui mane oriebaris?*' – later translated into English as 'How art thou fallen from heaven, O Lucifer, sun of the morning?' It is mentioned as part of a 'parable against the king of Babylon' in the Book of Isaiah, but the fall from heaven bit meant it was interpreted spiritually, and so the king of Babylon became designated as, or transposed into, the chief of 'the angels who kept not their first estate'. From this, it became the general view that Lucifer was

Satan's name before the Fall. The Latin word was adopted in all the English versions down to the seventeenth century, but in more modern revised versions in English 'Lucifer' has been replaced by 'daystar', which is far more in keeping with the appearance of Venus just before the dawn.

DEVIL'S ISLAND IS A PENAL COLONY OFF THE COAST OF COLONIAL FRENCH GUIANA

This is a popular error in so many different ways. Devil's Island became well known in the English-speaking world firstly when the unjustly convicted French army officer Alfred Dreyfus was sent there in 1895, and then more recently as a result of Henri Charrière's account of his escape. The place is synonymous with extreme brutality.

We can start by pointing out, according to official French documents, that 'Papillon' himself was a bit of a fabricator, and was never kept on the Île du Diable. This is not to say he wasn't in, rather than on, Devil's Island. Let me explain. The island is one of three in a group called the Îles du Salut, the others being the Île Royale and Île Saint-Joseph. There is a prison facility on each of the islands, as well as on the mainland at Kourou. Over

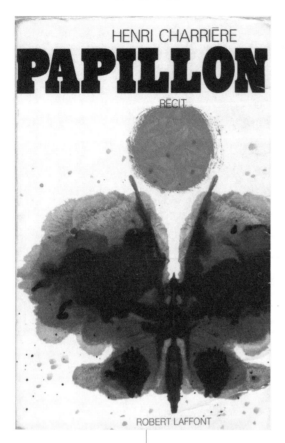

HENRI CHARRIÈRE
PAPILLON
RÉCIT

ROBERT LAFFONT

time the four facilities became known collectively as Devil's Island in the English-speaking world. The French call them the Bagne de Cayenne (Cayenne Penal Colony) after the main city of French Guiana. Papillon was kept at Kourou, so as stated was *in* but not *on* Devil's Island.

The second half of the commonly held belief that is wrong is that French Guiana, like many other French possessions around the world, isn't a colony. It's one of the twenty-six regions of France and consists of a single *departement d'outrer-mer*, or overseas department. It is an integral part of the French Republic, uses the euro as its currency and is even part of the European Union. It sends two deputies to the French National Assembly and one senator to the upper house. So, since the closure of Devil's Island in 1952, it might have become a great place to live and work – and any citizen of the EU can do just that if they so wish.

THE DAIQUIRI

The cocktail, or more accurately the family of rum-based cocktails, known as the daiquiri was supposedly invented in the Cuban city of Daiquiri and named after it. It became a widely enjoyed drink when it was associated with the writer Ernest Hemingway, who is said to have enjoyed his favorite tipple in the El Floridita bar in the Cuban capital, Havana.

But Daiquiri is only a village, fourteen miles east of Santiago de Cuba along the south coast of the island, and never has been a city. It did actually come to brief prominence as the focal point for the landing of American forces in the Spanish–American War in 1898, but this is merely of passing interest as the story behind the invention of the cocktail points to the probability that it wasn't even named after the village.

Daiquiri is also the name of a beach and of an iron-ore mine in the area, and it is after the latter that the drink is most probably named. The cocktail was supposedly invented in or around the early years of the nineteenth century, in the Venus bar in Santiago. A group of mining engineers from the USA was in the area, and one Jennings Cox, a manager working for the Spanish American Iron Company, is credited with coming up with the idea while entertaining some of his countrymen. The story goes that he ran out of gin, so the daiquiri was invented as he turned instead to rum. In all probability the drink came about by trial and error: rum is a natural partner for sugar and lime, and all of these ingredients are commonly available in that part of the world. Whatever the true explanation, it was the involvement of the boys from the iron-ore mine that gave the drink its name.

THE TANGO IS A SEXY DANCE

———— ❦ ————

Today I don't think many would disagree with that assertion; it has become a popular dance, involving many sultry looks and dramatic, swift movements. However, and I tread carefully in these more enlightened times, while agreeing that it actually developed in a very sexually charged environment, would it surprise the majority of people to learn that it actually started as a dance usually performed by two men?

It is generally believed that the tango began in the brothels of Buenos Aires and in those of Montevideo across the wide mouth of the River Plate. However, I tend to think that it was actually widely danced among the huge and growing immigrant working class, and those who wrote of the dance's origins, the literary classes, first encountered it in the brothels, one of the few places where the 'lower orders' would have had social contact with their 'betters'.

In the quickly developing cities of the nineteenth century a common

THE TANGO OF TO-DAY

problem was the lack of women. Prostitution was therefore a boom industry. However, shortages of women in general were mirrored by shortages of women in the brothels. This meant a common scene in and around brothels was queues of men waiting for the hard-working girls to become available. In exactly the same way that led a young Les Dawson to find to his shock that his employment as a pianist in Paris was actually a front for a brothel, the men were entertained while they waited. Brothels in Buenos Aires and Montevideo employed musicians and singers to play the popular music of the poor. (This then became popular among the more refined citizenship in the way essentially black music was introduced to the white population via rock and roll in 1950s America.)

Now, here's the rub. Clearly the prostitutes wouldn't have danced with the waiting men; the madams would have made damn sure they were maximising their earning potential elsewhere. So at the very times that the queues were at their longest, the girls just weren't available. But if music was being played it seems odds on the men would have used the opportunity to practise their dancing together.

THE TANGO IS A LATIN DANCE

Yes, I agree that the tango originated in a Latin country, but in the World Dance Council's internationally defined standards it isn't classified as a Latin dance. The five 'International Latin' dances are the samba, rumba, paso doble, cha cha cha and, most interestingly, the jive. The tango is classed as one of the five 'International Standard' ballroom dances, along with the slow waltz, Viennese waltz, slow foxtrot and quickstep.

CHA CHA . . . CHA

ow many times have you heard a reference to 'dancing the cha cha'? It might sometimes go by this name, especially in North America, but again we take our lead from the World Dance Council, who more correctly give it three cha's, not two.

FOXTROT

he name of this dance is not a reference to any similarities to the gait of a fox as it trots along. If you watch a fox as it moves, it utilises a low skulking lope rather than a lively hopping, skipping and jumping style.

Simply, despite some theories that beg to differ, as it was invented by the vaudeville actor Harry Fox, the origins of its name seem pretty obvious to me.

BELA LUGOSI WANTED TO BE BURIED
IN HIS DRACULA OUTFIT

———— ❦ ————

Lugosi lies in his film cloak in Holy Cross cemetery in Culver City, California because that is what his son and fourth wife thought he would have wanted. He wasn't so conceited about his success as the most famous of screen vampires that he instructed in his will that he was to be buried in his costume.

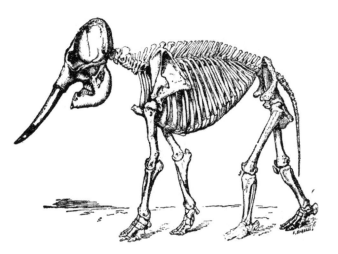

THE ELEPHANT'S THE ONLY ANIMAL THAT CAN'T JUMP

An idea probably based on the mistaken belief that the elephant is the only mammal with four knees; I refer to any museum with an elephant skeleton on display to disprove this strange idea. There are actually a number of animals (with legs) that can't jump. The list does include elephants, but also takes in sloths and hippopotami and a number of different types of burrowing rodents.

FRAY BENTOS ON THE PLATE

A joke popular with schoolboys, because the city that gives its name to a brand of corned beef is on the River Plate. As with these Latin quotes, '*Caesar adsum jam forte, Antonius sed passus sum,*' and

> *Caesar aderat forte,*
> *Pompey adsum jam,*
> *Caesar sic in omnibus,*
> *Pompey sic intram.*

it's probably the subject of food that make them popular. Fray Bentos is a

49

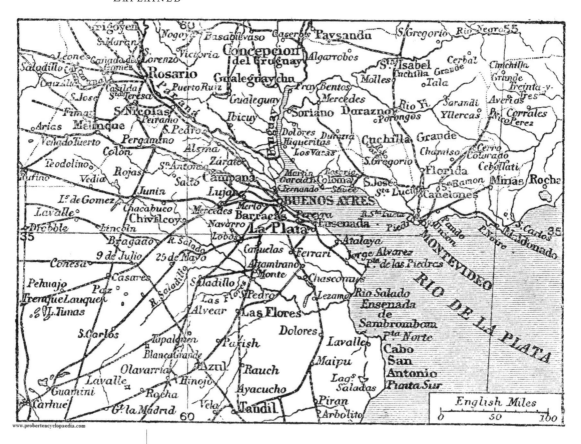

www.probertencyclopaedia.com

port in Uruguay, famous as the focal point for the processing of beef from the herds of the pampas around it.

The joke falls down if you look at a map and discover the town actually sits on the Uruguay River.

HUMBLE(D) PIE

— ❧❦ —

It is sweet serendipity that the phrase 'to eat humble pie' reflects the fact that a person being very apologetic does actually act in a humble manner. Not so sweet is the actual foodstuff from which the phrase derives. Although probably once thought of as a delicacy – but this in an age when the British hadn't honed their collective culinary abilities – an

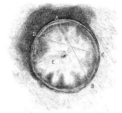

umble pie was indeed 'what it said on the tin': a pie made from umbles, otherwise known as deer's innards. In sharing out a deer's carcass, it was the rich that got the venison, and the poor that got the umbles. As the poor were usually deferential to the rich, umble-eaters were by nature humble.

SHIPS SAIL THROUGH THE PANAMA CANAL FROM EAST TO WEST FROM THE ATLANTIC TO THE PACIFIC

———※ ※———

They don't. They enter the canal from the Atlantic travelling due south, and then spend most of the time travelling east and south-east.

SURELY THE PANAMA HAT ORIGINATED IN PANAMA?

———※ ※———

Actually, it didn't, and who'd have thought there was a connection between Stilton cheese and Panama hats? It's the same story, essentially. The coach stop on the Great North Road became associated

with the cheese because that's where most people sampled it. The majority of Panama hats, in common with a lot of South America's exports, were firstly shipped to Panama before being sent on to Europe, Asia and North America. So the rest of the world thought that's where they came from, and in one way I suppose they did.

It's the triumph of the point of sale over the point of origin. A more proper name for the hat is a Jipijana, a town in Ecuador which was the centre of the hat trade.

WHERE IS THE DEAD CENTRE OF ENGLAND?

The cemetery furthest from the sea, I hear you jest. Actually, this distinction is generally claimed by a town in Warwickshire. In his recently published investigation into middle England – the social middle not the geographical one – entitled *Adventures on the High Teas*, the aforementioned Stuart Maconie visits Meridan, where there is a long-standing monument to the claim.

The Ordnance Survey – and what better body to be the arbiter? – recently decided to ascertain the true centre of the country. Look away

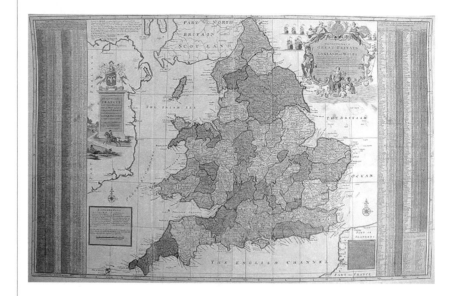

now, residents of Meridan, if you don't want to know the result. The OS declared that the grid reference of the very middle of the country is SP 36373.66 96143.05. This is in a field on Lindley Hall Farm in Leicestershire, eleven miles from the monument.

THE AZTECS DIDN'T HAVE THE WHEEL

Put another way, the Aztecs did not understand the principle of the wheel. Which is strange when put into context. The Aztecs has a more accurate calendar than their sixteenth-century European conquerers. They had cities with populations unheard of across the Atlantic since the days of Rome. Key to any great empire, they had a very sophisticated civil service. Their legal system was pretty good as well. So it seems a little strange that they didn't have any mechanical devices based on rotary motion, such as a potter's wheel.

We do them an injustice. It's just that they hadn't applied the principle to anything other than items such as children's pull-along toys. Pre-conquistador toys are in existence to prove this fact. I suppose it's a bit like the Chinese and gunpowder: it took a Western brain to transform something as fantastic as a means of detonating wonderful fireworks into a weapon.

MOTH-EATEN

As even the *OED* defines this as 'eaten away or destroyed by or as by moths', a large number of people think that it's the flying insects that cause the damage, when in fact it's the moth in its larval or grub stage that does the eating. Many moths do not eat at all after they reach their adult stage.

THE SCOTS HISTORICALLY WORE DIFFERENT TARTANS TO SHOW TO WHICH CLAN THEY BELONGED

The picture that comes down to us in films and stories about the great figures and events of Scottish history – Rob Roy, the Bruce, Culloden and Flodden to name but a few – is of proud fighters wearing their clan tartan with honour and pride. However, although tartan is known to

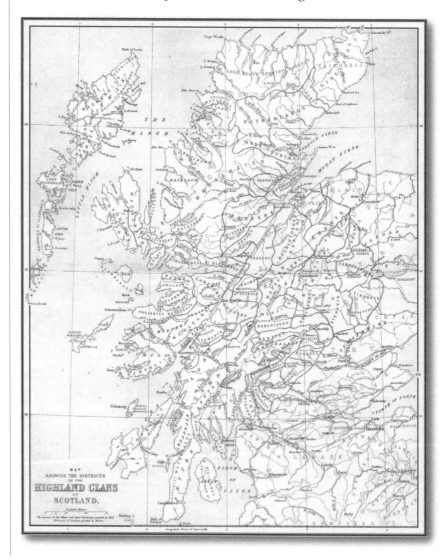

have been made and worn in Scotland from at least the sixteenth century, any uniformity in pattern showed the origin of the cloth rather than the affiliation of its wearers to any chief or clan. It is thought the natives of the glens and islands simply wore what they could get, meaning some sported two or three different tartans at once. Uniformity developed first in the British army, with the colonels of Highland regiments kitting out their troops in particular patterns. The Black Watch, formed in 1739, is considered the first example of this.

The whole idea of clan tartans only arose in the period following the visit of George IV to Edinburgh in 1822. That old romantic Sir Walter Scott had formed the Celtic Society of Edinburgh two years earlier, and frankly seems to have gone a little Caledonian crazy when Prinny came to town. He got the local worthies to turn out 'all plaided and plumed in their tartan array'. The king was painted in full Highland dress by Sir David Wilkie and the thing snowballed.

Books were published cataloguing the patterns, and the makers of tartan thought they'd get on the commercial bandwagon and invented clan tartans, in turn first documented in the *Vestiarium Scoticum* published in 1842. This was produced by two seemingly shady Welsh brothers, John Sobieski Hay and Charles Allen Hay[1], who claimed to be the grandsons of Bonnie Prince Charlie. They maintained their book was based on an ancient manuscript about clan tartans, but couldn't actually show anyone this ancient tome. Their equally dubious *The Costume of the Clans* came out two years later, just as Victoria and Albert were making their first visits to north Britain. Albert especially was an enthusiast and kitted out Balmoral Castle's interiors with tartan. He utilised the red Royal Stewart and the green Hunting Stewart tartans for carpets, while using the Dress Stewart for curtains and upholstery. The Queen designed the Victoria, and Albert produced the Balmoral, which is still used today as a royal tartan. The legend of clan tartans romantically originating in the mists of history was firmly established, which is ironic as the idea was popularised at the very point in history when the supposed progenitors of the stuff were being turfed out of their ancient lands in the Highland Clearances.

1   Just two of the various names used at various times by two men born John Carter Allen and Charles Manning Allen. Their claims to regality were quite breathtaking – both claimed on the 1871 Census that they had been born in Versailles.

QUEEN VICTORIA – BORN TO RULE A GREAT BRITISH EMPIRE

At over sixty-three years, her reign has been longer than that of any other British monarch to date.

Let us start with two connected axioms of British history: that Queen Victoria was born to rule a great empire, and it was a thing she did with such an all-encompassing influence that she lent her name to our greatest period as a nation. However, even without the arguments about her withdrawal from public life at the death of her husband Albert[1] in 1861, less than twenty-five years into a reign that lasted over six decades, the foundations of these supposed axioms are less secure than we are often led to believe.

Queen Victoria. Queen-Empress Victoria, even. Among other things too numerous to mention, she has had railway stations, streets, dams, docks, ships, lakes, bridges, a sponge cake, buildings, a number of universities (including Manchester University as discussed elsewhere in this book), hospitals, more than one medal, parks, the capitals of British Columbia and the Seychelles, and even two component states of Australia named after her, although we should note in the case of Queensland that this was not directly but through her title. As I have noted above, she even lent her name to an epoch in British history. Beginning with her ascension to the throne in 1837, the rest of the nineteenth century belonged to Victoria, and of course hers is a popular name for female babies from Penzance to Thurso even now, well into the twenty-first century.

Victoria: has any other name been so synonymous with or evocative of an expansionist victorious empire? At over sixty-three years, her reign has been longer than that of any other British monarch to date. She was surely named with her future as a queen and empress in mind. Except, as I said above, that on two major accounts this belief is wrong.

First: Victoria wasn't born to rule. In fact she was at her birth even further away from the throne than her great-great-granddaughter Elizabeth was at hers. It was the abdication crisis of 1936 that put the latter on course to become our current queen. Victoria faced a far more circuitous route,

[1] Who was really called Francis – Francis Albert Augustus Charles Emmanuel, to give him his full list of Christian names.

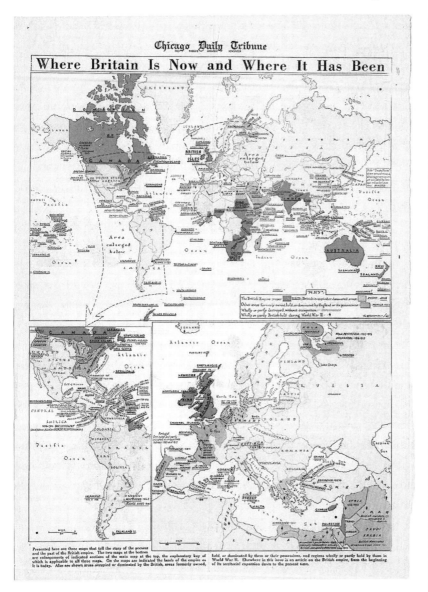

Presented here are three maps that tell the story of the present and the past of the British empire. The two maps at the bottom are enlargements of indicated sections of the main map at the top, which is applicable to all three maps. Also are shown areas occupied or dominated by the British, areas formerly owned, held, or dominated by them or their possessions, and regions wholly or partly held by them in World War II. Elsewhere in this issue is an article on the British empire, from the beginning of its territorial expansion down to the present time.

and was born into a life that promised the obscurity of being a minor royal of German origin in an era where such people were abundant. Born in 1818, she was the daughter of the fourth son of George III, one Edward Augustus, Duke of Kent. She was an only child, and came late in his life (he was already into his fifties) during the scramble to marry and produce offspring after the death of Charlotte, the only child of the Prince of Wales and his estranged wife Caroline of Brunswick in 1817. Ahead of the duke were three elder brothers (and an elder sister, who perhaps now would be thought to have been wrongly ignored). These elder brothers had collectively produced three offspring. However, all six were to die (with Edward Augustus himself dying to make a seventh) either before or during the seventeen years between the demise of George III and the elevation of Victoria. And even when she became heir presumptive at the age of eleven on the accession of her uncle William IV in 1830 (this due to his two offspring both dying in infancy) an act of parliament was passed to make her mother, Victoria of Saxe-Coburg-Saalfeld[1], Duchess of Kent, regent until the young Victoria reached her majority. It's a wonder that Victoria became famous at all, instead of her name dominating British history as it did (and does).

And here we come to the second reason why it is an amazement that we owe so much that is both good and bad to what is reverently referred to as the Victorian era. She wasn't christened Victoria; she was actually christened *Alexandrina* Victoria. Her proper forename was given in honour of one of her godparents, Tsar Alexander of Russia. As a child, she was called Drina by her family. What saved us from catching the 8.15 from Alexandrina to Brighton, eating Alexandrina sponge or learning at school that Africa's largest stretch of open water is Lake Alexandrina was her being formally styled from birth HRH Princess Victoria of Kent.

From what we know of her overbearing and manipulative mother, this seems to have been a result of her ego – ensuring her only child inherited her name, at least on a formal basis. This, incidentally, leads to the question of the second part of Victoria's name, a question that at one stage of her life caused her great consternation. Was she Victoria Hanover, or did she have another surname?

'SHE KEEPS∕A MOW∕WAY AND SHAN∕DON IN A PRETTY CABINET . . .'

───※ ❦ ※───

Talking of queens (his own self-deprecating joke, not mine), so sang Freddie Mercury on the regally named band's 1974 hit 'Killer Queen'. Great showman; terrible at pronunciation.

He got the Chandon part right, but Claude Moët had a Dutch name,

1 Born Mary Louise Victoria in 1786.

so the French practice of not pronouncing the final letter does not apply, and when asking for the champagne of this particular house one should tell the sommelier you require MOWETT or M'WET.

ALEXANDER THE GREAT
AND ERIC BRISTOW

There is a wonderful televised quote delivered in broad Geordie by the Cambridge alumnus and 'voice of darts' Sid Waddell: 'When Alexander of Macedonia was thirty-three, he cried salt tears because there were no more worlds to conquer . . . [Eric] Bristow's only twenty-seven.' Marvellous stuff, but this is a quote based on a misconception. We don't know if Alexander did actually cry, but it was exactly the opposite reason to the popular error that caused him to be upset. He realised he hadn't even conquered the area formerly controlled by the Persians, let alone the rest of Asia, the Mediterranean world and Africa south of Egypt. When a sophist called Anaxarchus pointed this out, Alexander responded, 'Do you not think it worthy of lamentation that when there is such a vast multitude of worlds, we have not yet conquered one?'

KANGAROO? I DON'T UNDERSTAND . . .

Captain Cook lands in New South Wales.
(From an old print, 1807.)

The common myth about the English name for this animal is that *Kangaroo* is Aboriginal for 'I don't understand you.'

James Cook was accompanying naturalist Sir Joseph Banks in the exploration of an area of northern Queensland when they happened upon the strange creature. They asked a local who just happened to be passing by what the animal was called. The local responded, '*Kangaroo*,' which they took to be the name of the creature. This story requires us to believe that the local understood English but chose to reply in his native tongue, and that the great men made the initial mistake.

This myth was disproved in the 1970s by John B Haviland in his research with the Guugu Yimidhirr. The English name derives from their word *gagangurru*, which denotes the grey kangaroo.

MRS WETTIN? OR IS THAT VICKY BROWN?

Having established that Queen Victoria was properly called Alexandrina, we now look at the question of her true personal surname. She has always been known to history as Victoria of Hanover, and it seems most people have simply accepted this: that is, the royal dynasty that she was born into was named Hanover. As with so many things in history, this simple assumption is far from being simple and indeed far from being correct; nor did her family name remain the same throughout her life.

Dynastic names are not family names, in the same way as the Duke of Westminster's surname is Grosvenor and the Earl of Portland is a Bentinck. Another way of looking at it is to say that Queen Elizabeth II's surname isn't 'The-United-Kingdom-of-Great-Britain-and-Northern-Ireland'; that's where she's queen of, and we haven't even included her dominions overseas, etc. However, more of Victoria's descendant when we discuss the surname of our current royal family.

When Victoria's direct ancestor George I, Elector of Hanover[1] accepted the British throne in the early eighteenth century, he was just one member of a very extensive noble family that had its origins in the eleventh century in Germany and two centuries earlier in what is now Italy. The German house of Welf is the older branch of the house of Este, known to have been in existence in Lombardy in the ninth century. In the early days of the Holy Roman Empire there was much interaction between the north and south of the empire, and none of the modern national boundaries. Via marriages, disputes and inheritances initially involving ownership of places such as Ferrara and Mantua, the Estes prospered, and this led in time to Welf IV beginning the family's dynastic activities north of the Alps. Moving through the dukedoms of Carinthia, Bavaria and Saxony, the Welfs evolved into a dynasty ruling the Duchy of Brunswick-Lüneburg. A cadet branch of this dynasty, the Calenberg line, ruled in Hanover until their support for Austria in its 1866 war with Prussia led to the latter annexing what was by then the Kingdom of Hanover.[2]

Throughout all this, the family name remained Welf, and from 1714

1   The title Prince Elector (*Kurfürst*), or usually just Elector, was given to seven noblemen and senior clerics within the Holy Roman Empire who were members of the council that elected the emperor. Hanover was given the accolade in 1692.

2   Victoria wasn't allowed to become Queen of Hanover, an extant kingdom in Germany at the time of her succession. This was because of Salic law, which meant women couldn't succeed to a throne. Her uncle, the Duke of Cumberland, became King of Hanover.

until Victoria's death in 1901 the United Kingdom was ruled by Welfs –
or some say until Victoria's marriage in 1840, when she married Albert
of Saxe-Coburg and Gotha, and became a Wettin. The Wettins, like
the Welfs, were much involved in the dynastic toings and froings of the
last millennium.[3] It was the Ernestine branch of the family – how these
families split to spread their influence – that numbered Prince Albert in
its ranks. In the late nineteenth century Victoria asked the College of
Heralds to determine the correct personal surname of her late husband.
Her dynasty had during its tenure been referred to as Hanover, Brunswick
or Guelph,[4] and she was unsure as to what surname her son should
use. They researched extensively, and came back to her with Wettin, or
von Wettin. Her personal papers tell us that this did not please her. She
decided that Bertie (Edward VII) and his descendants were to be members
of the house of Saxe-Coburg and Gotha, and that was the end of the
matter.

3   Wettins at various stages have ruled Poland, Bulgaria, Saxony, Belgium and of course
Great Britain, in the last case by being the father of a reigning queen's children (as in
Portugal also). They remain rulers to this day in Britain and Belgium. Even the short-lived
ruler of Mexico, Emperor Maximilian I, was a Wettin.
4   Through the support of the Welfs for the Pope in the disputes between the papacy and
the Holy Roman Empire, the Italian form of Welf, Guelph, was used as a generic term
for all the supporters of that side. The Emperor's supporters were the Ghibellines. Italy's
greatest poet, Dante, was a member of a faction known as the White Guelphs.

Well for her, yes, but for us, no. With the current ruling dynasty of the United Kingdom calling itself the house of Windsor, we know better.

There are other untidy edges to this story. Alexandrina Victoria Wettin née Welf should, if conventions had been followed correctly, have remained a Welf, as noblewomen do not assume membership of their husband's house. The College of Heralds do not seem to have followed their own rules. So perhaps she was just plain Drina Welf all along.

And if she did remain a Welf, one last twist to the story of her surname may be no more than a red herring. It is accepted as fact that in her later years Victoria became increasingly reliant on her Scottish gillie John Brown. So reliant in fact to the eyes of some observers, that stories abounded of a clandestine marriage. These remain unproven, but at the time the queen was disrespectfully referred to in some quarters as Mrs Brown, and was buried with mementos of both Albert (born Francis) and John Brown. So we might still speculate, in our more fanciful moments, that Drina Welf became Mrs Frankie Wettin, and then ended her days as plain old Vicky Brown.

'STOP ALL THE CLOCKS' ISN'T A POEM

Well, in its original form it isn't. Or in its second form come to that. 'Stop all the clocks' isn't actually its real name. It is commonly known by these opening words, but the work exists in two very different versions. The original version is in five stanzas. The four-stanza version, which appeared two years after the original, is the one we know from the 1994 film *Four Weddings and a Funeral*. The original five-stanza version was a parody of a political poem of mourning, and is actually part of a verse play entitled *The Ascent of F6*, written by W H Auden and Christopher Isherwood in 1936.

The later version was written to be sung by the soprano Hedli Anderson in a setting by Benjamin Britten. The original and this version share the first and second stanzas, but the endings are entirely different. The later one appeared in *The Year's Poetry, 1938*, an anthology compiled by Denys Kilham Roberts and Geoffrey Grigson in 1938. Auden included this version in his 1940 book of poetry, *Another Time*, as one of four poems headed Four

Cabaret Songs for Miss Hedli Anderson. The poem itself was actually entitled 'Funeral Blues'. Auden never used any other title for the work.

MANCHESTER UNIVERSITY
IS NOT A RED-BRICK UNIVERSITY

Most of us would accept the definition of a red-brick university as being one of the six founded in the industrial cities of England in the late-Victorian and Edwardian periods: namely Birmingham, Liverpool, Leeds, Sheffield, Bristol and the first of them, Manchester. The only problem is that Manchester University wasn't created until 2004. The history of higher education in Cottonopolis, as it was once nicknamed, is far from simple.

The origins of the august institution which is now the university are in Owens College, which was founded using a textile magnate's bequest in 1851. (I'm afraid at this point, as an alumnus of the University of Manchester Institute of Science and Technology (UMIST), I must point out that 'Owens' was used for years by students at my alma mater as a derogatory term for the main university down the road. This is because UMIST is actually older. We started as the Mechanics Institute in 1824, and

only linked into the main university as its faculty of technology in 1905, under the name of the Municipal College of Technology. But more self-indulgent point-scoring later.)

With the growth of the great industrial cities in the latter half of the nineteenth century, it became apparent that their centres of learning needed to be given a bit of a leg-up; Oxford, Cambridge, Durham and London were just not in the right locations for their vast and growing populations. So in 1880 a new university was founded 'for the north of England' in Manchester, and like a lot of large projects at the time was named after the Queen. Calling it after the city was avoided partly because it was established as a federal university with the hope that other colleges in northern England would get involved.

Owens joined immediately, University College in Liverpool in 1884, and Yorkshire College in Leeds three years after that. However, by 1904 Liverpool and Leeds both had independent university status, so an act of parliament amalgamated the remaining Manchester-based parts into the Victoria University of Manchester. The College of Technology remained financially independent, and although still the technology faculty of Victoria University achieved university status with its own chancellor and vice chancellor in the 1950s, changed its name to UMIST in 1966, and awarded Victoria University degrees until full independence in 1993. Only when these two universities amalgamated in 2004 could it be said that, perhaps at last, there was a University of Manchester.

YORKSHIRE WASN'T HISTORICALLY DIVIDED INTO JUST THREE RIDINGS

A lthough now much changed since the redrawing of political boundaries undertaken on our behalf by the Tory government of the early 1970s, it's pretty well accepted that Yorkshire used to be in three parts, namely the North, West and East Ridings. As the term riding is derived from an Old English word meaning a third, they had to do with only three of the four cardinal points, and south missed out. However, historically Yorkshire was divided politically into five parts, and this does not take into account all the self-determining boroughs that mushroomed during the industrialisation of the Pennine valleys and the growing ports in the nineteenth century forced by localised increases in population. So where were the missing two divisions?

One was the city after which the county was named, York. Founded

in AD 71 by the Romans (and probably occupied by the Brigantes before that) York has always stood alone, and was never incorporated into the Ridings system. A comparatively large and important urban area in both the Dark Ages and medieval period, it needed to guarantee its food supply. So here we have the other, lying to the west of the city, the Wapentake[1] of Ainsty. This was a collection of thirty-five villages bounded by the Nidd, the Wharfe and York's major river, the Ouse. Annexed to York for 440 years as a bread basket and hinterland for the kingdom's second city, it was not formally included in any of the Ridings until 1889. For the sake of convenience, over the years it was sometimes lumped in with either the East Riding or its more natural neighbour the West, but, a little like Berwick-upon-Tweed, nobody actually bothered to put the definitive tin lid on the issue until 1888, when it was finally and formally decided that it would join the West Riding by act of parliament the following year.

IS THE 'FOUR YORKSHIREMEN' THE FUNNIEST *MONTY PYTHON* SKETCH?

If you think it is you're mistaken, and this is nothing to do with me forcing my opinions on you. If you are a fan of the 'Lumberjack Song' or the demise of 'The Norwegian Blue Parrot' or the madness of 'Whicker's Island' then you might feel justified in arguing your point. However, the 'Four Yorkshiremen' isn't a sketch from *Monty Python's Flying Circus*. It was in fact first performed on television a couple of years before *Monty Python* burst on to our screens in 1969, as a sketch on the more obscure comedy *At Last the 1948 Show*, by the show's writers, who included two later Pythons, John Cleese and Graham Chapman, but intriguingly also Tim Brooke-Taylor and Marty Feldman.

1   Wapentakes were divisions of the area of England under Danish rule in the Dark Ages. These later became administrative sub-divisions within the county system. They are the equivalent of the hundreds (such as the Chiltern Hundreds of parliamentary fame) in those areas that remained under Anglo-Saxon control.

WHIP-MA-WHOP-MA-GATE
AND THE PILLORY

I'd be interested to know why some streets end up with such strange names. Hull has The Land of Green Ginger. London has its fair share, including Little Britain. Glasgow has Dobbie's Loan. I'm sure everyone knows a couple close to home, but it's one in York I'm interested in here, Whip-Ma-Whop-Ma-Gate.

There are two theories often attached to the origin of this fantastic name, but neither of them is correct, and there is also some debate as to where the street actually is. Its road sign is fixed to a low wall to the rear of St Crux church facing onto where Colliergate opens out into a wider space, so many take this as the correct location. Others point to the fact that the only dwelling, now numbered 1½ for the benefit of the modern tourist, is actually in a tiny almost alley-like thoroughfare connecting with the bottom of The Shambles, the historical street of the butchers. Some have it connecting with Stonebow and a street with the contradictory name of Pavement. It really is a corner for strange names.

The theory I grew up with is that it is where the city's medieval stocks or pillory was located, and a lot of whipping went on around there. One I heard some time later which also made sense is that, as it was next to a street full of butchers, it was where the livestock driven into the city from the countryside were whipped into pens just prior to slaughter. But all one has to do is read the sign kindly put up on the wall of St Crux by the York Civic Trust. It reads, 'WHIP-MA-WHOP-MA-GATE The Shortest Street in York. Known in 1505 as Whitnourwhatnourgate (and meaning 'What a street!') it was changed later into its present name. The footpath was paved in York stone by the York Civic Trust in 1985.' There is evidence that the Tudor name derived from the Anglo-Saxon *whit nour what nour*, which meant something along the lines of 'neither one thing nor the other'.

So there you are – nothing more than a modern rendition of a name from 500 years ago. There is no suggestion in the etymology that it has anything to do with whips in any shape or form, although I do apologise that I leave you with a puzzle. Just what was it about the place that made the Tudor residents of York and their Anglo-Saxon antecedents unable to decide what it was?

DICK TURPIN WAS NOT
SUCH A BRILLIANT HORSEMAN

———— ✠✠✠ ————

We all know the legend of the dashing highwayman Dick Turpin and his trusty horse Black Bess, who died of exhaustion after carrying her master to York in one 200-mile gallop, gaining him an alibi for a crime committed in London. By Turpin playing bowls with the lord mayor of York the day after the crime was committed, he obviously took himself out of the frame. Not so. Step forward William Harrison Ainsworth, a Victorian story writer who featured Turpin as a character in his hugely successful novel *Rookwood*. It's within the pages of this book that the legend that had grown up around Dick Turpin was set in stone.

Like most legends, there are elements of truth in the story. Turpin was involved with horses at the start of his criminal career, but as a horse thief, the activity for which he was ultimately hung. The evidence is that he followed his father into both butchery and inn keeping as a youth, but spent most of the first half of the 1730s in an Essex gang who, apart from stealing horses, poached deer and committed armed burglary. It was only after the capture of the majority of the gang in 1735 that he tried his hand at highway robbery, but this only lasted for a short time, and he then dropped out of public view.

When he resurfaced, he felt it advisable to travel north after a brief and messy period that ended with a murder, settling in the Humberside area under the alias of John Palmer. So his journey up-country was almost certainly taken at a far more leisurely pace than the legend would have us believe. Although posing as a trader, he was suspected of being a horse thief, was arrested, and as he was in the East Riding of Yorkshire at the

THE 7

TRIAL
Of the Notorious Highwayman
𝕽𝖎𝖈𝖍𝖆𝖗𝖉 𝕿𝖚𝖗𝖕𝖎𝖓,

At *York* Aſſizes, on the 22d Day of *March*, 1739, before the Hon. Sir WILLIAM CHAPPLE, Knt. Judge of Aſſize, and one of His Majeſty's Juſtices of the Court of *King's Bench.*

Taken down in Court by Mr. THOMAS KYLL, Profeſſor of Short-Hand.

To which is prefix'd,

An exact Account of the ſaid *Turpin*, from his firſt coming into *Yorkſhire*, to the Time of his being committed Priſoner to *York* Caſtle; communicated by Mr. APPLETON of *Beverley*, Clerk of the Peace for the *Eaſt-Riding* of the ſaid County.

With a Copy of a Letter which *Turpin* received form his Father, while under Sentence of Death.

To which is added,

His Behaviour at the Place of Execution, on *Saturday* the 7th of *April*, 1739. Together with the whole Confeſſion he made to the Hangman at the Gallows; wherein he acknowledg'd himſelf guilty of the Facts for which he ſuffer'd, own'd the Murder of Mr. *Thompſon's* Servant on *Epping-Foreſt*, and gave a particular Account of ſeveral Robberies which he had committed.

The SECOND EDITION.,

Y O R K :

Printed by WARD and CHANDLER Bookſellers, at their Printing-Office in *Coney-Street* ; and Sold at their Shop without *Temple-Bar, London* ; 1739. (Price Sixpence.)

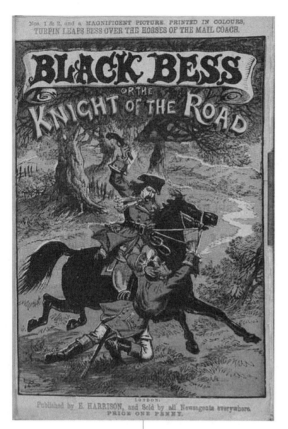

Nos. 1 & 2, and a MAGNIFICENT PICTURE, PRINTED IN COLOURS,
TURPIN LEAPS BESS OVER THE HORSES OF THE MAIL COACH.

BLACK BESS
OR THE
KNIGHT OF THE ROAD

LONDON:
Published by E. HARRISON, and Sold by all Newsagents everywhere.
PRICE ONE PENNY.

time, was taken to the county assizes, That is how he ended up in a cell at York castle. So, contrary to the legend, he didn't ride to York, but arrived there in handcuffs already charged with a crime.

Turpin's fate was sealed when he revealed his true identity in a letter to his brother-in-law while in custody, and he was hung on the aptly name Knavesmire in 1739. There is a gravestone in the churchyard of St George's that is reputed to mark his resting place, but like most things to do with this man, this is supposition or legend. The stories began immediately in the partly fictional *The Genuine History of the Life of Richard Turpin* released by Richard Bayes straight after the trial, and grew from there, with embellishments added throughout the eighteenth century until the legend was finally and comprehensively established by *Rookwood*.

Intriguingly, Ainsworth seems to have stolen the idea of Turpin's overnight journey from London on Black Bess from Daniel Defoe's account of an alleged episode in the life of Yorkshireman William Nevison (or John Nevison as he was also known) from 1676. Fleeing from Kent in the summer of that year after a bungled robbery near Rochester in which he was recognised, he caught a ferry to Essex, raced north on horseback in one overnight ride, met the lord mayor of York, and played him at bowls. When arrested and tried for the Kent robbery, the alderman supported his alibi, and amazingly Nevison got off. However, as we all know, criminals always get their comeuppance. Later in 1676 he was arrested for another crime and was transported to Tangier for five years. On his return, he couldn't help taking up highway robbery again, and in 1684 was hung, as Turpin was to be over fifty years later, in York, in Nevison's case for the murder of a constable near Wakefield.

HAVING A NIGHTMARE

——— 🙙🙚 ———

We presume that this has something to do with horses because a mare is of course a female horse. Although not the case, interestingly the term does derive from associations with the female sex. Just as in the north of England and Scotland especially, there are many streets that confusingly end with -gate because the old Nordic term for a street was *gata*, thus the word mare in this sense derives from *mara*, a word for a female spirit or monster that settles on a sleeping figure, producing a feeling of suffocation.

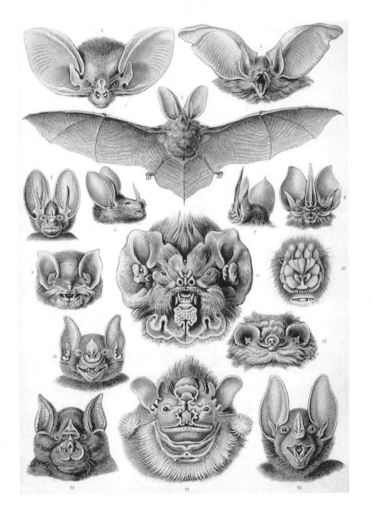

YE OLDE TRIP TO JERUSALEM

This famous pub is built hard by the rock on which Nottingham Castle sits. It is often celebrated as the oldest known continuously used public house in Britain. We read on its whitewashed outer walls it is the 'oldest inn in England', and its date of foundation is claimed as 1189. This is a significant date, as it is the year that famous crusader to the Holy Land Richard the Lionheart was crowned. By then he had already taken the Cross and was well on with his plans to sail. Could it be that this pub, if not the place he planned or even started his 'trip to Jerusalem', is named after the event?

I'm afraid we are going to have to deconstruct this romantic notion. The pub is only one of twenty that lays claim to be the oldest in England; indeed, there are two others in Nottingham itself that claim this title. The current building only dates back around 300 years, and although I accept it is built on older foundations, the Bingley Arms just to the north of Leeds can trace a proven history dating back to 953, with evidence suggesting it could date to 905, so I can't see the Trip winning that battle. Actually I think the pub has missed a trick by seemingly picking 1189 because of its link with the crusades. This is because the pub is also famous for its caves, which are carved out of the sandstone beneath the castle, the larger ones now being used as its rear rooms. There is also a network of caves beneath

the building that has been used as a brewery. As these seem to date from around the time of the known foundation of the castle in 1068, an alcoholic connection could have been easily made to this earlier date.

There is another popular error with regard to this hostelry, one based on modern English usage differing from the language of our forefathers. The word trip as used in the pub's name does not mean an entire journey. An older meaning of the word fits in far more sensibly with the purpose of the place. In this sense it meant a stop or a place of rest during a journey. Now that seems a far better idea.

The pub is only one of twenty that lays claim to be the oldest in England; indeed, there are two others in Nottingham itself that claim this title.

ROBIN HOOD – HALLAMSHIRE MAN!

A few years ago the good burghers of South Yorkshire caused a great deal of unrest among their equivalent city fathers in Nottingham, some thirtyish miles to the south. What foul calumny could they have committed to cause such outrage? Simple – they had named the newly improved Doncaster Sheffield Airport after Robin Hood. Whether or not he existed is of no consequence here. There is nothing more likely to arouse feelings in the hearts of true Nottingham men against other cities and towns than them claiming the legend of Robin Hood as their own. The evidence is there to rebuff anyone getting in on their act: Robin Hood's rival was the sheriff of Nottingham and modern Sherwood Forest lies close to the north of the city – QED.

Now, without getting into an endless debate as to whether Robin Hood was around at the time of Richard the Lionheart, or whether he was based on a real person who was possibly a nobleman, or why Maid Marian and Friar Tuck didn't appear in the earliest ballads about our outlaw hero, is there any justification in a bunch of modern-day Yorkshiremen muscling in on Nottingham's glory? As you might have expected when you started reading this, the answer is yes.

The early ballads do have him stirring things up in Nottinghamshire, especially in Sherwood Forest. Scholars will point however to the overall picture that comes from the surviving early ballads and rhymes, which suggests that he may have been based in the Barnsdale area. Barnsdale Forest is to the north of Doncaster in the historical West Riding of Yorkshire.

Another tradition dating back at least to the end of the sixteenth century gives Loxley (as in the numerous references to his supposed noble title, Robin of Loxley) as his birthplace. Loxley is a village that is now a suburb of Sheffield. Finally, his grave is claimed to be at Kirklees Priory near Mirfield . . . in Yorkshire.

So I can see why those in Sheffield and Doncaster felt quite justified in naming their shiny new airport after him. In addition, the geography of the adjacent counties in both medieval and modern times, as well as the political and economic set-ups, may point to Robin Hood's area of operations being a little away from the *city* of Nottingham. Let me explain. The city of Nottingham sits in the very south of the historic Nottinghamshire, which stretches northwards for thirty or so miles to the very edges of Sheffield. In modern times the northern part of Nottinghamshire, containing numerous industrial towns sitting on what was a major coalfield, has become quite different from the south. Coal mining, a giant industry by the Victorian era, was already beginning in a small way in the Middle Ages. A number of these industrial towns have always looked to Sheffield and the Hallamshire district in general as reflecting their landscape and life, not their county's capital to the south. Many are now in the Sheffield commuter belt. Indeed I speak from first-hand experience when I say that there is little love for Nottingham city among the citizens of the north of the county. Quite the opposite it seemed to me from the strong language contained in the opinions I heard expressed. It even extends to people from Newark, such as a close friend of mine, choosing to support Lincoln City FC rather than either of the teams in Nottingham.

We should also remember that the word sheriff is a contraction of shire reeve, the royal official responsible for keeping the peace throughout a shire or county on behalf of the king. Thus the sheriff of Nottingham's remit would extend over the entire county, not just the city. I would add to this the claim that at one stage Britain was once so heavily wooded that it was possible to pass from one coast to the opposite sea without having to descend from the trees. Even if there is only a thread of truth in this, it is highly likely that the remaining 423 hectares of Sherwood Forest around Edwinstowe are but a remnant of a royal hunting ground, the Shire Wood, which was so vast it would have stretched into neighbouring counties.

So may I suggest a compromise? Let us suggest to the warring factions that it was quite possible for Robin Hood to have operated in Sherwood Forest in Nottingham's northern, and Yorkshire's southern, borderlands, and for the jurisdiction of the sheriff to be very much active so far from the city which gave his office its name.

The city of Nottingham sits in the very south of historic Nottinghamshire.

CHESTER RACECOURSE

Chester's Racecourse, the 'Roodee', is a beautiful spot near the banks of the Dee within view of the city's walls. As there is evidence that racing took place there as long ago as the early sixteenth century, it is generally claimed that it is the oldest racecourse in the country. However, for this claim to hold water it requires the inclusion of 'continuously used'. This

is because there is also evidence that the scene of Dick Turpin's demise, the Knavesmire, was used by the occupying Romans to race horses, and as they arrived in AD 71 and left in the fifth century, that's about a thousand years ahead of Chester. I look forward to someone telling me the Druids raced horses at Cheltenham.

I'LL SWING FOR YOU . . .

A phrase often directed at me by my mother when I was younger, I took it to mean that if I was to be thoughtless enough to wander into her reach, then I would be the recipient of a well-aimed smack around the head as the result of her taking a swing at me. Before you condemn my mother as wicked let me reassure you that such a blow would have always been deserved, and indeed was regarded by me as mild retribution for some of the more serious domestic crimes I was capable of committing.

I was later to learn that there was a less direct but far grimmer origin for the phrase. Effectively what she was saying was that she was so angry she was capable of committing a capital crime on my person, and was willing to take the judicial consequences to the extent of going to the scaffold. *Collins Dictionary of Slang* dates this usage and meaning to the 1800s.

Recently it has also been suggested to me that the phrase can be reversed in part of its meaning, and I can see no reason to contradict this alternative. The phrase might also be used in the sense that a person is so besotted with another they would kill for their sake, and is prepared to be hanged as a result. In other words, a sort of older equivalent of the more modern 'I'd take a bullet for you'.

DICK WHITTINGTON

—❦❧—

As we think the pantomime must be based to some degree on truth, we tend to believe that a poor servant, thinking the streets of London are paved with gold, arrives there, buys a cat for a penny and sells it for a fortune, and ends up lord mayor and knighted. Many locations up and down England claim him as one of their own, and Highgate Hill has a statue of his cat to mark the spot where Dick hears Bow Bells telling him not to go back to the countryside and to try his luck in the capital again. The truth is that there was a Richard Whittington, who is recorded as being lord mayor of London in 1397/8, 1406/7 and 1419/20. Quite an important man then but as far as we know never knighted.

The evidence points to Dick being the reasonably well-off son of Sir William Whittington of Gloucestershire and his wife, the daughter of the sheriff of Gloucester. He improved on this reasonable start by using his business sense to become a successful textile trader or mercer, and by lending money to Henry V, who required finance for his wars in France. He comes across in the pantomime as being a nice fellow, and this part should be believed as among his charitable donations he helped rebuild Newgate Prison and Bart's (St Bartholemews's Hospital).

THE NOT-SO RIGHT HONOURABLE
LORD MAYOR OF BRISTOL

—❦❧—

Civic dignity is at stake here, so I'll tread carefully. It seems a reasonable supposition that if a town is made a city, then the mayor automatically becomes the lord mayor (or in the case of Scotland, lord provost). In actuality, the title of lord mayor or lord provost is a dignity that in modern times is granted separately from city status and by letters patent, and is less

common than city status. There are currently twenty-three lord mayors in England and Wales, only three of which (London, York and Bristol) are styled with the title Right Honourable rather than the supposedly less dignified Right Worshipful.

London and York were already using 'Right Honourable' by the 1600s. A lot more lord mayors were then created in the 1890s to reflect the growing status and size of the new industrial conurbations. However, it wasn't clear if these new lord mayors could simply start calling themselves 'Honourable'.

The trouble started when the Garter Principal King of Arms at the time thought the newly created lord mayors of Liverpool and Manchester should become 'Right Honourable's. The lord mayor of Bristol quietly adopted the title at about the same time. Ten years later the next king of arms decided that a mistake had been made. The lord mayors of Liverpool, Manchester (and Bristol) simply ignored him and continued to use the prefix. The matter came to a head in 1921 when the King visited Liverpool. To avoid any potential embarrassment the government felt it necessary to write to the city council to outline that as the lord mayor didn't have George V's express permission to call himself 'Right Honourable', he couldn't use it. Leading Lancashire citizens were miffed, especially seeing that the honorific had been formally granted to the lord provost of Glasgow in 1912 to give him equal status with the lord provost of Edinburgh, and the lord mayor of Belfast was also so honoured in 1923. When a professor at Liverpool University, the MP Herbert Woodcock and the entire Corporation of Manchester demanded the dignity to be applied to all lord mayors, the home secretary replied thus in 1932:

> The only Lord Mayors and Provosts in the United Kingdom who are entitled to be styled 'Right Honourable' are the Lord Mayors of London and York and the Lord Provost of Edinburgh, who have had the privilege from time immemorial, and the Lord Provost of Glasgow and the Lord Mayor of Belfast on whom it has been conferred by grant in modern times. If it has been used in other cases, this has been done through a misunderstanding and without authority; and whenever the attention of myself or of my predecessors has been called to such unauthorised use, or enquiries on the subject have been made, it has always

been pointed out that the style could not be used without His Majesty's permission.

The number of lord mayors and provosts allowed to refer to themselves as 'Right Honourable' now numbers six; Cardiff was included when the city was declared capital of Wales in 1956. To this day, the lord mayor of Bristol continues to ignore the rules.

ORDER IN COURT!

It was that wonderful broadcaster Marcel Berlins that put me on to this common misconception. I read a rather good article by him in which he paid tribute to a recent drama about the pioneering barrister William Garrow, who is credited with the creation of modern cross-examination. Understanding him to be not a little controversial, the dramatist created many scenes where Garrow tries the patience of the judge and those present in court, resulting in various degrees of uproar. The judge then responds to these disturbances by calling for order and banging his wooden gavel furiously to mark his authority.

And there's the problem. English judges don't use gavels, nor have they ever done so. I'm afraid that in attempting to heighten the drama of court scenes, British TV dramatists, producers and directors quite often import a little bit of the USA.

WHY GOING TO THE SMALL CLAIMS COURT IS A BAD IDEA

—— ❧ ❧ ——

So the builder you hired has left the job half done, isn't answering your calls, and you are getting increasingly frustrated. You've bought a CD player that doesn't work, but the shop refuses to take it back and refund your money. While you were away on holiday your neighbour organised for the council to come and cut down a lovely tree that happens to be on your property. No problem. You will take them all to the Small Claims Court.

The only trouble is it doesn't exist. To paraphrase the government's website, when people talk about the Small Claims Court, what they really mean is the special procedure by which one can pursue a smaller claim through the county court system.

. . . ALLEGEDLY

—— ❧ ❧ ——

Contrary to its overuse on a whole raft of light-hearted news shows on television and radio, adding the word allegedly to the end of a slanderous statement does not negate the slander. This is just not a defence that can be used in law. If it could, it would be easy to make the most extreme and damaging comments about a person without having to take any regard of the consequences.

The reason a show host or panellist is not taken to court by the subject of their comic barbs is either that what is said is actually true, or that they fear they would look foolish by pursuing the case.

CAN THE POLICE TRAVEL
IN FIRST CLASS FOR FREE?

———— ❧❦❧ ————

I saw a postman get onto a one-man bus after his morning shift the other day. Quite rightly, I suppose, as a public servant who had probably spent the last few hours in the rain (falling heavily at the time), he didn't pay the driver but just found a seat. His uniform was his fare. This reminded me that I'd recently been informed by a friend that throughout the UK policemen had a long-standing right to travel first class on the railways for free. Delving into this question when I got home, I found this wasn't the case at all.

The right to travel free does exist for some police officers, but it is purely down to arrangements between the local force and the train company. The right to first-class travel is not enshrined in any schemes I've come across. Among the many agreements, official and unofficial, the most extensive is for Metropolitan Police officers, who thanks to an agreement with the railway companies can travel free up to seventy miles from London. This extended an existing scheme for officers travelling free on London Underground and London buses, and was introduced to combat a recruitment and retention problem exacerbated by the high cost of living in the capital after the government took away the police housing allowance. This is the real reason for the scheme, not, as is widely believed, that an officer, either on or off duty, is expected to use his powers as a constable to combat the perceived increase in violent conduct on public transport and attacks on staff.

So, however annoying or admirable you think such arrangements are, the right to travel for free by rail does exist for some officers. I'm also convinced that some officers flash their warrant cards at railway staff in first-class compartments. It's then up to the individual railway staff member to decide if they should take a leaf out of 'Dirty Harry' Callaghan's book and face down the cheeky traveller with the question, 'Do you feel lucky?'

IS BRITAIN'S BUSIEST RAILWAY STATION
IN CLAPHAM?

— ⚜ ⚜ —

**SURREY
Iron Railway.**

The COMMITTEE of the SURREY
IRON RAILWAY COMPANY,

HEREBY, GIVE NOTICE, That the BASON at
Wandsworth, and the Railway therefrom up to *Croydon*
and *Carshalton*, is now open for the Use of the Public,
on Payment of the following Tolls, &c.

For all Coals entering into or going out of their Bason at Wandsworth,	*per Chaldron*,	3d.
For all other Goods entering into or going out of their Bason at Wandsworth	*per Ton*,	3d.

For all GOODS, carried on the said
RAILWAY, as follows, viz.

For Dung,	*per Ton, per Mile*,	1d.
For Lime, and all Manures, (except Dung,) Lime-stone, Chalk, Clay, Breeze, Ashes, Sand, Bricks, Stone, Flints, and Fuller's Earth,	*per Ton, per Mile*,	2d.
For Coals,	*per Chald. per Mile*,	3d.
And, For all other Goods,	*per Ton, per Mile*,	3d.

By ORDER of the COMMITTEE.
W. B. LUTTLY,
Clerk of the Company.

Wandsworth, June 1, 1804.

Clapham Junction railway station deals with more than one hundred trains an hour outside peak times, as the conduit for services from both Waterloo and Victoria to and from all points south. Therefore, as one of the busiest stations in Europe – at least using number of trains passing through as the benchmark – it can justifiably be claimed as the busiest in the UK.

Pride in this fact among the people in Clapham might be regarded as a little misplaced, however, as the station isn't there. Clapham is in the borough of Lambeth and covers the postcode sw4, as well as parts of sw8, sw9, sw11 and sw12. Clapham Junction station is in sw11 but in the borough of Wandsworth.

LLOYD'S OF LONDON IS THE WORLD'S
BIGGEST INSURANCE COMPANY

— ⚜ ⚜ —

Any analysis of this claim is pretty pointless as Lloyd's isn't a company. It is a market where an association of individuals (the famous 'names') and companies offering financial backing and underwriting come together to insure and reinsure risks. It may compete with insurance companies but was incorporated as a society by an act of parliament in 1871. To say there's such a thing as a Lloyd's policy is like saying the Stock Exchange sells stock.

THERE ISN'T A NOBEL PRIZE FOR ECONOMICS

———— ❦ ————

Nobel Prizes were first awarded in 1901 in five categories. Since 1969 the Sveriges Riksbank has awarded an internationally renowned prize in economic sciences in memory of Alfred Nobel. It is announced annually along with the prizes in physics, chemistry, physiology or medicine, literature and peace. It is awarded along with the others at the annual Nobel Prize award ceremony.

Technically, it's not a Nobel Prize like the other five, as it wasn't established by Nobel but rather in his memory, but who am I to take anything away from any of these great achievers?

WHY DO SOME TOWNS CALL THEMSELVES CITIES WHEN THEY DON'T HAVE A CATHEDRAL?

———— ❦ ————

There is a traditional belief that the presence of a cathedral means a town is in fact a city. This sometimes incorporates the idea that it has to be a diocesan cathedral. It follows that the reverse is also the rule: that a town without a cathedral cannot call itself a city. Now, although this was the traditional and commonly used criterion in the past, there are no actual pre-requirements for a conurbation to be created a city. It becomes a city when it is granted that status by a reigning monarch, and that's all that's needed. The traditional belief seems to have grown out of Henry VIII creating six new diocesan cathedrals in 1540 during the establishing of the Church of England, and making their locations cities at the same time. Even the *Encyclopaedia Britannica* fell into the trap in the early twentieth century, wrongly elevating the towns of Southwell and St Asaph to city status.[1]

1   Around the same time, in 1898 in fact, Sir Ebenezer Howard founded the Garden City Movement in Britain, which represented a new approach to town planning. In 1903 Letchworth Garden City was founded in Hertfordshire. This was followed in the 1920s

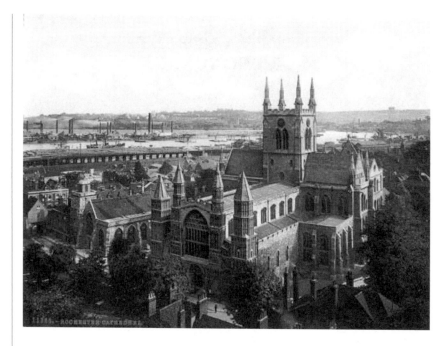

The unwritten rule on the need for a cathedral was well and truly ignored in 1889, when Birmingham successfully applied for city status based on the size of its population and the fact it had governed itself well for a good number of years. The parish church did become a cathedral in 1905, but sixteen years after its parish had become a city. The large county boroughs of Bradford, Kingston-upon-Hull and Nottingham followed a similar course in Victoria's diamond jubilee year. On the other hand there is the case of Guildford, which although having a diocesan cathedral and despite applying on numerous occasions still has not achieved city status. Surrey is actually a county with no cities in it at all. The town of Rochester in Kent had city status until 1998, when it was accidentally stripped of this under government reorganisation. By the time Medway Council noticed this in 2002, it was too late. Like Guildford, the town has now begun petitioning for city status, in this case for reinstatement of something it once had.

---

by Welwyn Garden City, in the same county. At no stage does it seem that by including City in the names of these two settlements there was an attempt to presume city status. Although nowadays Letchworth generally ignores the latter part of its original title, anyone passing through its station on the East Coast railway line can clearly see that Welwyn Garden City has retained its full original name.

Although Edward VII and his government tried to lay down three criteria – a minimum population of 300,000, a 'local metropolitan character' and a good record of local government – there was no requirement for a cathedral. Actually, Edward VII's rules have been ignored on numerous occasions and for various reasons since, so don't really have any bearing anyway. The modern criteria appear in a memorandum issued in 1927 by the Home Office.

> If a town wishes to obtain the title of a city the proper method
> of procedure is to address a petition to the King through the
> Home Office. It is the duty of the Home Secretary to submit
> such petitions to his Majesty and to advise his Majesty to the
> reply to be returned. It is a well-established principle that the
> grant of the title is only recommended in the case of towns of
> the first rank in population, size and importance, and having a
> distinctive character and identity of their own. At the present
> day, therefore, it is only rarely and in exceptional circumstances
> that the title is given.

In fact, a town can now apply to the lord chancellor, who then makes recommendations to the sovereign. City status is granted on special national occasions, such as coronations, royal jubilees, or recently the Millennium.

LONDON AND NEW YORK ARE ON THE SAME LATITUDE

I've been blessed with a good sense of geography and an ability to read maps, so I'm always surprised when I hear this old chestnut. It is quite astonishing how many people on both sides of the Atlantic believe if you want to travel from one city to the other then it is only a matter of travelling due east or due west.

The latitude for London is 51 degrees 32 minutes north, and that of New York 40 degrees and 47 minutes – a difference of more than ten degrees of latitude. London is actually further north than most of the major cities of Canada; New York is just a little to the south of Barcelona. Alas for New

It is quite astonishing how many people on both sides of the Atlantic believe if you want to travel from one city to the other then it is only a matter of travelling due east or due west.

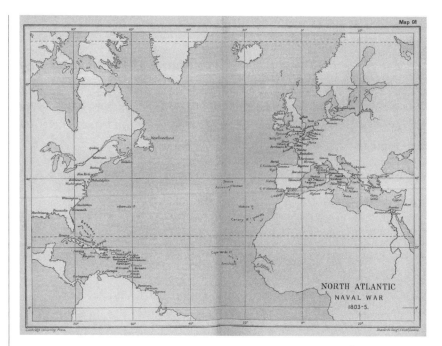

Yorkers but luckily for Londoners, because of the forces of nature and their effect on the weather, neither of these cities shares a climate with its transatlantic counterparts on the same degree of latitude.

THE SHORTEST DISTANCE
BETWEEN TWO POINTS ISN'T ALWAYS
A STRAIGHT LINE

All right, all right, Euclidian geometry is quite clear on the matter: the shortest distance between two points is a straight line. However, I would argue that, like most things mathematical, geometry's logic comes from the fact it exists neatly within its own limited and somewhat exclusive definitions. Life is actually a little bit more flexible and uncertain for the majority of us on a day-to-day basis.

The captains of transtlantic planes and ships have another idea. These navigators would say that a straight line is not the shortest distance between two points on the east and west shores of the ocean. When seen on a map, the line they travel is actually curved – it looks like a segment of a circle.

This 'great circle route' looks like this because map are two-dimensional – flat representations of the three-dimensional earth. Actually, if the route was marked by a wire stretched over the waves and you were viewing it from above then it would be a straight line, but then again you could argue that a truly straight line would actually go under the seabed and the water above it. It is a matter of the parameters of definition.

The above explanation doesn't follow Einsteinian physics. According to the great man, if using the terms of his theories a straight line will ultimately meet itself. But please don't ask me to explain that here.

THE TOWER OF LONDON AND RUDOLPH HESS, AND RONNIE AND REGGIE

The standard belief is that Rudolph Hess (Heß in German), following his rather bizarre flight to Britain in 1941 at the height of the Second World War, was thrown into the Tower and thus became the last prisoner to be held there. This seems a little strange perhaps, the Tower being associated with figures from medieval and Tudor history rather than Nazis. Hess wasn't however the last in a line including among many others John Balliol, Sir Thomas More, Sir Walter Raleigh and Guy Fawkes; in fact other German prisoners were held there throughout the Second World War. I suppose it might be right to say that because of his importance as the deputy leader of his country, Hess was the last prisoner *of the state* to be held there.

So who was or were the last? Students of the London underworld are keen to point out an incident that occurred in 1952. Twins Ronnie and Reggie Kray had decided they couldn't be bothered to report for national service. Once arrested, they were held for a few days in the Tower, eleven years after Hess, the fortress being used in part as a military prison. The frustrating thing is that it cannot be said with any certainty that these celebrity criminals were the last either. Even the Historic Royal Palaces site tells

us it was Hess, despite evidence of the Krays' temporary incarceration. So for once I have to tell you that although the deputy to the Führer can be disregarded, I cannot offer the name of the real holder of the accolade.

GET CARTER IS A STORY SET IN AND AROUND NEWCASTLE

The 1971 film called *Get Carter* is set there, that is without doubt, so I'm not trying to be clever by saying I'm referring to the 2000 remake, which takes the action to Las Vegas. I'm actually referring to the novel on which the film is based.

The power and the quality of the film reflect the fact that at that time Newcastle was the perfect place to shoot it. The local council was seen as visionary, with the old city being bulldozed to allow a bright new tomorrow to take its place. There was a lot of money and even glamour associated with the north-east of England. Where better for Michael Caine to give one of his most powerful performances?

The film's producers remained very true to Ted Lewis's marvellous story from the original book, but if they had remained true to the original location, all that glamour, corruption and cash would have been swimming around . . . Scunthorpe. In *Jack's Return Home* the ruthless, even amoral London hard man goes back to his hometown 'somewhere near Doncaster'. Although not named specifically, it's a steel town, so Scunthorpe is the primary candidate for the book's setting.

Actually I might be wrong thinking that swapping the location was unfair on the citizens of the north Lincolnshire town. They might now have a thriving tourist industry – like those of Whitby, thanks to *Dracula*, and Thirsk because of *All Creatures Great and Small* – but it's surely a good thing their town isn't forever associated with an underworld of snooker halls, massage parlours and teenage pornography.

ST TRINIAN'S . . . AND THOSE GIRLS' PINAFORES

E ven in the recent modern episodes added to the four original St Trinian's films of the 1950s and '60s, the senior girls at the school look a lot different to the pupils of the lower school. Not for them the pigtails, thick socks, crushed boaters and voluminous pinafore dresses of the junior oiks; they are sexy, short-skirted and be-stockinged. The film-makers might have played on the well-worn and clichéd image of the 'knowing' schoolgirl, but actually the contrast is founded in practical reality.

At many girls' private schools in the post-war years, the pupils (please don't ask me to call them students) were from families living with the deprivations and shortages caused by the recent conflict. Their daughters still needed educating, but corners could be cut when kitting them out. New girls arrived at the school gates on their first day in oversized pinafores into which they would grow. By their third or fourth year, the same dresses now actually just about fitted. By the time they got into senior school, they were inadequate to cover their blossoming womanhood. So it was less to with make-up, and more to do with make do and mend.

NYLON = N(EW) Y(ORK) + LON(DON)

W hat a wonderful, adaptable invention nylon is. It was first used commercially for the bristles of toothbrushes. In another form, it soon became the means by which many a US serviceman stationed in Britain during the Second World War (or, as the Americans would have said, World War Two) gained the favours of the young ladies of these islands. So what a wonderful coincidence that it was named after two of our great cities.

If only it was true. A statement from DuPont, the company where nylon was created, stated as early as 1940 (five years after its invention) that the name of Wallace Carothers' creation came from the arbitrary use of 'nyl', to which was added the fabric-sounding suffix -on, as in cotton or rayon. Probably more accurate is the story that they actually wanted to call it No-Run but thought better of what was an unjustifiable claim, then played about with letters until they reached 'nylon'. So the idea that it was named after New York and London is as unfounded as the story that it represented the initial letters of the patriotic 'Now You've Lost, Old Nippon,' referring to the resulting decline in the need for silk from Japan.

DIAMOND ISN'T THE HARDEST NATURAL SUBSTANCE

I sense a sharp intake of breath over this claim. For years we have regarded the diamond as such a rare and extraordinary thing, something so beautiful it can be worn as jewellery but so useful it can be used to cut through rock and steel like butter because it is the hardest thing known to man.

I can remember a photograph in a copy of *The Guinness Book of Records* I was given forty years ago showing a diamond being scored by the element boron. This seemed to stick in my mind at the time as proof of the superiority of boron, but I will look into that and report back to you in the future. Without doubt though we are now aware of a natural substance that is harder than diamond, and this is a substance called lonsdaleite. It is an allotrope of carbon just like diamond and graphite, but has a different structure. It is sometimes called, because of its closeness to the former

champion, the hexagonal diamond. It forms when meteorites that contain graphite fall to earth. Huge heat and stress on impact transforms the graphite into diamond but – here's the interesting bit – it retains graphite's hexagonal crystal lattice structure. It was identified for the first time in 1967 at the site of the Canyon Diablo meteorite, as microscopic crystals associated with diamond.

Actually, there is another substance in addition to lonsdaleite that appears to be harder than diamond. Tests undertaken by an international team in Shanghai found wurtzite boron nitride (Ah! The boron photo from all those years ago might have some truth behind it) withstood 18 per cent more stress than diamond. Lonsdaleite could withstand 58 per cent more.

Just for the record, wurtzite boron nitride is formed during volcanic eruptions, and as it is stable in oxygen at higher temperatures than diamond, it might just replace diamond as the cutting agent on drills. I wonder what it looks like when worn around the neck.

COMPASSES DO NOT POINT TO THE MAGNETIC NORTH POLE

E veryone knows that a compass points to the magnetic North Pole, which is in a very different place to true north. But of course a compass points to the former, I hear you say. What point is a compass if it's inaccurate? Well, pretty useful actually because usually there is no need to have something that is perfectly accurate, as in most uses you are not heading for the North Pole. You need a reasonable approximation of north so that, using the clues around you in the landscape, you head in the direction you want to go.

That accepted, I hope, it's for me to advise you that a magnetic compass aligns itself with the earth's magnetic field at a given location. This not only can be displaced from true magnetic

*If you were heading
for the North Pole
and relying on your
compass, prepare
to follow a slightly
irregular path. And
keep your ear on the
news.*

north by local vagaries in the field, it can change for any given location from year to year. So as magnetic lines of force are unlike the perfectly straight but artificial lines of latitude and longitude, they will give you a pretty accurate approximation and nothing more. Indeed, if you were heading for the North Pole and relying on your compass, prepare to follow a slightly irregular path. And keep your ear on the news. The theory is now that the earth's flow of magnetic force has over the millennia inverted a number of times, so at these times in the very distant past all compasses pointed south.

WHAT'S THE NEWS?

Ignore the fact the cardinal points are usually recited in the order north, south, east, west, giving the nonsense word nsew; the word news neatly reflects the gathering of information from the four corners of the world. Well, if the world had corners. Only the word is from the family of words that also gives us the word new as in novel. Quite simple really.

POSH

————— ❧❦ —————

The idea persists that the word posh is tied up with the idea that wealthy seafarers could pay a little extra to ensure their cabin was on the cooler, shadier side of the ship when they were either toing or froing between Great Britain and India. 'Port Out, Starboard Home', goes the mantra. And, say the more knowledgeable of us, the Peninsular & Oriental Steam Navigation Company, now usually just referred to as P&O and the main carrier on the route, stamped the tickets for such cabins with the letters POSH, hence the word. Neat but wrong, because George Chowdharay-Best looked into this idea in the *Mariner's Mirror* nearly forty years ago and found no evidence of it whatsoever.

So, where did the word come from? Here's what I think. It *was* the posh who could afford the better cabins, but the word is more likely to have come from their wealth and the display of it rather than their maritime sleeping habits. The word was recorded in an 1890 dictionary of slang, and again in 1902 and 1912, to mean a dandy, as in a well-dressed man. So as with many words, especially slang expressions, it was probably just invented, or derived from terms and prejudices now all but lost.

We know P G Wodehouse used a variant of it, 'push', to describe a waistcoat in Cambridge at the turn of the twentieth century. The Grossmiths in that wonderful book *Diary of a Nobody* actually used the word even earlier than Wodehouse, in 1892, but as a surname. 'Frank . . . said . . . he had a friend waiting outside for him, named Murray Posh, adding he was quite a swell.' So, I conclude, the word started out being associated with money and evolved to take in notions of being upper class and smart – especially in the military. At the outbreak of the First World War Jack Mann, writing as E C Vivian, alluded to British cavalrymen making a point of wearing 'posh' clothing – 'articles of attire other than those issued by and strictly conforming to regulations'. Dandies to a man, I shouldn't wonder. Then again, the word could also be from a Urdu or Persian term (then, like now in English, slightly derogatory) for a person

*In 2002 the UK Patents
Office confirmed that
when Peterborough
United FC lodged an
application to register
their nickname Posh, a
counter-claim had been
registered.*

dressed in white. This leads us helpfully to a modern tale that reached the inner pages of a few of our national dailies.

In 2002 the UK Patents Office confirmed that when Peterborough United FC lodged an application to register their nickname Posh, a counter-claim had been registered. One Mrs Victoria Beckham was attempting to put a copyright on her nickname within the Spice Girls. Posh Spice's solicitors wrote to Peterborough to advise them to stop using the nickname as it was an infringement of Mrs Beckham's rights. Six years later, the *Peterborough Evening Telegraph* reported,

> Girl power has finally come up trumps in a long-standing battle between Peterborough United and Victoria Beckham over the nickname Posh. Today Peterborough United chairman Darragh MacAnthony revealed he had given up the rights to the Posh nickname to Victoria – but was quick to add that it's not all doom and gloom. Mr MacAnthony said that he had managed to secure Victoria's superstar husband David Beckham to appear in two of Peterborough United's pre-season friendlies.

Unfortunately, as this article appeared on 1 April, a question arises as to its truthfulness. The fact is that Victoria's challenge had been overturned almost immediately, on the basis that Peterborough United had been using the name since the 1920s, over half a century before Mrs Beckham née Adams had even been thought of by her parents.

It's of interest to note there are many other diverse uses of the word as a noun rather than an adjective. The *OED* gives us these other meanings, sadly now mostly discarded and unused. These include:

- A halfpenny, or by derivation a coin of small value, or just money in general.
- A child's name for porridge in Scotland and, perhaps derived from this, a term in the north of England for a soft, decaying, rotten, pulpy mass. I hear Dr Johnson's comment about oats being eaten by horses in England and by the populace in Scotland echoing down the centuries.
- A variant of bosh and tosh, in so much it means rubbish or nonsense. We northerners are also supposed to use the variant pash in this sense, but this is, as we more correctly say, pish and tush.

BEFORE COLUMBUS,[1] EVERYONE
THOUGHT THE WORLD WAS FLAT

— ❧ ❧ —

This idea is so widespread that I was actually taught that the crews in Columbus's three ships were close to mutiny, fearing that they would fall off the edge of the world. If they were about to mutiny, I proffer the idea that it was more to do with pay and conditions than fear of their imminent demise – if I know anything about mariners, it's that they are a pretty unfanciful and practical lot, and damn good trade unionists as well.

The fact of the matter is the theory the world is a sphere was put forward in ancient Greece in the sixth century BC, and proved by Ptolemy in the second century AD. Indeed, part of his argument was based on the fact that the masts of a ship became visible before the hull when it was sailing towards the viewing point. What is perhaps ironic is that Columbus based his

---

1   Christopher Columbus is obviously an anglicised version of his name. If he was Genoese (and there's some dispute as to this) he would have been known locally as Christoffa Corombo. In standard Italian he was Cristoforo Colombo. To one of his sponsors, the Catalan king Ferdinand, he would have been Cristòfor Colom; Ferdinand's Castilian wife Isabella would have called him Cristóbal Colón. The Portuguese had him as Cristóvão Colombo, and the soon-to-be-grateful Catholic Church would have referred to him in Latin as Christophorus Columbus.

plans to sail to the Orient in an occidental direction on Ptolemy's incorrect calculations of the size of the earth. Following these, Columbus thought the distance between the Canary Islands and Japan would be less than two and a half thousand miles. So his opponents at court or on board ship might have just thought he was just biting off more than he could chew.

CHARLES LINDBERGH WAS THE FIRST PERSON TO FLY THE ATLANTIC NON-STOP

I am taking nothing away from the achievement of this aviator, but I laud him as the first person to fly the Atlantic non-stop – solo. William Alcock and Arthur Whitten Brown were the first known to have achieved the feat of getting across the Pond non-stop, flying from Newfoundland to Ireland in 1919, eight years ahead of Lindbergh. Not only that, but as Ripley of *Believe it or Not* fame pointed out in a cartoon that created enormous indignation and drew over 2,000 letters and telegrams of complaint, sixty-four others had also completed the task in the interim, making Lindbergh the sixty-seventh. The others had flown by dirigible, thirty-one in the British R-34 in 1919, and thirty-three aboard the German LX-126 in 1924. Actually, the R-34 flew back as well, so we could say Lindbergh's flight was the ninety-eighth time a person had achieved the feat. But surely that would be just a little churlish, would it not?

AIR POCKETS DON'T EXIST

What is the likelihood of a random hole in the atmosphere? About as likely as the transporter on *Star Trek*. In the latter's case, what you'd be trying to do is occupy the same space in the universe with two atoms at one time. I don't think I'd like to be around to observe the consequences of that one.

The frightening sudden drop in altitude experienced by aeroplane passengers is due to a massive downdraught in the atmosphere. A hole in the atmosphere, a vacuum, is just not possible.

AIR POLLUTION ISN'T SUCH A BAD THING

W ell, a little bit isn't. Think about it. A completely pollution-free atmosphere wouldn't allow raindrops to form. The drops have to take shape around small particles in the air. No hygroscopic (cloud condensation) nuclei, no rain.

THE WRIGHT BROTHERS ACHIEVED
THE FIRST POWERED FLIGHT

So say the FAI, the international governing body for aeronautics and air sports, and arbiters as to world records in the area of flight. Well, actually they don't. They stress that in their view what Orville and Wilbur Wright achieved at Kittyhawk (actually they say it was at Kill Devil Hills just to the south of Kittyhawk), North Carolina in December 1903 was 'the first sustained, controlled, powered heavier-than-air manned flight'. That's a lot of qualifications, and with a lot of justification.

As long ago as the fifteenth century Leonardo was designing powered aircraft, and since the Montgolfiers sent a couple of intrepid pioneers into the air in 1783 (please note the Montgolfier brothers were clever men – clever enough to send two other Frenchmen up in their place) human flight had been a reality. Although this flight was sustained (it lasted over five miles), it wasn't controlled. The French were also the first to achieve sustained and controlled flight, in 1884 with a military airship called *La France*, which was also powered. The only criterion to be achieved now was that all this had to be done in a 'heavier-than-air' aircraft.

Gliders (heavier than air) had been whizzing around the sky for some years, but were not powered. One had definitely achieved flight near Scarborough in 1853, although there might have been earlier, unrecorded flights such was the general interest in aviation in the nineteenth century. Like the Montgolfiers, Sir George Caley sent someone else up in his craft

for the flight near Scarborough – to wit, his coachman. Contemporaries of the Wright Brothers Samuel Langley and Gustave Whitehead were also in the chase. The Smithsonian Institute actually asserts that the former's aircraft, *Aerodrome*, was the first machine 'capable of flight'. It is also just possible, although there are no photos, that Whitehead flew in a heavier-than-air machine as early as 1899. He even claimed to have flown seven miles over Long Island Sound in 1902. Contemporary newspaper reports in at least three different newspapers and affidavits sworn later on in the 1930s all attest to his achievements. So we are left with the idea, very much as in the case of Elisha Grey with the telephone or Joseph Swan with the light bulb, that the Wrights might just have been given the credit for an invention that history has subsequently ascribed to others.

FAX MACHINES NEED
A TELEPHONE LINE CONNECTION

The text message and the email are the favoured means of interpersonal communication now, with wireless technology the norm. (This might already be a little out of date, what with the speed with which technology develops these days.) The history of communication is the chronology of the means by which we have improved and quickened the means of passing on a message: the letter, the telegraph, the telephone, the telex, the fax, the email, the text message. And since the telegraph each new development has taken the technology of the previous one and improved on it. Only the pantelegraph seems to have bucked this obvious progression.

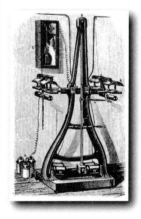

Ignoring the argument as to who invented what first, the first patent for what we now call the telephone was issued to Alexander Graham Bell in 1876, only thirty-two years after Inocenzo Manzetti put forward an idea for a 'speaking telegraph'. However, in the middle of this period, well in 1865 actually, another Italian by the name of Giovanni Caselli persuaded the French government to use his pantelegraph machine to introduce the first commercial fax service between Paris and Lyon. I make that eleven years before the telephone.

HENRY FORD – INVENTOR OF
THE PRODUCTION LINE

The Ford Motor Company became one of the biggest manufacturing companies in the world because of the genius of its founder, Henry Ford. True. He was a genius because he realised the fastest way to build his cars was using a production line. Also true. So he invented the production line. False.

I don't want to take anything away from a man of immense commercial ability (apart from being cruel enough to call his son Edsel and then naming a very unsuccessful model after him), but as with most cases of great success he 'borrowed' ideas. He borrowed from Ransom Olds, who had brought production-line automobile production to the USA, increasing output at his plant five-fold between 1901 and 1902 by the introduction of a production line. What Ford did was come up with the idea of conveyor belts bringing component parts to the main belt to keep the line moving. The importance of this innovation can be seen in the fact it reduced the time taken to produce one of his Model Ts from a day and a half to just ninety-three minutes.

We have to go back into history to see where Olds might have got his ideas. There is very strong evidence that the manufacture of the 8,000-strong 'terracotta army' in third-century-BC China was achieved by production-line methods. Components were made in various factories (each with a manufacturer's mark, as a sort of early quality-control mechanism) and then brought together to be assembled in situ. The Venetian Arsenal lays claim to the first modern production line, where in the sixteenth century 16,000 workers could make an entire ship in one day. Benjamin Franklin, Eli Whitney and Marc Isembard Brunel all had a part to play in the development of the production line. Ford was later to outline the influence of the already well-established meat packing industry around Chicago on motor manufacturing. In fact, it wouldn't be an exaggeration to say that by the time Ford came up with his refinement a whole raft of manufacturing and processing industries were using production lines to make goods for their increasingly populous and consumer-led markets.

POCAHONTAS WAS A BEAUTIFUL YOUNG WOMAN AND WAS MARRIED TO JOHN SMITH

My young daughters currently believe this, but as they get their history from Disney films at the moment I don't blame them. Most Disney films based on historic themes tinker with the truth, that being seen as a necessity when creating a story that will appeal to all.

Actually, I have even heard it said that Pocahontas didn't really exist. She was a real person, but that's about all that can be verified about her young life. Our problem is that the man she was supposed to have rescued from execution was well known as a bit of an embellisher. It is John Smith's account that has become the accepted truth, mainly because we don't know if Pocahontas ever told her own story. Smith wrote a book entitled *A True Relation of Such Occurrences and Accidents of Note as Hath happened in Virginia*, which was published in 1608. There is no mention of Pocahontas's act of bravery in this. It's not until he published *The General History of Virginia* in 1624 that the story appears. Other reasons for questioning the veracity of his account include that he was quite complimentary about Pocahontas's father Powhatan (actually a title; his real name was Wahunsunacock) in the first volume; by the second he had decided that he was dealing with a savage.

It is also possible that what Smith experienced was a ceremonial mock execution after being 'adopted' by his hosts. These seem to have been common among the tribes in that area. Smith either later, on his return to England, chose to make the episode a little bit more exciting for his readership, or just plain didn't get it. He does tell us one thing that is often forgotten: at the time of the incident Pocahontas was eleven years old, not a young woman as often portrayed. The rest of the embellished legend is down to us, the public. If she rescued him, surely she did it for love, and would have wanted to marry him. She actually married a gentleman called John Rolfe, and was quite the celebrity when she came to England in 1616. Sadly, probably due to the rigours of breathing the miasma of London, she fell ill. On a ship bound for Virginia, which had only managed to get as far as Gravesend, she died and was buried there in 1617.

On the question of her beauty, of the many representations of her fairness most are not contemporary and of course quite idealised. Simon de Passe's contemporary engraving of her is actually not very flattering. And the statue erected to her memory in the graveyard of St George's church in Gravesend suffers from what might be called the Braveheart effect. For evidence of this phenomenon, study pictures of the much-reviled statue of Sir William Wallace inspired by Mel Gibson's film, which was formerly in the car park of Stirling Castle.

As a coda to her tale, she did have a son, Thomas, who includes in his descendants a large number of Virginia notaries, including Nancy Reagan, Edith, wife of President Woodrow Wilson, and the astronomer Percival Lowell.

WHEN IS A MOHICAN HAIRCUT NOT A MOHICAN HAIRCUT?

All the time in the United Kingdom, actually. The style that we in the UK and most other English-speaking Commonwealth nations call a Mohican should actually be named after the Iroquois-speaking enemies of the tribe described in J Fenimore Cooper's great novel. The Americans (and by local association the Canadians) know what they're on about here. It is properly called a Mohawk.

THE GIRL GUIDES WERE FOUNDED
BY AGNES BADEN-POWELL

The Girl Guides have always been there at the side of the Boy Scouts. We in the modern age believe girls can do things just as well as boys.

Unfortunately, Robert Baden-Powell initially wasn't so enlightened. He wrote *Scouting for Boys* with no notion that someone as fluffy-headed as a girl might read and be inspired by it. So, after a successful camp for twenty-one boys at Brownsea Island, he organised a major rally at Crystal Palace in 1909. Imagine his surprise when a group of girls from Berkshire turned up and told B-P exactly what they thought about being excluded. Suitably impressed, if taken aback, he asked his sister to head up a new 'sister' organisation. So it seems that a small group of plucky girls were the moving force behind what is now the massive World Association of Girl Guides and Girl Scouts, and should be commended and celebrated for it.

Actually, in a way they are. To my knowledge this first guide company became known as the 1st Pinkneys Green Guides (Miss Powell's Own), and they're still going all these years later down in Maidenhead.

WILLIAM WALLACE
WASN'T A NATIONAL HERO

Post Mel Gibson's 1995 film *Braveheart* he might be, but a bit like Weems's version of the life of Washington (see later), it's a good story with some of the truth missed out for effect. *Some* people knew what a patriot he was, those being mainly antiquarians, the nobility, the merchant classes and those educated to grammar-school level, but until modern times the majority of the Scottish public were probably dimly aware of the National Wallace Monument near Stirling and that was about it. In a similar story to the invention of clan tartans in the nineteenth century, it was a Victorian surge in Scottish identity (safely ensconced within the cradle of United Kingdom unity 'neath the monarch) that highlighted his short brutal career as a smiter of the English.

Wallace wasn't actually as common as Gibson portrayed him. Rather than being a rough-and-ready, kilted, claymore-wielding scrapper, he was born a member of the lesser nobility and was well educated, speaking Latin and French. He would not have been thought a good candidate for the Church (as he was) without the ability to apply himself to his studies. At one point in the film he does speak French, but this sits oddly with the rest of Gibson's portrayal.

The opinion of the vast part of the Scottish populace didn't really count for a jot in the thirteenth and fourteenth centuries; it was the voice of the landowners that mattered. His temporary title Guardian of Scotland came from the few, not the many. Wallace might have been a player in the politics of the time, but the nobles of Scotland, as in many other countries, were so fractious and divided that even without the interference of Edward Longshanks from England, Wallace would have been as despised as he was feted. It all depended on which camp you belonged to at the time, and the members of the different factions shifted faster than the sands in the Moray Firth. He was actually shopped to the English by a fellow Scot. The current concept of Wallace as national hero should be replaced with the concept of 'temporarily the right man for whoever were the overdogs at the time'.

BORIS JOHNSON – A TRUE ENGLISHMAN

———— �֍ ————

What an archetypal Englishman Boris is. Blond, an alumnus of Eton and Balliol, a member of the Bullingdon Club at the latter and firmly in possession of a silver spoon on which he may chew. Why, his huntin', shootin' and fishin' ancestors must go back to William the Conqueror himself.

Actually, and I don't wish to display any political affiliations at this point, in a practical sense he is genetically ideally suited to be the political leader of the social melting point of modern multicultural Britain that London has become. His ancestors compete with those of Peter Ustinov[1] in their diversity.

Alexander Boris de Pheffel Johnson (Is there a clue already in that exotic name?) was born in New York, not England. Through his maternal great-grandmother he is descended from a German prince, one Paul of Württemberg. This makes him a descendant of George II, and in turn James I. So, like the royals we have at the moment, a good sprinkling of Germanic and Scottish genes can be presumed. His father's side is even more 'exotic', if I may use that epithet. He is a great-grandson of Ali Kemel Bey, a liberal Turkish journalist and the interior minister in the last government of the grand vizier of the Ottoman empire. So internationalism, politics and journalism from very diverse sources seem definitely to have been bred in the bone with Mr Johnson.

Alexander Boris de Pheffel Johnson was born in New York, not England.

GUY FAWKES WAS NOT HUNG, DRAWN AND QUARTERED

———— ✷ ————

I regard fellow Eborite (he was from York) Guy Fawkes as the only man to enter parliament with honest intentions. Although he was not the ringleader of the Gunpowder Plot, ten years of experience as a soldier

---

1   Peter Alexander Baron von Ustinow was born in London of Russian, German, Swiss, Italian, French and, it is claimed, even Ethiopian ancestry.

led to him being put in charge of the explosives, and as it was he who was caught in the cellars of the House of Lords, it is he who is the most celebrated of the conspirators today.

After a trial in January 1606, and following what was probably severe torture during a spell in the Tower of London, he was condemned with the other seven survivors to be hung, drawn and quartered. They were taken immediately from Westminster Hall to the yard outside, where a gallows had been set up. Now, just to remind you, the purpose of hanging, drawing and quartering was the severe 'discomfort' of victims. They were not hanged until dead, so they were still alive when disembowelled and emasculated, and their entrails and genitalia burned before their eyes. Last to mount the scaffold, Fawkes clearly decided that enough was enough and jumped, breaking his neck and so effectively depriving the authorities of their revenge.

PIRATES ALWAYS SPEAKS LIKE THIS . . .

September 19 is Talk Like a Pirate Day, when usually normal people walk around talking in nothing but the present tense and saying things like 'X marks the spot', 'Avast', and 'Arghhhh'. Clipped sentences are delivered in a strange growling non-specific West Country drawl.

There is no evidence that on becoming a pirate a seafarer would start talking like this. Although accepting that the talk of pirates in the *Boys' Own* stories of the previous hundred years might have been influential, it seems the idea is an invention of the 1950s. I would suggest it's mainly due to the popularity of Robert Newton's marvellous portrayal of the fictional pirate Long John Silver in Disney's version of Robert Louis Stevenson's brilliant yarn, *Treasure Island*. Both the *Boys' Own* argot and that of Newton seem to be based on the English of the West Country, which was long associated with seafaring and especially with smugglin', while the modern pirate dialect also seems based on that of Cornwall and neighbouring counties, but there is no real correspondence with what one would have really heard. I prefer the rather more refined take given to us by Johnny Depp in the *Pirates of the Caribbean* film series. 'Damn yer eyes, argh-argh.'

RED INDIANS SCALPED THEIR VICTIMS

I rather see the Native Americans as the victims. That aside, this barbarity with which white settlers supposedly had to contend is an inverted fallacy. It was the whites who were responsible for the spread of scalping. If I may be more specific, we can blame the Netherlanders.

Scalp bounty was initiated by the Dutch colonial authorities. Their settlements were under constant attack, and this encouraged their settlers to take a very direct approach to solving the problem. Later, as British influence spread, it was adopted by them as well. For example the rate was a significant £12 a scalp in Massachusetts in 1703 and rose to an astronomical £100 by 1772. That's a fortune in today's money; using the average earnings index, it's equivalent to just over £135,000 pounds. Further north, the French encouraged inter-tribal genocide to gain control of the fur trade, paying the Micmacs of Nova Scotia a bounty for every Beothuk scalp they could produce. Even as late as the mid-nineteenth century, Apache scalps were worth money ($250) in at least one county in Arizona.

Scalping was not widespread among the Native American tribes, and in the majority of cases the white man introduced the practice to the natives. The Cree and Teton Dakotas were scalp hunters, but to one of the more warlike tribes, the Navajo, even touching a dead body was taboo.

THE BATTLE OF
THE GREASY GRASS RIVER

Using the principle that the victors have the right to name the battle, then this is the correct name for the battle of the Little Big Horn. It's how Crazy Horse knew the river, anyway. Also, it wasn't a Native American ambush on the troops of the vainglorious George Custer, but rather an overwhelming response to an attack on their settlements by his forces. Finally, Sitting Bull didn't get involved; he stayed in the hills making medicine.

BATTLES ARE ALWAYS NAMED
BY THE VICTORS

—⚜—

To continue the theme of the previous piece, I think it is generally accepted that this is the case. It would certainly make sense and would seem fairest if whoever won got to decide by what name events would be remembered. Then again, history has never been sensible or fair. The problems started with the battle of Gaugamela, which was fought between Alexander the Great's troops and those of the Persian Empire in 331 BC. It is also referred to as the Battle of Arbela.

From that time onward the practice of having two names, with sometimes the losers' choice being the more readily accepted one, has gone on. Starting a by-no-means-comprehensive list, we have the Battle of Ligny in the Waterloo campaign. I believe the French refer to this 1815 clash of arms as the Second Battle of Fleurus, but as I seem to remember Napoleon won, it's funny we use the defeated Prussians' name for it to this day. Actually, I've always found the French name strange as well, as it wasn't the second but the fourth battle there, the earlier ones occurring in 1622, 1690 and 1794. Then again, fifty-one years later the boot was on the other foot. In 1866 the Prussians beat the Austro-Hungarians in the main battle of the Seven Weeks' War. Despite their crushing victory, the Battle of Königgrätz, as the victors called it, has become known to posterity as Sadowa, the losers' name. I shouldn't be surprised about anything to do with this conflict, though. This very short war is also called the Austro-Prussian War, the *Deutscher Kreig* (German War), the Unification War, the German Civil War and the *Bruderkreig*, or Fraternal War. That's six different names for a war that lasted seven weeks.

In addition, we have the mishmash of names thrown up during the American Civil War. The Union used creeks and rivers to name the battles, the Confederacy usually plumped for the nearest towns. Thus the two battles of Bull Run are also known as the First and Second Battles of Manassas. The bloody battle of Antietam (Creek) is also the battle of Sharpsburg. At least they could agree on Gettysburg, but perhaps only because the North for once chose to use the name of the town!

I might upset some of our older salts when I say this, but I think the

Despite their crushing victory, the Battle of Königgrätz, as the victors called it, has become known to posterity as Sadowa, the losers' name.

worst case of a battle being misnamed took place in the First World War. Although in the grand scheme of things it didn't resolve many questions, whichever way you look at the results of the events of 31 May and 1 June 1916 it was a German win. As such, what is called the Battle of Jutland over here is more correctly remembered across the North Sea as the *Skagerraktschlacht*, or the Battle of the Skagerrak.

FDR NEVER WALKED AFTER 1921

This misconception is almost a total flip of the original unspoken deception in which the American people were involved. Franklin Delano Roosevelt was undoubtedly a great peacetime and wartime leader, elected as US president for the first time in 1932, and the only man elected to the office four times. He steered his country through the Great Depression of the 1930s, and through World War Two (I bow to the American usage on this). Nowadays we presume, as we now know he was struck down with polio, that for years the American populace was complicit in the pretence that FDR could still get around. However, with the hindsight of history, we know that he couldn't walk and the whole thing was a politically necessary charade. This is not totally correct, however.

A disease, generally thought to be polio but possibly Guillain–Barré syndrome, struck FDR as early as 1921, and indeed caused paralysis from the waist down. He was already a successful politician, having been elected a state senator in 1910, and holding the post of assistant secretary of the navy from 1913 to 1920. He ran unsuccessfully for vice president in 1920, and was heading for high office when the disease struck.

What to do? Although using a wheelchair in private, he managed to convince the public of his fitness, using a car with hand controls rather than foot pedals and only appearing in public already standing, usually leaning carefully on one of his sons or aides. He was so successful in this deception that his illness never became the issue it could have been, and in quick succession, in 1929 and 1933, he achieved first the office of governor of New York and then that of the president of the United States. Throughout his long tenure, the deception continued. In the wartime photographs

taken of the big three (Roosevelt, Churchill and Stalin), the leaders are always sitting down, and this was because the American leader couldn't stand. We couldn't let the Nazis make hay with that one, could we?

But he could walk, and he did walk. It is documented that, soon after being struck down, Roosevelt learned to walk short distances by strapping iron braces to his legs and hips, and supporting himself with a cane. There is proof of this. There is film of FDR walking to take the oath of office at his inauguration in 1933. A brave man, indeed.

THE ASHES IS THE OLDEST INTERNATIONAL RIVALRY IN CRICKET

———— ⁂ ————

The first and the best of rivalries in international sport, never mind cricket. Whenever we beat the Aussies at this game, medals are handed out like confetti. Grown men weep. Babies are named after the men of the matches. Scenes of unbridled joy, reminiscent of those seen in the

In Affectionate Remembrance
OF
ENGLISH CRICKET,
WHICH DIED AT THE OVAL
ON
29th AUGUST, 1882,
Deeply lamented by a large circle of sorrowing
friends and acquaintances.

R. I. P.

N.B.—The body will be cremated and the
ashes taken to Australia.

capital on the news of the relief of Ladysmith, are seen the length and breadth of the land.

Well, perhaps I exaggerate. My wonderful history master Mr Stewart – and I would never contradict him – indicated that, in his words, 'there was even copulation in the streets' after the news came through from the Second Boer War. And we thought the Victorians were reserved. To get back to the point, beating the Aussies does feel good though, doesn't it? If only we could repeat the feat in rugby league.

Even though the Ashes didn't come into being until 1882, England and Australia have been taking strike at each other since a match in Melbourne in 1877. So, to reiterate the point, it is the first and the biggest of rivalries. Then again, what should we make of a match that took place in 1844 in Bloomingdale Park, New York? Billed as the 'United States of America versus the British Empire's Canadian Province', perhaps this is the oldest rivalry in international cricket? For the record, Canada won by twenty-three runs.

PEARL HARBOR WASN'T AN AMERICAN DISASTER

To paraphrase FDR, another day that 'lives in infamy' in American hearts (apart from losing at cricket) is 7 December 1941. This was the date of the Japanese attack on Pearl Harbor in Hawaii. A lot of US Navy tonnage was sunk as the warships were caught like sitting ducks, and the theory goes that if the Americans had been at sea, the losses would have been less.

Admiral Chester Nimitz has expressed a different view. While accepting the attack on Pearl Harbor was a huge blow to US morale, he pointed out that if the US Pacific Fleet had been at sea it would have faced a Japanese task force that could travel at least two knots an hour faster. In addition, the Americans with one carrier (well out of the way at the time) would have

not had the air cover to cope with six Japanese carriers all carrying a full complement of aircraft. Not only that, but the ships sunk at anchor were in a shallow port, and many were raised and repaired. If they had been sunk at sea, the losses in tonnage and men would have been irrevocable, even possibly fatal to the USA's war effort in the Pacific.

STALIN, GENGHIS KHAN AND ATTILA WERE GOOD LEADERS

The master of purges and the gulag, the creator of the greatest world empire of its time and the Scourge of God. Have I lost my senses? They killed, nay murdered, millions between them in their lust for power. At one stage I would have probably agreed with your scepticism. I would now on reflection take a more complex view.

A doubt as to the soundness of my initial view, my British view, was created in my mind a few years ago at a major European quizzing event. The British Isles were well represented, as were the Low Countries, Scandinavia and the Baltic States, all well-established hotbeds of quizzing.

At one stage I found myself sitting next to the solitary Hungarian who had made his way to Blackpool. He introduced himself as Attila. I was taken aback. I enquired as to his 'unusual' name, only to be told with good humour that in Hungary it was quite common. Attila the Hun is not just revered by the Magyars, but in Turkey and other Turkic-speaking countries in Asia. In fact, he's a bit of a hero. So it is with Genghis Khan (pronounced CHINGGIS KAAHN, if you like), who is regarded by the Mongols as the very symbol of their culture. As with Attila, it is not just among his own kinfolk that he is hero worshipped, but on a much wider basis among the peoples of central Asia. The third of our triumvirate, Uncle Joe, similarly finds a lot of supporters throughout the former Soviet Union. How can this be so, taking their reputations in the West into account?

I believe it is not just down to jingoism and macho nationalistic posturing; being great military leaders they are seen as great warriors. Away from the battlefield, they were all genuinely loved by many people, to a greater or lesser extent. Whatever the reality, the one thing they are now seen to have done by their descendants (in the case of the first two) was forge a strong indivisible nation from many parts and engender a collective feeling of nationhood. And in the case of Uncle Joe? Well, one must remember that for twenty years before his rise to power Russia had been in turmoil. The times called for stability. It may have required ruthlessness, but he gave the people what they wanted. He was then seen as saving Russian, even Slavic, culture by winning a war against a massive Teutonic onslaught.

MUSSOLINI MADE THE TRAINS RUN ON TIME

If there is one thing twentieth-century fascist organisations were good at it was propaganda. When he came to power as Italian prime minister in 1922, Mussolini needed a symbol to show the Italian people and the world that the new regime was beneficial and above all else efficient.

Now for this image to take hold, he needed something that had been poorly organised. The railways were perfect. Chaotic and badly maintained because of the privations of the First World War (Italy had fought with the

Japanese and the Allies against Germany and the other Central Powers), they were improved, with Mussolini claiming the credit. There were two problems, however. Firstly, by 1922 most of the improvements had been already instigated, so all he was doing was taking the credit for the hard work of others. Secondly, first-hand accounts of the railways under Mussolini's Fascists also tell us that actually the service wasn't anything to write home about. Still, if the facts get in the way of the legend, print the legend.

TALKING OF TIME . . .

Since the emergence of the railways, time has been standardised throughout Britain. We all know that in 1847 local mean times around the United Kingdom were abandoned by the railway operators in favour of Greenwich Mean Time, and by taking this action the network effectively imposed GMT on every other walk of life.

Being Britain, the home of the eccentric, there were of course a couple of exceptions. Don't set your watch by the clock on Tom Tower at the entrance to Christchurch College, Oxford. Local mean time was five minutes behind that in Greenwich, and when everyone else around them followed the railways' lead, this college decided to carry on in its own sweet way.

Even royalty got in on the act. Edward VII decided that the clocks at Sandringham should be set so that if he had to live by the strictly timed protocol of country house life, he was going to make it work to his advantage. So Sandringham Time ran half an hour ahead of time outside the gates of the estate to maximise the available shooting time in winter. His son George V carried on the tradition, but Edward VIII brought it to an end.

THE LEAGUE OF NATIONS WAS SUCCEEDED BY THE UNITED NATIONS

The League of Nations is the precursor of the United Nations. I for one disagree with this assertion. For one body to be replaced by another there must be succession and transition. One body comes into existence when the other ceases, and the aims and structures of the two organisations must be similar enough for this to be a progression. I am not trying to argue that there wasn't a seamless transition; on the contrary, depending on how you look at it, there was a six-year gap between the two, or the organisations actually coexisted for nearly six months. The UN was simply different from the League.

The League, which grew out of the Treaty of Versailles, reached its peak in the mid-1930s with fifty-eight members, which is hardly representative of the entire family of nations. I might be a little harsh here. The majority of countries were members at one stage or another during its existence, but its changing membership hindered the League from having have a real say-so on the world stage. I also draw attention to a similar flaw that in my view was the clincher: the United States of America, the country whose president had been so keen to create the League, never joined.

ORIGIN OF THE LEAGUE OF NATIONS

January 8th, 1918. Fourteen Points laid down by President Wilson as the basis of world peace. (*)

January 25th, 1919. League accepted in principle.

April 28th, 1919. Covenant adopted.

January 10th, 1920. League came into being; Secretariat established in London.

January 16th, 1920. First meeting of Council at Paris.

November 1st, 1920. League Headquarters moved from London to Geneva.

November 15th, 1920. First Meeting of Assembly at Geneva.

Woodrow WILSON

(*) THE FOURTEENTH POINT :

" A General Association of Nations must be formed under specific covenants for the purpose of affording mutual guarantees of political independence and territorial integrity to great and small States alike."

So, probably doomed to fail from the start, the League of Nations held its first general assembly in Geneva in November 1920. Less than nineteen years later at the outset of the Second World War it was effectively dead in the water. So if we take its demise as occurring in 1939, it could not have been succeeded by the UN as there was to be a six-year hiatus before the United Nations came into existence. Interestingly though, what the assembly actually did in 1939 was to transfer enough powers to the secretary general to allow the League to continue to exist in a legal sense, even if the Palace of Peace in Geneva remained unoccupied for the majority of the period of hostilities.

The transfer of powers meant that at the end of the Second World War the League of Nations was still in existence. It actually held its last assembly in April 1946, and wound itself up on the 20th of that month. So what of the UN? The idea of the UN arose because of the abject failure of the League to prevent the recent global conflict. Its originators weren't going to re-create the League, because all that would have meant was repeating failure. It had to be based on at least some different structures and ideals. Plus, there was no time to hang around once the Axis powers were in retreat. So the UN didn't succeed the League; it was already in existence. It officially came into being in October 1945 on the ratification of its charter by the five permanent members of its Security Council, now including the United States, and a majority of the other forty-six signatories. It held its first assemblies the following January in Westminster Central Hall. Fingers crossed, it has also, to date, despite some scares, managed to avoid the abject failure of the League of Nations in avoiding world conflict.

As a coda to this article, I was interested to note someone the other day advancing the commonly held idea that one of the interesting things about the United Nations is that Switzerland is not a member. I'm sorry to burst his bubble, but Switzerland joined in September 2002.

The League of Nations actually held its last assembly in April 1946, and wound itself up on the 20th of that month.

THE BRITISH EMPIRE AND THE COMMONWEALTH OF NATIONS

As with the League of Nations and the United Nations, the 'transition' from the first to the second of these international organisations wasn't simply the replacement of one with the other. In fact, an empire

and a loose confederation of equally minded but independent nations are actually so different that it is fallacious to talk about a succession.

I also make reference to dates. The term Commonwealth is an old one when used to refer to those territories and nations that were part of the British empire. As long ago as 1926, Balfour's declaration at that year's Imperial Conference suggested Britain and its dominions had equal status and were in no way subordinate one to another in any aspect of their domestic or external affairs, though all accepted a common allegiance to the Crown. The Statute of Westminster in 1931 tried to formalise things, but as Australia, New Zealand and Newfoundland had to ratify the statute for it to come into effect, despite the former two doing so in 1942 and 1947, Newfoundland, then separate politically from Canada, never did.

The retreat from Empire grew apace after 1945, and in 1949 'British Commonwealth' became just 'Commonwealth'. The retreat wasn't a single or simple event, by which one day Britain had an empire, and the following was part of a commonwealth. Some territories and dominions remained under direct rule well after others had gained independence either under the Crown or not. The UK's continuing sovereignty over fourteen overseas territories is a vestige of its empire.

We definitely fought the Second World War as Britain and the empire. Even as late as the 1950s the Conservative government was suggesting that Britain relied on the continued existence of the empire to retain its role in world politics. The first British Empire games were held in Hamilton, Canada in 1930. These became the British Empire and Commonwealth games in 1954, and it was not until 1970 in Edinburgh that the name of this tetra-annual sporting festival dropped the 'Empire'. 'British' was finally dropped in 1978.

So again, as with the previous piece, two organisations often thought to be the succeeded and the successor are actually separate things with different aims and structures and have coexisted together. The British empire hadn't disappeared by the time the Commonwealth came into existence.

Anomalies abound to this day. Canada and Australia, among a number of other Commonwealth members, remain kingdoms. Although the current British monarch is the head of the Commonwealth, there is no guarantee that her successor as British monarch will be. Some Commonwealth countries have their own royal families, such as Brunei and Tonga. Mozambique and Rwanda were never part of the British empire, but are now in the Commonwealth.

SALADIN WASN'T AN ARAB, OR EVEN TURKISH

Saladin roi d'Égypte

As Islam emerged in, by Western reckoning, seventh-century Arabia, I originally assumed Arabs still ruled the Middle East when the crusaders arrived to recover the Holy Land for Christianity. Later I discovered that the Seljuk Turks had become the dominant Islamic people in the region at least a hundred years before Richard the Lionheart arrived, so it was easy to imagine that his arch-rival Saladin, or Salāh ad-Dīn Yūsuf ibn Ayyūb to be more accurate, was a Turk.

He wasn't either of these things. He was a Kurd, which is something very different.[1] The area known as Kurdistan sits on the borders of modern Turkey, Iraq, Iran and Syria, and is populated by a people who have been there a very long time, possibly since the days of the ancient Medes. With an estimated population in the area of over twenty million, they have a very strong case for their claim to be the biggest nation on earth not to have their own country.

So I had made two wrong assumptions. One, that in the same way the Muslims had classed all crusaders as Franks, I had fallen into the trap of classing all Muslims at the time as Arabs. I now know there aren't too many people of Arabic ethnicity in the world's largest Muslim country, Indonesia. Two, I had assumed that if a power invaded and conquered another area, that territory was immediately and totally transformed, culturally and ethnically. I now know that despite the flow of world events and the adaptation of new cultural influences, on the whole people remain pretty fixed in the place where their ancestors lived before them.

1 Saladin's name in his native tongue is Selah'edînê Eyubî.

DID WASHINGTON CONFESS TO CUTTING DOWN THE CHERRY TREE?

I was taught a moral lesson at school. As a child, George Washington cut down his father's cherry tree, and instead of trying to cover up the fact when confronted with his crime, he did the right thing, stood up to his full height, and declared, 'I cannot tell a lie, it was I.'

Unfortunately – perhaps not for Washington but for those of us who have had this story drilled into them – all the evidence points to this being a fabrication or at least, if we are generous, an unproven anecdote of dubious pedigree. Now we cannot criticise the author for misinforming us; he was following an accepted convention of the time, that of building up moral incidents to enliven the biographical narrative of the hero in question. At the time the readers of such tales expected it. But it is the degree to which this particular author insisted on including such exaggerations (again I'm probably erring on the side of generosity as to their truthfulness) that sticks in the craw of the modern reader, now used to veracity when reading about the people who have shaped our history.

Washington's cheerleader was called Mason Locke Weems, known to posterity as Parson Weems. A good and religious man no doubt, he was a theologian who served as an Episcopalian minister in Virginia soon after the death of Washington at a church where both his hero and his hero's father had served in the vestry. Already interested in writing and publishing, he was forced through financial hardship to concentrate on a new career as a book agent and author. His major work was *A History of the Life and Death, Virtues and Exploits of General George Washington*, and it is in chapter two of this mighty tome that he quotes 'an aged lady' who claimed to be a cousin of the great man in question. He refers to her report as an anecdote that was too true to be doubted.

Now, it's not beyond reason to suggest young boys, given the wrong tools, can be very destructive. But the assertion that George faced his father with 'the sweet face of youth brightened with the inexpressible charm of all-conquering truth' and declared, 'I can't tell a lie, Pa; you know I cannot tell a lie. I did cut it with my hatchet' ascribes unbelievable cherubic qualities and a command of the English language far beyond that of an average six-year-old to a boy who in adult life was described by Weems as the 'greatest man that ever lived'.

This, along with other questionable anecdotes, has to lead us to the conclusion that Weems's expansive and creative imagination is the cause of many young boys, when facing the dilemma of whether to confess to a crime, assuming that the generous attitude of Augustine Washington will be extended to them, only to find disappointment and confusion in the retribution dealt to them by their own parents.

It's worth noting in passing that Weems's other works included a *Life of Benjamin Franklin, with Essays* and the *Life of William Penn*, both of which also paid glowing if exaggerated tributes to some of the creators of the United States of America. But it is for his dubious account of the cherry tree incident that he will be best remembered.

BEECH TREES DON'T GET HIT BY LIGHTNING

———— ✂✁ ————

This is one that came over from America, and was reported in a letter published in the 1820s, supposedly based on the observation of Native Americans during storms in Tennessee. In this letter it is claimed that the American beech is 'never known to be assailed by atmospheric electricity'. I just hope the author never put it to the test by sheltering under one.

LIGHTNING NEVER STRIKES TWICE
IN THE SAME PLACE

Another dangerous fallacy probably not believed by a large number of people today but still hanging around in some pub lounges and four-ale bars. In fact, the opposite is the case. Lightning is a discharge of electricity. When this happens, like all electric currents, it will follow the path of least resistance. As air is a poor conductor, the flow will seek out a high tree or building to help it on its way to the ground. If lightning never strikes twice in the same place, why do construction engineers bother maintaining the lightning conductors they put on tall buildings after it's been struck once?

SHEET LIGHTNING

I don't want to upset those astraphobics and brontophobics out there, but of the estimated sixteen million lightning storms every year, not one of them includes sheet lightning. There are many different descriptions for different types of lightning, be it cloud to cloud, ground to cloud or cloud to ground. There can be bead lightning, ribbon lightning, forked lightning, staccato lightning, heat lightning, dry lightning, rocket lightning, positive lightning, ball lightning, even elves! I won't go on. The sheet-lightning storms I thought I watched over the Vale of York as a boy I now know to be cloud-to-cloud lightning merely exhibiting a diffusion of brightness across the surface of a cloud, the actual bright discharge of the lightning being hidden within.

TORNADOES – UK V. USA

—⁂—

We all probably know that a tornado is a fast-moving rotating column of air, usually with a funnel-shaped cloud that extends to the ground. A lot of us have seen the film *Twister*, and failing that we've seen *The Wizard of Oz*. Yearly, we see news reports of the terrible destruction caused in that area of the USA called Tornado Alley.

So would it surprise you to find out that tornadoes are five times more likely to hit the UK than the USA? I thought it might. We get about one hundred a year here, which is about three times as many as we used to think. The reason why we see them as an American problem is simple – size and destructive effect. In the UK the largest would probably be a few tens of metres wide, with winds of up to 120 mph. That's not to say British tornadoes don't cause significant damage. Spare a thought for Selsey in West Sussex. In 1998 one hit the town and caused £10 million of damage. It was hit again in 2000, when two people were injured and more than half a million pounds of damage was caused. In general though, it's that the majority of them in the UK are just not seen or recorded. The US uses Doppler radar technology to detect tornadoes, and with good reason. Over there, they can be half a mile wide and have winds of up to 300 mph.

The US uses Doppler radar technology to detect tornadoes, and with good reason. Over there, they can be half a mile wide and have winds of up to 300 mph.

A SUNTAN IS HEALTHY???

—— ✼✼✼ ——

*Until recently a tan was
actually seen as a sign
of low status – proof
of outside labour rather
than a sophisticated
urban existence.*

Try telling that to the worried parents of those teenage children who have developed an addiction to sunbeds. The only thing a tan shows is that the body is doing its utmost to adopt a protective device against further damage from ultraviolet rays, be they natural or from a UV lamp. It's trying to protect itself because any form of radiation is ultimately dangerous to humans and other animals.

Until recently a tan was actually seen as a sign of low status – proof of outside labour rather than a sophisticated urban existence. Hence the derogatory American term redneck.

By the way, if this frightens you into only going outdoors when it isn't sunny, I'm sorry to tell you that even moderately thick cloud cover doesn't filter out the sun's ultraviolet rays.

THE STANDARD FOR UK MAINS ELECTRICITY IS SET AT 230 VOLTS

—— ✼✼✼ ——

Hold hard. It is surely 240 volts in the UK. It always has been since we've had a mains supply, and if you tested the flow in your home, you would find that it registers at 240. That, however, is not the standard. Along with kilograms and straight bananas, here's more ammunition for opponents of the EU to fire off.

Voltage harmonisation took place throughout the EU in 1995. Yes, I missed it as well. All mains supplies are now nominally set at 230 volts plus or minus 10 per cent at 50 hertz. The word nominally and the parameters of the tolerances are key here. They mean that no change in voltage is currently required by those who previously supplied at 220 or 240 volts. This will allow countries to continue to supply the same voltage until generating plants are replaced in the future, when they will be built to supply electricity at 230 volts. Don't worry that any future changes will cause your hairdryer to explode. Equipment used in the EU is now, or at least should be, designed to accept any voltage within the specified range.

PEOPLE WHO WEAR SUNGLASSES
ARE POSERS

—❧❦❧—

Well, on a sunny day it's downright sensible to protect your eyes. Otherwise, I admit they might be, in as much as wearing them indoors or on a cloudy day is probably an attempt to look cool. But if such individuals are trying to emulate their Hollywood heroes, however, they're blind to the facts.

The practice of wearing sunglasses didn't start as a fashion statement in Hollywood, but rather as a common-sense response to damage caused by the extremely bright lights used in the film studios. The actors just got into the habit of wearing them all the time.

MONSOON WEATHER
CAN BE DRY

—❧❦❧—

We know that a monsoon occurs in the monsoon season, is a torrential downpour lasting for weeks on end, and comes as a blessed relief from the drought that preceded it. Well, we know half the story.

The word derives from the Arabic word *moussem* meaning season, and a monsoon is actually a wind. There are two seasonal winds called a monsoon. The one we most associate with the name blows into India from the Indian Ocean to the south-west from April to October and is responsible for over four-fifths of that country's rainfall. The one that blows from the opposite direction, the north-east, comes from the drier interior of Asia, starting high above the Tibetan Plateau. It's this wind that carries the dust and causes the drought experienced in the other half of the year.

'WHITE CHRISTMAS' ISN'T ABOUT BEING IN THE SNOW . . .

Of course it is. What else makes a Christmas white? In the UK what Christmas holiday would be complete without sitting down to watch the 1954 film musical of the same name? Bing Crosby, Danny Kaye, Rosemary Clooney and Vera-Ellen start singing, and it starts snowing.

Think again. It's quite the opposite. The singer is *dreaming* of a white Christmas. In Vermont, where the musical is mainly set, there's not much need for you to dream of a white Christmas; you get one just about every year, and damned inconvenient it can be at times I bet. So it's erroneous to associate the song with being in a winter landscape. The song is about being in much warmer climes. Irving Berlin possibly wrote the song in Arizona, or in Los Angeles, two locations not noted for their snowfall. And take the opening verse, which is often omitted from performances and recordings.

> The sun is shining, the grass is green,
> The orange and palm trees sway.
> There's never been such a day
> In Beverly Hills, LA.
> But it's December the twenty-fourth,
> And I am longing to be up North . . .

The song initially came to prominence in *Holiday Inn*, a film made twelve years before *White Christmas*, and won an Oscar.

. . . AND 'JINGLE BELLS' WASN'T ORIGINALLY ABOUT CHRISTMAS

Again, I'm sorry to raise howls of protest by being a killjoy. The song was actually patented in 1857 as 'One Horse Open Sleigh'. Rather than a song about Christmas, the original lyrics, often missed out in large part, recount the story of a young beau taking a certain Fanny Bright for

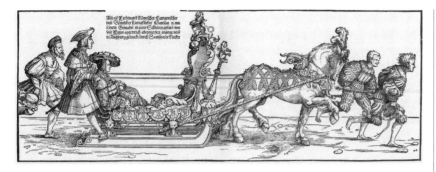

a sleigh ride only for them to come a cropper. He's then ridiculed by a passing man only for the singer to advise the beau to 'go it while you're young' – don't let one setback stop you having a bit of fun.

It is a song about the winter landscape, not Christmas. It is possibly the association of Santa Claus with a sleigh that has fixed the Christmas connection in place. In fact, it is this connection that led to the song being the first to be broadcast from space. It was part of a prank by Gemini 6 astronauts Stafford and Schirra on 16 December 1965. They reported they had seen an object looking like a satellite going from north to south, probably in polar orbit. It comprised a command module and eight smaller modules in front, with the pilot of the command module wearing a red suit. At this point, they produced a smuggled harmonica and sleigh bells and broadcast a rendition of the song.

ANTIFREEZE

It follows that if diluted antifreeze, which is the form in which most commercial brands are sold, offers some protection, it would be a smart move to get some undiluted ethylene glycol and use that, allowing you to maximise the protection for your car. In fact the manufacturers are conning us, are they not, doubling their profits by selling us a diluted product?

However, diluted antifreeze works to about minus 35 degrees Celsius, a far lower temperature than usually assails the UK. Use it pure, and it will be a useless slush soon after the temperature drops below zero.

WHERE'S THE DRIEST PLACE ON EARTH?

A desert is defined as having an annual average precipitation of less than 250 millilitres. So shall I suggest the Sahara? Actually, that's far too obvious. It has often been suggested that the Atacama Desert in South America has a more severe climate, so perhaps that's there where we will find it.

We are barking up the wrong tree. We presume that all deserts are hot. They are not, as the definition is based not on heat but, as stated, on precipitation. Surprisingly, the two biggest deserts in the world are in the Arctic and the Antarctic, which are similar in size but both at least 50 per cent bigger than the Sahara.

The winner of the accolade of the driest place on earth goes to the southern continent. It is estimated that the McMurdo Dry Valleys in Antarctica haven't seen rain in two million years.

ICELAND

—⊰❦⊱—

By definition, this is a very cold place and lies within the Arctic Circle to the north-west of mainland Europe.

Neither of these assertions is true. To deal with location first, only one island off its northern coast, Grimsey, actually touches the Arctic Circle. Geologically, Iceland is actually defined as a 'hotspot'. It sits in an area of widespread geological activity, has many volcanoes and geysers, and most households enjoy inexpensive electricity and hot water supplied from hydroelectric and hydrothermal sources. The name of the capital, Reykjavik, translates into English as Bay of Smokes. Beyond this, the North Atlantic Current ensures that its climate is far milder than many places on the same latitude around the world. It is of interest to note that the last year the sea on even the northern coast of Iceland froze over was as long ago as 1969.

The name of Iceland's capital, Reykjavik, translates into English as Bay of Smokes.

SOLSTICES AND EQUINOXES

—⊰❦⊱—

These are the facts as understood. In the northern hemisphere, the winter solstice (21 December) is the shortest day of the year in terms of hours of daylight; the summer solstice (21 June) is the longest. The spring equinox (21 March) and the autumnal equinox (21 September) are days of equal hours of light and dark.

This is not quite the reality. Due to leap years, the dates can vary. For example, a summer solstice can occur on 20 June and a winter solstice on 22 December. The spring equinox can occur on 20 March, and the autumnal equinox actually occurs on either 22 or 23 September.

Also, the tipping point where the hours of daylight and darkness are exactly the same actually occurs a few days before the spring equinox and a few days after the autumn one.

CATS HATE WATER

—❧✦❧—

If a believer in this idea thinks it applies it to big cats, they should travel to the jungles of Asia and see what fun tigers have splashing about. If they want to say all *domesticated* cats hate water, then they should visit the east of Turkey around Lake Van. Among many fascinating characteristics, the Turkish Van cat loves to play in the water and will join you in the bath or try and help with the washing-up. Known as the 'swimming cat', they also retrieve items from the water, and have been described as dogs in a cat's skin because of their unusual personalities.

SNOWFLAKES

—❧✦❧—

No two snowflakes are alike; they are perfectly symmetrical and if refrozen after melting will resume the exact form they had prior to melting. Well, one out of three isn't too bad. The true part is that no two snowflakes are identical, unless this occurs by some unbelievably unlikely, nay freakish chance. That is because it is estimated that each flake contains around 10 to the power of 18 water molecules, and it is impossible to recreate the conditions in which snowflakes form so perfectly and on such a small scale that all those molecules can be arranged into two exactly matching patterns. The large number of molecules in each flake is also one of the major reasons they are never perfectly symmetrical. They appear so to the naked eye because, as Kepler and Descartes both found out as long ago as the seventeenth century, they have hexagonal symmetry – visual symmetry, yes, but perfect symmetry, no. Finally, the idea that a snowflake will reform in exactly the same shape – that the water contained in the flake has a memory – is pure fantasy. But I have to admit they are magical things.

A GOOGLE

——— ❧❧ ———

As a quick aside on large numbers, I have to correct a mistake I heard someone make the other day. I didn't have the heart or the bravery to tell him to his face, so here is my belated cowardly correction. The person in question was talking about a very popular Internet search engine, and asked, 'Do you know what it's named after?' He didn't give his friend the chance to reply. 'A google is the number 1 to the power of 100.'

Oops. Not so, I'm afraid. This is a common misunderstanding about the term 'to the power of'. As an example, 3 to the power of 3 is 3 x 3 x 3, which is 27. To break this down, 3 x 3 is 9, and 9 x 3 is 27. Likewise 2 to the power of 3 is 8, as it is 2 x 2 x 2. However the number 1 has a certain property: it doesn't matter to what power you multiply it, it's always 1. So 1 x 1 x 1 x 1, etc. done a hundred times still gives the same result as 1 x 1. It'll never get any bigger.

What he should have said is that a google is 1 followed by 100 noughts, which is a completely different thing. In fact, when nine-year-old Milton Sirotta gave the number its name, he was actually describing a number that is higher than the estimated number of protons in the universe.

ALL POLAR BEARS ARE LEFT-HANDED

——— ❧❧ ———

Returning to the snow theme, it is widely believed that all polar bears are left-handed. How could such a strange idea arise? There is no scientific evidence that this is so. It seems this wrong-headed notion derives from the separate idea that when hunting in the whiteness of the Arctic, the polar bear tries to fool its prey by running into the attack with its right paw covering its supposedly highly visible black nose, leaving its left paw to do the actual killing. How bizarre! To think a polar bear attacking its prey

would deliberately lessen its chances of a kill by slowing itself down by running on three legs. And if left-handed, why doesn't it use its left paw to cover its nose as this is obviously the more difficult and delicate task it has to undertake? I'm now waiting for the video evidence to flood in and prove me wrong.

POLAR BEARS HAVE WHITE FUR

The second commonly held error that I have found relating to the polar bear is the more reasonable idea that it has white fur. Its fur does appear white, I cannot deny that. Also, I do not claim that polar bears have such an understanding of physics that they have deliberately adapted their fur to their conditions, but it does seem that Mother Nature, through the wonderful process of evolution, has done just that for them.

Each shaft of hair is actually totally pigment-free. In addition, because each shaft has a hollow core, light falling on the bear's fur is scattered and reflected, just like what happens with the ice and snow it lives among. The fur is merely reflecting the full spectrum of light and the whiteness around it. Polar bears look whitest when they are clean and in bright sunlight, especially after moulting. Before moulting, the build-up of oils on their fur from seals they have killed can make them look yellow. Bears in zoos have been known to turn green due to colonies of algae growing in the hollow hair shafts. This discoloration could actually be made to appear even stranger, perhaps psychedelic, if one was brave enough to shave off patterns of fur to expose the polar bear's skin. That happens to be black.

BEARS DON'T HIBERNATE

— ❦❦ —

I was very impressed by a recently released Disney film entitled *Over the Hedge*. It was very funny, and in contrast to the anthropomorphism exhibited by its animal characters actually contained a scientific truth that is usually not appreciated. In the film a raccoon endeavours to steal the food of a hibernating bear, only to accidentally wake him up while simultaneously destroying the food store. The bear then gives him a week or so before he wakes up properly to get every single item back.

The ease with which RJ wakes Vincent is the key. Bears might be torpid during much of the period of cold weather, but the body temperature, rate of breathing and heart rate of a true hibernator will drop significantly; it is very difficult to wake them or indeed for them to wake themselves. Bears on the other hand do not truly hibernate and can, as correctly shown in the film, be very active very quickly.

PADDINGTON BEAR

— ❦❦ —

Echoes here of Rolihlahla Mandela ending up being known to the world as Nelson, although on this occasion it is a fictional example. Found at the eponymous station by the Brown family, a lot of us assume that as a bear, however anthropomorphised, Paddington arrived without a name. Actually, a visit to his website informs us he did have a name in 'Darkest Peru' – it was Pastuso.

WHALEBONE IS THE BONE OF A WHALE

— ❦❦ —

Whalebone does not come from the skeleton of a whale, and indeed isn't bone at all. Its alternative name is baleen, and it comes from the filtering structure found in the mouths of most whales, used in feeding to sieve small animals out of mouthfuls of seawater. This structure consists

of two parallel rows of flat, flexible, comb-like plates in the upper jaw. Baleen is actually composed of the protein keratin, the substance which makes up horn, scales and claws on most animals that have them, and in humans, hair and nails.

THERE ARE MORE ANIMALS
AWAY FROM HUMAN HABITATION
THAN CLOSE TO IT

If you really want to commune with nature, you should get as far away from the city as possible. Not only will there be fewer humans, but more chances to see species of wild animals other than us.

I refer you again to Disney's film *Over the Hedge*. The storyline includes the suggestion that human eating habits, especially the tendency to waste food in the Western world, actually attracts animals to us as food is more plentiful. Also, the deeper and darker the woods, the fewer opportunities there are to forage for naturally occurring foods. There are far more opportunities in gardens, fields, wetlands, in the wake of a fishing boat, etc.

Just ask a rat or a seagull.

DARWIN NEVER USED THE TERM 'EVOLUTION'

Darwin has come down to us as the founder of the theory of evolution. This is strange because I have been unable to find any evidence of him originating the use of the term. He also didn't coin the phrase 'survival of the fittest'. He definitely put forward a theory that we now generically call evolution, but his ideas were based on other areas of science such as geology. He used the term 'natural selection' in the title of his major work. He also widely used 'descent with modification'. Evolution derives from a word meaning unrolling, and this was not really what Darwin meant. He didn't see evolution as a form of progress. His terminology derives from and is influenced by the likes of Hutton, Smith and Lyell, and by the works of Thomas Malthus.

Actually, evolution is a term that at the time was more associated with Alfred Russell Wallace, whose theory of evolution was nearly identical to the theories of Darwin. Wallace was to put forward his theory at a conference, and Darwin's friends asked the organisers for a few minutes just before Wallace was to speak to read aloud excerpts from some of Darwin's letters and notes to them that dealt with the theory of natural selection. Therefore Darwin's theory was presented first and he received the credit (or blame, if you are a supporter of intelligent design) for the theory of evolution. In 1859 *The Origin of Species by Means of Natural Selection or the Preservation of Favoured Races in the Struggle for Life*, better known as *The Origin of Species* was finally published and his name was made.

MOLES ARE GOOD FOR THE PLANTS

Moles cause visual disturbances to a manicured garden feature that isn't exactly natural in the first place.

I've probably upset millions of gardeners. I expect to receive a mountain of mail containing everything from condescending pity through to full and forthright explanations of my mistake to vitriolic hate. I'll explain why I believe my assertion to be right.

Firstly the diet of moles is made up of insects, worms and other invertebrates; they don't eat plants. Worms aside, they eat a number of invertebrates that are actually harmful to plants. As to their tunnelling, there is benefit in this as they aerate the soil through their activities. Why many gardeners think they are harmful is, apart from occasionally exposing roots that shouldn't be exposed, that they ruin lawns. So, to put the real case, moles cause visual, aesthetically undesirable disturbances to a manicured garden feature that isn't exactly natural in the first place.

A COOT IS BALD

The coot is not bald, nor is the bald eagle, which actually features the often derogatory description in its name. If one were to look closely at the head of, say, a vulture or a condor, one would see more evidence of a lack of feathers, and thus baldness. So where does the idea come from, and why are these two species singled out for attention? It is, if you pardon the avian quip, a chicken-and-egg situation. Modern man sees the modern term 'bald' in modern human terms. We ascribe anthropomorphic qualities to the coot and the eagle through our modern usage of the word.

However, if we look at the origins of the medieval English word balled, meaning ball-like, which when applied to the human head meant hairless, we get to the nub of the matter. Although the word might have developed into something that meant smooth, there is evidence in many languages, from Dutch through to French and German to Welsh (and according to the *OED* even Greek) that bald originated in a term meaning 'shining white'. This was especially applied to horses with white patches on the forehead. A coot is a black waterfowl with an immediately noticeable white blaze from the top of its head to its beak. The bald eagle is instantly recognisable for the bright whiteness of the feathers on its head compared to the rest of its plumage.

TU-WHIT, TU-WHAT?

Shakespeare is partly the culprit for this misconception. I refer you to a lovely song from *Love's Labour's Lost.*

> When icicles hang by the wall
> And Dick the shepherd blows his nail
> And Tom bears logs into the hall
> And milk comes frozen home in pail,
> When blood is nipp'd and ways be foul,
> Then nightly sings the staring owl, Tu-whit;
> Tu-who, a merry note,
> While greasy Joan doth keel the pot.

An owl never calls, 'Tu-whit, tu-who.' 'Tu whit' is better represented by 'ke-wick', and 'tu-who' is more accurately 'hoo-hoo-oooo'. This latter sound is a male territorial call. Therefore, 'Ke-wick', 'Hoo-hoo-oooo' is most likely a male answering a female or another male. So it's two birds in the bush that you hear, not one.

There are a few other misconceptions with regard to owls. They are usually all talked of as Strigidae because they are of the order Strigiformes, but barn owls are a separate family from the 'typical owls' of the Strigidae family, and are of the family Tytonidae. Like the bald eagle not being bald, the screech owl is maligned by humans – it doesn't screech. Lastly, many also think that it's too bright for owls to be active in the daytime. This is not the case at all. They have very good eyesight whatever the conditions. Some varieties do hunt during the day, but as their prey is usually nocturnal and it's easier to be stealthy at night, it's a choice rather than a necessity.

NOTHING ON EARTH HAS EVER SEEN A BRONTOSAURUS

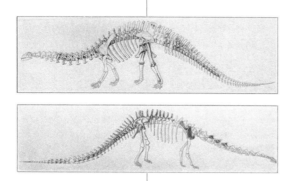

That's because it never existed. There was a dinosaur called an apatosaurus, a sauropod that lived about 150 million years ago in the Jurassic period, and yes, it was enormous, being twenty-three metres long when fully grown, and weighing in at over twenty metric tonnes. Let me outline the story of the thunder lizard that never was.

In 1877 Othniel Charles Marsh introduced one of his findings to the world as *Apatosaurus ajax*. Two years later, he introduced a more complete specimen that he had found. He thought this a new and totally separate genus and called it *Brontosaurus excelsus*. Over two decades later Elmer Riggs thought *Brontosaurus excelsus* was similar to *Apatosaurus ajax*, so similar, in fact, he concluded that it belonged in the same genus and reclassified it as *Apatosaurus excelsus*. So, according to the rules of the International Code of Zoological Nomenclature, as *Apatosaurus* was published first it had priority as the official name. *Brontosaurus*, being what is referred to as a junior synonym, was officially discarded.

So despite the evidence from my childhood dinosaur books, the brontosaurus didn't last for millions of years; it lasted for just twenty-four.

GIVING CLEOPATRA THE NEEDLES

—❦❦—

There is actually no connection between Cleopatra VII, lover of Mark Antony and Julius Caesar, and any of her so-called needles. She was born in 69 BC and died before she was forty. The Cleopatra's Needle on the Thames Embankment (its twin is in Central Park, New York City) was made for Thutmose III. He was around about one and a half thousand years earlier than the famous queen. To add insult to injury, as a descendant of the Macedonian general Ptolemy, Cleopatra wasn't even a relative of Thutmose.

GYPSIES ORIGINATED IN EGYPT

—❦❦—

Gypsy. The old, and I apologise if taken as derogatory, name for the Romani people. The etymology could not be clearer – they originated in Egypt. The French *Gitan* and the Spanish *Gitano* derive in exactly the same way. Now, this sort of supposition might have been acceptable in the simpler times of the sixteenth century when the term came into use, but we are more sophisticated now, are we not? So why do I still hear that the origin of the Romani people is clearly expressed in this now outmoded term for them, and that their ancestors were expelled from their homeland for hiding and harbouring the baby Jesus?

It might surprise those who still cling to this belief that the linguistic and genetic evidence points to the Romani originating in the Indian subcontinent and starting their migration west in the second half of the first millennium. This move, probably born out of conflict, was only the first of a series of sadnesses in their history. Persecution of the Romani continues in the countries throughout which they are now spread, sometimes covert, often very open. They also featured in one of the greatest and most tragic historical ironies of the twentieth century. As we all know, not only Jews were herded into the concentration and extermination camps of the Third Reich; the Gypsies were one of the other groups stripped of their citizenship and persecuted. So how strange that they had a far better claim to be called Aryan than the Nazis who perpetrated the Holocaust.

ARYANS WERE PURE-BLOODED, BLUE-EYED AND BLOND

Aryan describes a group of peoples inhabiting the Iranian plateau who moved into northern India.

A total fabrication made up by a group of occultists masquerading as a political party in Germany in the middle of the twentieth century. In the proper ethnic sense, Aryan describes a group of peoples inhabiting the Iranian plateau who moved into northern India. They include Indians and Iranians among their descendants but not the Nordic and Germanic people of Europe. Linguistically, as Aryans spoke the Indo-European mother tongue, they are related to us because languages as diverse as Greek and Hindustani can be included in the group termed 'Aryan', but that's all.

The 'pure-blood' theory is also nonsense. Ceaseless migrations and counter-migrations mean that every single race or group on the planet has mixed within it the genes of other groups to a lesser, or more likely greater, extent. In the words of a good friend of mine, 'It's a wise man that knows his own father.'

STONEHENGE

John Aubrey has a lot to answer for, what with the cost of policing and the number of film crews that turn out to cover the annual shindig at Stonehenge. Every year at sunrise on the summer solstice upwards of 30,000 hippies, sun worshippers and Druids gather to celebrate. Now the hippies and sun worshippers I can understand – what better excuse for a party in the majestic surroundings of Stonehenge? The Druids, however, I don't quite get. What are they are doing there, unless they wrongly believe that their ancient forebears built the place?

Aubrey, interestingly the biographer of the philosopher Thomas

Hobbes, had a great love of megalithic rings, and, in fact, there is a feature at Stonehenge, the Aubrey Holes, named after him. It was he who popularised the idea in the seventeenth century that the Druids built the great monument in Wiltshire, an idea which persists to this day.

There are two major flaws in this. The main tenets of the Druidic religion, according to the Romans, were metempsychosis (the trans-migration or resurrection of the soul), human sacrifice and reverence for various aspects of the natural world, especially oak trees and mistletoe. The Roman suppression of Druidism came to a head in Britain in AD 60 when soldiers crossed over into Anglesey and destroyed the Sacred Groves. It was only news of Boudicca's revolt back in the south-east that stopped the invaders from totally destroying the Druids' last base. So it was a reverence for living things, a sort of animism, that inspired the Druids, not the building of huge stone temples or the like. Woodhenge, about two kilometres to the north-east of Stonehenge, would have been much more to their liking.

The second point is that we have no evidence of the Druidic religion existing before the second century BC (or BCE, if you prefer). The stone megaliths (and the wooden ones for that matter) that dot our landscape are prehistoric and therefore much older than the Druids. In fact, it is thought that Stonehenge has been a sacred site for nearly 5,000 years, with the current locally sourced Sarsen stones and Welsh bluestones dating back to between 2,600 and 1,600 BC. The ancient Druids probably looked at Stonehenge and, in the same way that we react nowadays, said to themselves, 'I wonder why they built that?'

HITLER NEVER HAD A HIDEAWAY
CALLED THE EAGLE'S NEST

On his fiftieth birthday in 1939, Hitler was given a mountain retreat called the Kehlsteinhaus near Berchtesgaden, which had been commissioned by Martin Bormann. Although Eva Braun's sister Gretl had her wedding reception there, nothing else of any significance seems to have happened at this house. It was not even Hitler's Tea House, as it sometimes has been wrongly labelled, as he preferred to have his afternoon tea at the nearby Mooslahnerkopf Teehaus. He is thought to have visited the property no more than ten or so times, usually for less than an hour. However, he did receive the departing French ambassador André François-Poncet there in October 1938, and it is this diplomat who is often credited with calling it the Eagle's Nest. There is no evidence that Hitler ever used such a grand-sounding name for a place in which he obviously had such little interest. Even the French didn't pick up on this nickname; it is generally only in English-speaking countries that it seems to be referred to as the Eagle's Nest.

It is possible that the error has been compounded by a mix-up in people's minds as to the identity of the house, as Hitler did actually have a hideaway (known as the Berghof) on the same mountain. He had a completely different attitude towards this place, and it is estimated he spent more time in the Berghof than anywhere else during the Second World War. He also had one of his many command complexes near Bad Nauheim, further to the north in Hesse. This the Nazis called Adlerhorst – the Eagle's Nest.

There is no evidence that Hitler ever used such a grand-sounding name for a place in which he obviously had such little interest.

WHO DO YOU THINK YOU ARE KIDDING, MR FLANAGAN?

Let me confess to a guilty pleasure – I am a fanatical fan of the timeless comedy of the TV sitcom *Dad's Army*. But watching the episodes when originally broadcast from 1968 to 1977 I made a misinformed assumption that still persists in places today. I believed the theme song, 'Who do you think you are kidding Mr Hitler?', was not just a wartime song, but a wartime recording.

I knew enough to realise the singer was Bud Flanagan, and I associated him with the antics of the Crazy Gang, stalwart raisers of morale throughout the Second World War. However, unknown to me, they remained popular for decades after that, their last performance together being at the Royal Variety Performance of 1967. Sadly, Flanagan died the following year, but his last recording, a pastiche of his songs from the Second World War, was the *Dad's Army* theme song, with lyrics by the series deviser and co-writer Jimmy Perry and music by Derek Taverner.

ARTHUR LOWE AND JOHN LE MESURIER

Another popular error associated with *Dad's Army* is that when Jimmy Perry, and later David Croft, developed the show, John Le Mesurier was approached to play the pompous Captain Mainwaring, and Arthur Lowe was asked to play his sergeant. They then however picked up on the additional comic effect they could achieve with the social-climbing middle-class bank manager being in charge, with his sergeant being both his inferior at work and in the military, but annoyingly far, far his superior socially.

Neither Croft nor Perry has given credence to this, although there were a few changes to the cast of *Fighting Tigers*, the original working title of the show. Jimmy Perry actually wrote the part of the spiv with himself in mind, but was persuaded to relinquish the role to the wonderful James Beck. Also head of comedy at the BBC Michael Mills suggested they add a Scot to the cast. And the actor they originally felt could fill the size-six-and-a-half boots of Captain Mainwaring? Jon Pertwee, then of *Navy Lark* fame, and soon to be the third incarnation of the Doctor.

HITLER WAS A VEGETARIAN

Or so he would have had the world believe. However, there are many, sometimes comic, anecdotes and documents that point to the fact that he both deliberately and unknowingly broke the rules by which a modern self-professed vegetarian would operate. Hitler, also publicly projected as a teetotaller and a non-smoker, was particularly impressed with the diet of the Roman legionary, and thought his soldiers should eat similarly. He seemed sincere in his desire to eradicate cruelty to animals, and the same Nazis who implemented the Holocaust brought in the most forward-thinking animal welfare laws known in the world at that time. So

much for the 'positives', if such a term can be used to describe the man and his regime.

The negatives are far more entertaining. Robert Payne published a biography in 1973 in which he claimed Hitler had a fondness for Bavarian wurst and caviar but at the same time avoided fish. In the 1990s it came to light that chef Dione Lucas had worked in pre-war Hamburg and often served stuffed squab (young pigeon) to an appreciative Hitler. The *New York Times* produced evidence in 1996 that he ate ham. His cook often added animal broth and fat to his meals. His dietician Marlene von Exner apparently despised vegetarianism, and from 1943 secretly added bone marrow to his diet. The clincher is that, with the full knowledge and agreement of Hitler, his physician for the last nine years of his life, Theodor Morell, injected him with 'elixirs of youth' containing in varying degrees cardiac muscle, placenta, liver, pancreas, prostate glands, adrenal glands and even bovine testosterone. So, despite what he said, I don't think he was what we would now call a vegetarian.

LUTHER PINNED THE 'NINETY-FIVE THESES' TO THE DOOR OF WITTENBERG CATHEDRAL TO START THE PROTESTANT REFORMATION

———— 8✠3 ————

Martin Luther published the 'Ninety-Five Theses on the Power and Efficacy of Indulgences' in 1517. He actually nailed them to the door of All Saints Church,[1] which had been used for some time as a university noticeboard. Therefore, his actions appear not to have been as dramatic in real life as in the story that I grew up with.

The majority of Protestant sects date their separation from the Catholic Church to this time, if not specifically to Luther's protest. However, Luther was lancing a boil that had been swelling since at least the fourteenth century, a process originating in the ideas of the Englishman John Wycliffe and the Bohemian Jan Hus. His aim was not to set up a separate Church,

---

1 Commonly known as Schlosskirche or the 'Castle Church' It is also known as the Reformation Memorial Church.

but cause a reformation of Catholicism. Radicalism and politics were to transform these modest aims and lead to widespread inter-religious (rather than inter-state) conflict in Europe until the Treaty of Westphalia in 1648. Another reason to reject 1517 as the start of the Reformation is that the brethren Churches – the Unitas Fratrum and the Moravian Brethren – trace their doctrinal origins back to the aforementioned Jan Hus.

MINSTER
MEANS BIG CHURCH

York Minster, Beverley Minster, Selby Minster, Southwell Minster. The Midlands and north of England are dotted with huge churches that as a matter of honour are given the title Minster to reflect their sheer size. But, as with a lot of things in life, size isn't everything.

The word is first found in royal foundation charters of the seventh century, and corresponds to the Latin *monasterium*, meaning monastery. It could actually designate any settlement of ecclesiastics living in a community under a charter and following the obligation of maintaining the daily office of prayer. Minsters declined from the tenth century because of the systematic introduction of the parish church system, but the title remained an honorific for a wide range of Church establishments – cathedrals, monasteries, collegiate and even parish churches – that had their origins in an Anglo-Saxon foundation.

So the modern practice of using the term for any large or important church is off the mark, especially bestowing the status of minster on an existing parish church.

CATHOLIC PRIESTS CAN'T
BE MARRIED

I'd better tell that to an acquaintance of mine. I think she'll be a little upset that her marriage to her husband, a Roman Catholic priest, is invalid by the laws of that Church. You will respond that it's obvious why this anomaly exists: they were married before he converted to Catholicism. In this case, yes, you're right, but the picture is a little more complex than that.

Most married Catholic priests actually belong to the Eastern Catholic Churches, also known as the Eastern Rite, found in countries like Ukraine, the Czech Republic, Slovakia and Hungary. These priests live and work where western European Christianity and eastern European Christianity meet. Their Churches are under the jurisdiction of the Vatican and they recognise the authority of the Pope in Rome. However, their traditions are much more in line with the Eastern Orthodox Churches, where although monks are celibate, parish priests are not just allowed to marry; they are expected to, and to produce children. Some estimates have the ratio of legally married to unmarried priests in the worldwide Catholic Church as one in every five, even though the official line is that celibacy is a requirement.

In the West, including North America, the usual explanation for a married Catholic priest is that he was formerly a minister in another denomination such as the Anglican or Lutheran Churches. In such a case he applies to a local bishop, who then submits a special application to the Pope. If accepted, he is certainly not expected to divorce or separate from his spouse, so his wife becomes the parish priest's wife. This exception to the celibacy rule has been in force from the early 1980s.

Some estimates have the ratio of legally married to unmarried priests in the worldwide Catholic Church as one in every five.

IT'S HERESY TO CALL YOUR BABY SON JESUS

I know there are thousands if not millions of agnostics and atheists out there who won't have the slightest interest in this. I talk rather to the more religiously minded people who call themselves Christians. If they have doctrinal evidence that a child cannot be called Jesus by its parents, then try telling that to the people of the Spanish- and Portuguese-speaking parts of the world, a far more religiously observant population on average than that of the English-speaking regions. As well as noting that it's a common surname in Portugal, I'd especially like to see someone argue the case with the Mexican Jesús Martinez – he's a boxer.

ST PATRICK CLEARED IRELAND OF SNAKES

Again possibly of interest only to the faithful, but it has been a long-standing belief among those who believe in the miracles of the saints that this is, as you might say, gospel. However, if you don't think this story holds much water, it still leaves the intriguing question of why Ireland doesn't have any native snakes, whereas neighbouring Great Britain does.

The reason the island of Ireland has to make do with the common lizard as its only reptile is the effect on its fauna of the ice ages. There are a number of other native non-reptilian species that Ireland lacks, among them moles and weasels. Their absence is down to the bridge of land and earth that linked Ireland to Great Britain disappearing about 12,000 years ago. The Irish Sea, as it is now called, all but stopped the immigration of any species that had not reached the island by then. However, the bridge that linked Great Britain to continental Europe didn't disappear until 5,000 years ago. Cold-blooded reptiles were among the last species to reach the British Isles as the ice receded, and even if they fancied a trip to the Emerald Isle they could get no further than the Welsh and Scottish coasts.

U2 ARE NOT AN IRISH BAND

If we base our argument on the fact that they were formed in Dublin, then our contention is unfounded. That makes them Irish. Bono Vox (Paul Hewson), their lead singer, was born in Dublin. So was Larry Mullen, the drummer around who the band coalesced in the 1970s. However, the Edge, aka David Evans, was actually born in Barking to Welsh parents who moved as a family to Dublin a year later. The fourth member of the band, Adam Clayton, was also born in England, in Chinnor, Oxfordshire, five years before his family also moved to Ireland. However, he retains his British passport, and thus his British citizenship, making U2 an Anglo-Irish band.

'WHEN IRISH EYES ARE SMILING'

What a lovely old Irish folk tune, drifting down to us through the mists of Hibernian musical history. Well actually, like Scotland's new unofficial national anthem 'Flower of Scotland', it's not quite as antique as it seems. Nor is it very Irish.

With lyrics by Chauncey Olcott (from Buffalo, New York) and George Graff, Jr (a native of Manhattan of Dutch and German descent), and music composed by Ernest Ball (Cleveland, Ohio), it first appeared in Olcott's production *The Isle O'Dreams*. He first sang the song in the show in 1912, less than a hundred years ago – in New York.

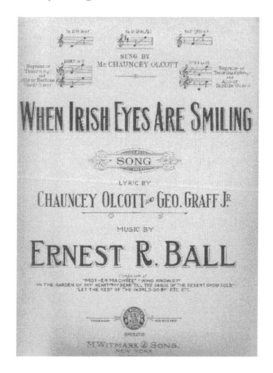

SCOTLAND'S OFFICIAL NATIONAL ANTHEM IS STILL 'GOD SAVE THE QUEEN'

Although the Scots have been belting out 'Flower of Scotland' at major sporting events since the 1990s (it was written in the 1960s), 'God Save the Queen' remains the national anthem in law. Well, actually it doesn't, as there is no official national anthem for the United Kingdom. So 'Hen Wlad Fy Nhadau' (or 'Glan Rhondda'), written in the 1850s, is also not the official anthem of Wales, despite being sung at official openings of the Welsh Assembly. An amusing aside here is that in 1993 newly appointed Welsh secretary John Redwood was publicly filmed opening and closing his mouth in a bizarre fashion during a rendition of 'Land of My Fathers', clearly not knowing the words (and unable to mime). John Major tells us in his autobiography that the first thing Redwood's successor at the Welsh Office, William Hague, did on being appointed was to find someone to teach him the words. He later married his teacher, Ffion Jenkins.

So, when an anthem is needed for one of the constituent countries of the UK at, say, an international sporting event, alternative songs are often used because they can be.

- England has used 'God Save the Queen' but also 'Land of Hope and Glory' (at the Commonwealth Games), 'Rule Britannia!' and, especially at rugby league matches, 'Jerusalem'. This last song has also been used since 2004 at England (and Wales) cricket matches.
- Scotland either uses 'Flower of Scotland' or traditionally at the Commonwealth Games, 'Scotland the Brave'.
- Wales, as stated, uses 'Hen Wlad Fy Nhadau'.
- Northern Ireland uses the 'Londonderry Air' ('Danny Boy') at the Commonwealth Games.

DE VALERA ALSO WASN'T IRISH

——⅋⅋——

That symbol of Irish independence from the United Kingdom and founder of Fianna Fáil, Eamon de Valera also served as both Taoiseach and president of Ireland, but was born a citizen of the good old United States of America. He was a New Yorker actually. His mother was born in Ireland but the matter of his father's origins is a little more obscure. De Valera himself claimed his dad was Juan Vivion de Valera, but couldn't seem to decide if he was Spanish or Cuban. One historian suggests he came from the south-west United States, so he could have been American or a Mexican immigrant.

De Valera also had what is now called a 'journey' towards the name by which he is remembered. His birth certificate stated he was George de Valero, with his father named as Vivion de Valero. George de Valero had become Edward de Valera by 1916 at the latest. Eamon appeared after this.

BRITANNIA WAS CREATED IN THE EIGHTEENTH CENTURY

——⅋⅋——

Britannia is the symbol of Great Britain, the counterpart of Marianne in France, the female personification of the nation. If Great Britain brought about her creation, then she can't be any older than about 300, when Great Britain was created from the union of the kingdoms of Scotland and England.

IX

The Romans referred to the British Isles as Insulae Britannicae even before they invaded temporarily in 55 BC and 54 BC and then again successfully and permanently in AD 43. Following their settlement here, the Romans created the province of Britannica, although it never covered the entire island. It was during the reign of Hadrian that a female personification by the name of Britannica began appearing on coins. Quickly promoted to a goddess, early portraits showed her as a beautiful young woman wearing a helmet, wrapped in white and rather racily with her left breast exposed. She soon started to be depicted sitting on a rock, holding a spear and leaning on a shield. I think any of us being asked to describe Britannica would come up with something very similar.

BAGPIPES ARE SCOTTISH

Love 'em or loathe 'em, the bagpipe (singular according to the *OED*) is usually blamed on the Scots. Being a fan, I thank the ancient Persians or whoever it was that invented them. The evidence is the Persians then introduced it to the Romans, who in turn spread it throughout their empire and beyond, so that there are varieties of bagpipe as far afield as Spain (there is an international bagpipe museum in Gijon), the Balkans, Italy, France, Anatolia, Scandinavia and the Low Countries. They appear quite often in the paintings of Breugel, Bosch and other Flemish and Dutch artists.

The Romans also introduced the bagpipe to the British Isles, where the main variations now are the Irish Uilleann, the Northumbrian Smallpipe, and perhaps now the most famous internationally, the Great Highland Bagpipe.

COOL BRITANNIA

Tony Blair, or at least his spin doctors, has or have been credited with the creation of this term for the fresh young arts culture contemporary to the political changes attempted by New Labour in the 1990s. I like to think that bands like Blur and Oasis, most commonly cited as leaders of this movement, might recoil from the fact that the *OED* tells us the phrase originated with the trad-jazz-influenced art school group the Bonzo Dog Doo-Dah Band. It was the title of the first track on their first album *Gorilla* released in 1967.

BRITAIN HAS NOT BEEN INVADED
SINCE 1066

———— ❧❧ ————

This is a matter of pride for the British, or rather the inhabitants of Great Britain, especially the English. We seem to have no problem with the earlier Romans, the Anglo-Saxons (and the Jutes), and finally the Normans. I think we see these invaders as actually adding something to the national character; that is to say, we are the sum of these invaders of the first millennium.

Then total national amnesia sets in for the next thousand years. We draw attention to the defeat of the Spanish Armada in 1588, and the fact that we managed to keep both Napoleon and Hitler at bay,[1] mainly due to our sea power. However, our sea power has let us down on a number of occasions. Let me point out some highlights of what is, I'm sure, not a fully comprehensive list.

We like to concentrate on the battles of Poitiers, Crécy and Agincourt in our accounts of the Hundred Years War with France, but like to omit that on four separate occasions in the 1300s Portsmouth was sacked by raiding Frenchmen. During the little-discussed seventeenth-century wars against the Dutch, the enemy sailed up the Thames, burned Sheerness, raided our major dockyard at Chatham and even captured the royal barge. We gloss over the fact that James II had 7,000 Frenchmen in his army when he tried to get his throne back in 1690, but the major fight in that conflict was in Ireland and we (that is a Dutchman we had invited to be on our side) won with the help of a mishmash of European Protestants in the ranks of the home side. The American admiral John Paul Jones raided Whitehaven of all places in 1788 during the American War of Independence, but as it's a little out of the way, let's not pay much attention to that. We do like to celebrate, however, the ramshackle landing of troops of revolutionary France at Fishguard in 1799, and the wonderful story of them mistaking the Welsh women in their red shawls and stove-pipe hats for British troops.

For good measure, we also tend not to count the incidents involving William of Orange and Bonnie Prince Charlie because the first landing

During the seventeenth-century wars against the Dutch, the enemy sailed up the Thames, burned Sheerness, raided our major dockyard at Chatham and even captured the royal barge.

---

1 Although, of course, the Channel Islands were occupied right to the end of the Second World War, being bypassed by the invading allies in 1944.

was by invitation and the second we regard as a family spat. My conclusion is that history has been far more complicated than we would like to admit, and what we should say is we have not been successfully *occupied* since 1066.

CABAL

First appearing in Charles II's reign, this word refers to a small exclusive committee or council. It originated from his Committee for Foreign Affairs, which effectively managed the government and was a precursor of the modern cabinet. It's a word made up of the first letters of the surnames of the five members of this committee: Clifford, Arlington, Buckingham, Ashley and Lauderdale.

Whoever spotted this serendipitous connection was truly a wit but didn't invent the word. It was borrowed from the French and descended from Hebrew; the name of the modern celebrity-attracting Jewish discipline Kabbalah comes from the same root. Anyway, the five members of the Cabal don't appear in order of their importance. In addition, Clifford became Lord Chudleigh, which still fits, but Arlington's surname was Bennet; Buckingham was really George Villiers; Ashley's proper name was Anthony Ashley Cooper, 1st Earl of Shaftsbury, who just happened to call himself Lord Ashley; and Lauderdale was John Maitland, 1st Duke and 2nd Earl of Lauderdale, and 3rd Lord Thirlestane. I call on any Scrabble experts out there to come up with some new words based on this surfeit of newly available initials.

DOOMSDAY AND DREAD

We often alter the correct spelling of the 1086 Domesday Book, describing it as the Doomsday Book. In doing this, we ascribe to it a sense that is quite wrong. It has nothing to do with a day on which everyone is doomed. It's from the Old English *dom*, which has more to do with judgement – and not in the biblical sense – than being doomed. The main purpose of the survey was to determine who held what land and therefore owed what taxes under the Anglo-Saxon king Edward the Confessor. By basing tax liabilties on the status quo before the conquest of 1066 the Normans sought to give their system a basis in law and established fact. The *dome* or judgement of the assessors was to do with their accounting or reckoning, although it was doom-laden in the sense it was final with no appeal. What was written down was the law and that was that.

A similar misunderstanding due to a change in the meaning of a word occurs in the original epistle dedicatory that introduces the 1611 King James Bible: 'Great and manifold were the blessings, most *dread* Sovereign, which Almighty God, the Father of all mercies, bestowed upon us the people of England, when first he sent Your Majesty's Royal Person to rule and reign over us.' While not suggesting the king was a Rastafarian (with accompanying hairstyle), was James I to be dreaded as we understand it in the modern sense? The answer is no; what we would say today is 'revered king' or if we were truly down with the kids, 'awesome'.

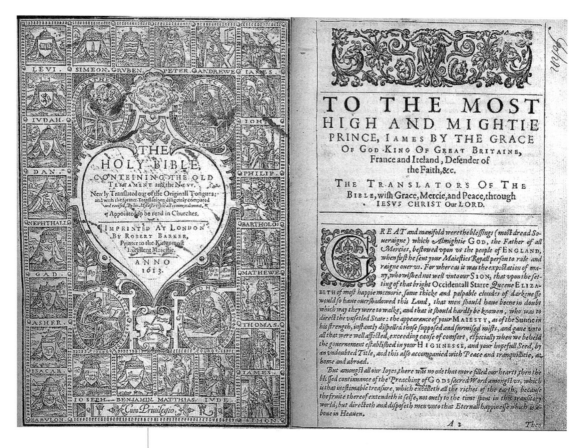

Returning to the original subject, the Domesday Book actually isn't one work but two, the bigger and more detailed Little Domesday, which covered Norfolk, Suffolk and Essex and thought of as a first attempt, and the more convenient and less detailed Great Domesday, which covered the rest of England with the exception of the as-yet-unconsolidated northern counties of Cumberland, Westmoreland, Northumberland and Durham. Cumberland and Westmoreland were mostly part of the Scottish Kingdom of Strathclyde at the time, and the Bishop of Durham had sole taxation rights in his fiefdom as well as probably most of Northumberland. Significantly, London and Winchester (among other towns) are missed out too, probably due to their size and complexity as urban areas. Without the omitted places as outlined above, the total value of property in England in 1086 was about £75,000. Also of interest is the fact that the Domesday Book tells us 80 per cent of the cultivated land at the outbreak of the First World War was already in use in 1086.

THE FRENCH KING
OF ENGLAND

— ✠ ✠ —

I can recite the list of the Kings and Queens of England, and can even make a reasonable stab at the dates. There are of course some anomalies in the generally accepted list. One such is the question of whether Henry II's mother, Matilda (or Maud in some sources), ruled in her own right during her war with the usurper King Stephen? Another is do we include Lady Jane Grey's nine days before Bloody Mary won her birthright? But putting these aside for a moment the mnemonic I grew up with reads like this.

> Willie, Willie, Harry, Stee,
> Harry, Dick, John, Harry Three,
> One-to-Three Neds, Richard Two,
> Harrys Four, Five, Six, then who?
> Edwards Four, Five, Dick the Bad,
> Harrys Twain, Ned Six (the lad).
> Mary, Bessie, James, you ken,
> Then Charlie, Charlie, James again.
> Will and Mary, Anne of Gloria,
> Georges (four!), Will Four, Victoria.
> Edward Seven next, and then
> Came George the Fifth in 1910.
> Ned the Eighth soon abdicated,
> So George Six was coronated.
> Then Number-Two Elizabeth,
> And that's all, folks (until her death)!

Only there's someone missing from the second line – King Louis.

Every former schoolboy of my age or thereabouts knows the story that in 1216 King John lost his treasure in the Wash, the large bay on the coasts of Lincolnshire and Norfolk, that is; not his local launderette. There are arguments as to the veracity of this story, but most scholars would not argue with the assertion that he was in the middle of yet another

spat with his barons at the time. He had been forced to seal[1] Magna Carta the previous year, and as he didn't like its terms was fighting a civil war. Whether or not you think the story of the lost treasure is true, it does beg a question. If John was fighting a civil war as the king, surely his power base would have been his capital, London? So why was he gallivanting around the countryside instead of sitting safe in the Tower of London? The fact is, another king was sitting on the throne in the capital at the time.

By 1215 some of the most important barons in England had had enough of John, and with the support of the French Dauphin and Alexander II King of the Scots, they took London in June. John was forced to agree to Magna Carta, but as soon as the barons left London he renounced it, plunging England into civil war. As the Pope was on his side for once, he was confident of success. Sadly for him though, he couldn't hold on to London and had to take to the country. The Dauphin invaded in 1216, and was proclaimed king in London in May of that year with the support of the barons. This is the missing Louis, King of England.

Things changed quickly later that year when John died from dysentery. His nine-year-old son Henry was next in line for the throne, and as the royalist side thought he'd be more acceptable to the barons he was swiftly crowned Henry III in late October 1216. English support for Louis collapsed and he returned to France, where he eventually ruled as Louis VII. Back in England, the medieval equivalent of the airbrush was utilised, and Louis was removed from the list of English monarchs.

CULLODEN WAS NOT THE LAST BATTLE
ON BRITISH SOIL

The last Jacobite rebellion[2] ended when the English finally defeated the Scots (I'll cover this other common misunderstanding next) in 1746 at Culloden near Inverness. This was the last battle, to date at least, to take

---

1 I can find no evidence that John couldn't read and write, which is often given as the reason the charter was sealed. This is not the reason why. A seal was a recognisable symbol of authority, especially in a society where the majority were illiterate.

2 Contrary to the popular error that 1745 saw *the* Jacobite rising, this was only the last in a series of rebellions, the most serious previous one of which was in 1715.

place on British soil. Only it wasn't. I'm not referring to the Easter Rising in Dublin in 1916 against the rule of the British. Nor am I trying to make out that the inner-city riots of 1981 or those against the poll tax in 1990 should be classed as battles, even if they did have most of the characteristics of one. I'm highlighting instead an event that took place in 1781 on the island of Jersey.

I'm perhaps being a little controversial in claiming that Jersey is British soil. I know there are those who will argue that as it is not part of the United Kingdom, and the island is not British, an interesting point to debate in the pubs in Douglas on the Isle of Man. But if Jersey is British, then it was the site of the last battle on British soil, because in that year in the streets of St Helier 2,000 men under Major Francis Peirson defeated a force of 1,000 Frenchmen under the Baron de Rullecourt, who had invaded to help their allies the American revolutionaries. Little known to the rest of us, the event is actually well commemorated by the islanders, and there is a painting by John Singleton Copley in London's Tate Britain dramatising the death of Major Peirson. However, if you can't get to the Tate there is another place you can see it, as it appears on the Jersey ten-pound note.

AT CULLODEN THE ENGLISH
DEFEATED THE SCOTS

The last battle on mainland Britain is generally thought to be the massive and final defeat of Bonnie Prince Charlie's Highland Scots by an English army under the command of the Duke of Cumberland. Generally true, but perhaps sadly for Scots today there was an element of Scot fighting Scot. It would be more accurate to call the victorious side a British government army, as of its sixteen infantry battalions, one was Irish and four were Scottish.

THE BIGGEST VOLUNTEER ARMY

I heard on a TV documentary the other day the British army of the First World War described as the greatest volunteer force ever raised. I took this to mean that the narrator thought it was the finest, because it certainly wasn't the biggest ever raised.

That accolade goes to the Indian Army, which by the end of the Second World War stood at 2.5 million, a figure supposedly achieved totally without conscription. It is generally recognised that the Indian Army was also the biggest volunteer army during the First World War as well, with over 140,000 seeing active service on the Western Front alone.

THE MARATHON

The long-distance foot race now known as the marathon, run over a
distance measuring (using imperial rather than metric) 26 miles and
385 yards, is named after the exploit of the Greek soldier Pheidippides.
In 490 BC he took news of the victory over the Persians at the Battle
of Marathon to Athens, which happened to be that distance from the
battlefield. Tragically, after running the entire distance without stopping
he burst into the Athenian assembly, exclaimed, 'Nenikékamen,' ('We have
won') and then collapsed and died.

The story seems to be an amalgam of legends and semi-legends, and
the belief that Athens and Marathon are just over twenty-six miles apart by
road also needs to be corrected.

The tale outlined above comes down to us from Plutarch's first-
century-AD work *On the Glory of Athens*, written a good 500 years after
the event. However, he actually gives a choice of different names for the
runner, Thersipus, Eucles or even Erchius. When Lucian rewrote the
story in the second century AD, the runner became Philippides, which is
close to Pheidippides but, as they say, no cigar. Perhaps Lucian had read
one of the manuscripts of the seminal account of the Greco-Persian

*It wasn't until 1921
that the International
Amateur Athletics
Federation fixed the
distance as that which
had been used at the
London Olympics in
1908.*

Wars by Herodotus. In this the famed ancient Greek historian tells us of Pheidippides (in some manuscripts Philippides), but has him running away from Athens in the direction of Sparta to ask for help, being refused, and then running back to tell the Athenians that they were on their own. This is actually a distance of over 150 miles – each way! There is no mention of a messenger leaving the battlefield at Marathon; in fact, Herodotus tells us that because they feared a Persian naval raid on Athens, the majority of the exhausted army decided to hightail it back home, arriving there the same day. What fixed the composite legend rather than the true story in the minds of modern readers was Robert Browning's 1876 poem 'Pheidippides'. By default this has been taken as historic fact.

Now we turn to the route and the distance. The first problem here is that there is a mountain in the way if you want to run directly from Marathon to Athens. The route that the modern road between the two follows is around twenty-six miles, so we take it this was probably the distance measured by Michel Breal when inspired to invent the modern marathon. The alternative route, if a little shorter at around twenty-two miles, has some very steep climbs and descents.

The first modern marathon, at the 1896 Olympics, followed the legendary route and measured forty kilometres. From the 1900 games up to the 1920 Antwerp Olympics the marathon varied between 24.85 and 26.56 miles; the only thing that mattered was that all the competitors took the same route. It wasn't until 1921 that the International Amateur Athletics Federation fixed the distance as that which had been used at the London Olympics in 1908. Initially it had been planned that this race would start at Windsor Castle, finish at the White City Stadium and run for forty kilometres, and this looked set to be the standardised distance once the authorities got round to agreeing on it. But, in true British style, a few late amendments were necessary.

Complaints about tramlines and cobbles caused the race to be re-routed across the rough ground of Wormwood Scrubs, and it was then agreed that it would start at Queen Victoria's statue at Windsor Castle. These alterations lengthened the course, and so a new distance of twenty-six miles was settled on, with an additional lap of the track at the end, another 585 yards and 2 feet. Two stories exist as to why things were changed further. One is that the start had to be moved so that the King, suffering from a cold, could watch the start from his window. More believable is that by changing the stadium entry to be used by the athletes at the end of the race and the direction of the final lap (from anticlockwise to clockwise) to improve the view for the Queen and the rest of the spectators, the route became 26 miles and 385 yards, the modern standard distance. So millions of runners at marathons around the world now run what is effectively an arbitrary distance to celebrate an event that probably never took place.

THREE HUNDRED SPARTANS – AND THEN THERE WERE THE OTHERS

Another legendary event in the struggle between the Persians and the Greeks was the heroic stand at Thermopylae in 480 BC of a mere 300 Spartans against a horde of Persian invaders. It has inspired the spending of many Hollywood dollars and is held up as perhaps the greatest example of selfless courage against overwhelming odds.

Not wishing to undermine the heroism of these brave men by one jot, King Leonidas actually had a few more troops at his disposal than just his 299 fellow Spartans. Most versions of the tale forget that as well as his own troops Leonidas had probably up to 900 soldiers drawn from the people who lived as subjects of the Spartans, the helots. Four hundred Thebans stayed as well, and 700 Thespians also refused to leave with the other

Greeks who were able to fight another day. So over 2,000 men probably fought to the death in the narrow pass.

Now before you imagine that the Persians found themselves in a pitched battle with a large Greek chorus, I need to advise you that the brave but now forgotten Thespians were citizens of Thespiae, a city in Boeotia. The theatrical use of the word derives from the name of the legendary first actor, Thespis.

SPARTA WAS NOT A STATE
OF ANCIENT GREECE

Not to the Spartans anyway. We see the Spartans as an ancient symbol of upright citizenship, living a harsh personal regime that helped their state to become a major military power in the ancient Greek world. These were people who left their newborn children on hillsides all night to see if they were tough enough, and used iron bars as coinage to stop anyone gathering a large amount of personal wealth. This is all very well documented. But if we brought one of the citizens of the ancient city via

the use of time travel into our modern world, he might take us to task as to the accuracy of using the term Spartan to describe the place he had come from.

During the archaic and classical periods of ancient Greece, the city of Sparta dominated an area known as Laconia. Full citizens either living in the city or in the surrounding countryside called themselves Spartiates[1], but there were other settlements in Laconia populated by non-citizens. In fact, the strength of the state and its military machine was based on a social structure in which the majority of inhabitants were not citizens. These Lacedaemonians or Perioeci[2] (a term that translates as 'about-dwellers') were also regarded as part of the state. And then there were the helots, a class of serfs living in conditions close to slavery.

Therefore the Spartiates were simply the ruling class named after the dominant city in the region. The state, however, was called Laconia. This can be see in any illustration of its soldiers. Unlike the hoplites from other states in ancient Greece, where a certain amount of individuality was tolerated, all the shields of Laconian soldiers bore an inverted chevron. This was the Greek letter lambda, standing for Laconia.

These were people who left their newborn children on hillsides all night to see if they were tough enough, and used iron bars as coinage to stop anyone gathering a large amount of personal wealth.

METAPHYSICS

The *OED* defines metaphysics as 'the study of phenomena beyond the scope of scientific enquiry' and relates to the 'the science, doctrine, or theory of spirits or spiritual beings'. It is this sense that comes down to us from works such as Kit Marlowe's *Faustus*, when he writes, 'These Metaphysickes of Magicians, And Negromantike bookes are heauenly'.

However, this is a modern misinterpretation that has developed in contrast to the origins of the word. When he first used the term, Aristotle did mean those things that are 'beyond', but not those things that transcend the natural world and are in the realm of the supernatural. In the philosophical sense, metaphysics is the branch of philosophy

---

1 The Spartiates were also known as the Homoi oi (those who are alike). These were trained soldiers. Their dominance as a fighting force is even more impressive to us when we find that they only numbered 8,000 at their height.

2 Also Perioikoi.

dealing with the first principles of things, including questions about being, substance, time and space, causation, change and identity. There is nothing supernatural there, I think. In the works of Aristotle he followed the section called Physics with a section called Metaphysics. In Greek, *meta* means following, so metaphysics in its original sense meant that which comes after physics.

THE ANCIENT GREEK WORLD WAS FULL OF STATUES OF PURE WHITE MARBLE

The ancient Greeks did use white marble to make a large number of beautiful statues, which are still admired today for their artistry and workmanship, and we laud them for the purity of their work. Only we are looking at these works of art with a modern eye.

The ancients loved to paint and decorate their work, and the more colourful they could make them the better. The use of gold and ivory was widespread. It's only over time that, due to wear and theft, what we see today has evolved. We now generally prefer clean lines in art, so it might be equally disappointing to the modern eye to note that the Celtic crosses standing in churchyards up and down the land, and indeed the walls of the churches themselves, were once festooned with colour, only for it to disappear over time – and with the help of Puritans armed with whitewash in the seventeenth century.

A BELFRY IS A PLACE TO KEEP BELLS

Not in the original sense of the word. Although the etymology from the original German is a bit shady, the word when first used in English meant a penthouse. And that's not penthouse as in luxury top-floor flat but as in siege tower. The meaning was then extended to watchtowers of various types, and in turn to the tower of a church. As it's usually in the tower of a church that the bells are kept, the usual modern usage has come to denote this. This arose after the word was already in use in English.

BELL WEATHER

— ❦ ❦ —

From the French *belle* and weather, hence originally an indicator of good weather, and now in developed euphemistic senses a harbinger of news or events, both good and bad.

Nothing that fancy, I'm afraid. We shouldn't mix our Anglo-Saxon and our French so carelessly. The word is actually spelt bellwether, and originated with the practice of hanging a bell around the neck of the lead sheep in a flock so the others followed. So bell not *belle* and wether not weather, as in male sheep or ram, usually a castrated one. The word now means leader, not harbinger.

BATS HAVE RADAR

— ❦ ❦ —

They don't have radio detection and ranging; that was developed by human beings. What a bat has, as does a dolphin, is the ability to use echolocation, which is more akin to sonar.

ST THOMAS À BECKET

— ❦ ❦ —

Thomas à Becket was the troublemaker murdered on the say-so of King Henry II with the words 'Will no one rid me of this turbulent priest?' There are a number of fallacies here.

First, what of the name? It seems that Thomas Becket, as he was known to his contemporaries, became Thomas à Becket around the time of the Reformation, centuries after his assassination. This was possibly done to make his name sound like that of the later German theologian Thomas à Kempis, so as to gain some extra kudos from the brilliant continental churchman. Second, what of Henry II's words? I'm with the noted historian Simon Schama on this one, who cites the words of Becket's contemporary biographer Edward Grim. He in turn quotes the at that time sickly king as saying, 'What miserable drones and traitors have I nourished and brought

When Becket decided his privileges had been usurped by the Archbishop of York and the Bishops of London and Salisbury, he excommunicated all three.

up in my household, who let their lord be treated with such shameful contempt by a low-born cleric?' Other variations have come down to us including the commonly believed one.

The third point I would make is that Becket the churchman wasn't always the tragic, ascetic figure he appears in the common memory. He played politics and had been stirring it up for years. After an international education in civil and religious law, and a career as an envoy to Rome, he was appointed by Henry as his chancellor, a secular post, on the say-so of the Archbishop of Canterbury, Theobald. He relished this role, and supported the king totally as a close friend and courtier, even enforcing Henry's right to tax the Church. On the death of Theobald, Henry saw his chancellor as a means of further extending his control over every aspect of his kingdom, with the Church being especially on his mind. But Becket the archbishop was a very different kettle of fish to Becket the chancellor. He was already unpopular within the Church because of his earlier activities, but that didn't stop him seeking to establish his authority and resisting Henry's attempts at royal control. His new asceticism also made him very unpopular at court, where he was seen as ungrateful by Henry. He was soon forced to flee to France. While there he even managed to fall out with Pope Alexander III, who favoured a more diplomatic approach to resolving the differences between the Church and the English crown. However, now on the point of being excommunicated, Henry II let him back into England.

Unfortunately, Becket just couldn't stop himself acting far too big for his mitre. When he decided his privileges had been usurped by the Archbishop of York and the Bishops of London and Salisbury, he excommunicated all three[1] and then continued excommunicating his opponents in the clergy. Henry, now ill and in Normandy, probably wasn't in the mood for all the annoying news of Becket's activities back in England. However, the quote from Grim could be the king merely having a sideswipe at his retainers while feeling off colour. It doesn't seem to have been a direct

1   A practice adopted from the French kings by Stephen of England (c. 1096–1154), and Henry II was to have the heir to the throne crowned as a sort of junior king during his father's reign. Henry the Young King was the second but eldest surviving son of Henry II, and it was his coronation at York in 1170 by the Archbishop of York and the Bishops of London and Salisbury that caused Becket to excommunicate them. As the Young King died before his father, he does not appear in lists of English kings and queens.

order to get rid of Becket. Nevertheless, it was taken by some as a royal command to face down or assassinate Becket, and four knights, Reginald Fitzurse, Hugh de Morville, William de Tracy and Richard le Breton, set out to confront the archbishop. On 29 December 1170 they arrived at Canterbury. According to the monk Gervase of Canterbury and Grim, an eyewitness, they put their weapons under a tree and concealed their mail coats under their cloaks before entering the cathedral to challenge Becket. The knights told

Becket he was to go to Winchester to account for his actions, but he refused. It was not until he refused their demands to submit to the king's will that they retrieved their weapons and rushed back inside to cut him down.

So, to conclude, we remember this churchman by a misnomer and as the godly victim of a cruel king when in fact he was, for the period, getting nothing but his comeuppance for his obstreperousness and ingratitude to his former employer.

Still, Becket the ascetic had the last word from beyond the grave. For whatever reason, political or spiritual, Alexander III canonised Becket only three years after his death. His shrine remained a popular site of pilgrimage until its destruction was ordered by Henry VIII, and we should be thankful to Becket indirectly for that masterpiece of English literature *The Canterbury Tales*. In a way, he even got his own back on a personal level. Facing revolt by his sons and blamed for the martyr's death, his nemesis Henry II felt it politic to humble himself by paying public penance at Becket's tomb.

TWO SMALL Fs

I trawled through the electoral register the other day, inspired to check a question raised by Mr Mulliner from the stories of P G Wodehouse. I found about a hundred households under the name Ffrench and five(ish) named Ffinch. There are many variations due to double-barrelling, and indeed one source I found claims to have a database with at least a hundred different surnames that begin with two small fs.

There's something aristocratic in the sight of a name starting with two small fs, but unlike the guardian of Mulliner's wife Angela, Sir Jasper ffinch-ffarowmere[1], I fear the belief that such a name indicates Norman ancestry is wrong. It is born more out of ignorance than bloodline.

It seemingly began in the eighteenth century with a misunderstanding of the manuscript form of the capital F, which resembles two lower-case fs joined together. *The Complete Peerage* (1926) saw through the affectation developed after this initial mistake: 'This ffoolish ffancy, which is aggravated if the F be written Ff [as it is in the electoral register], has happily not been repeated by any member of the peerage, and, considering the spread of education, is not likely now to occur again.' All that said, by bringing up this rebuke of one of his ancestors, I doubt if I will be invited to Castle ffrench, the home of Robuck John Peter Charles Mario ffrench, 8th Baron ffrench in Galway, in the near future.

'STEWART' IS SCOTTISH, 'STUART' IS ENGLISH

As you might gather, this has been a particular bugbear of mine throughout my life, particularly on the occasions I have been asked, 'Do you spell it the Scottish or English way?'

While not dragging the two people I am aware of called Stuert into the argument, I would like to point out that Stewart and Stuart are both Scottish in origin, and English as well, and in a way French. The royal house which ruled Scotland from 1316 until 1714, and England from 1603 until 1714, actually used both forms at different times over its regnal career.

Stewart was and is a Scottish surname and is now much used as a forename. Linguistically it is Old English, derived from *stigeweard*, the genitive prefix *stige* meaning sty, and the suffix *weard* meaning guardian or warden. So the name started as one given to a pig man, which was actually quite an important job back then. The progenitor of the Stewart dynasty is believed to have been a knight from Brittany who came to England after the Norman Conquest. A few generations later his descendants relocated

---

1 Who lived at the fictional ffinch hall, ffinch, Yorkshire, and pronounce each 'f' separately.

to Scotland and were given the title high sty-ward. The title became a name, which then transmuted into Steward and finally Stewart.

After the marriage of the sixth high steward, Walter Stewart, to Robert Bruce's daughter in 1315, the course was set for his son to become Robert II and start the ruling dynasty. The family ruled under this name until the middle of the sixteenth century, when Stuart was introduced as a variant French spelling of the old name. James V was married to two Frenchwomen, Madeleine of Valois (daughter of King Francis I) and Mary of Guise, who was the mother of Mary Queen of Scots.[1] His untimely death when Mary was only six days old led to attempts by Henry VIII of England to promote a widely unpopular dynastic match between Mary and the future Edward VI. James's prior efforts to reinvigorate the Auld Alliance paid

off, because the more attractive offer of marriage to the French Dauphin was accepted, and at the age of five Mary and her mother sailed for France. She spent the next thirteen years there, where she was known as Marie Stuart. She married, became Queen of France and was widowed in rapid succession between 1558 and 1560. After her return to take up her thrown in Scotland the following year, she brought the new spelling with her.

'DISNUMERATE' IS A DYSLEXIC SPELLING

I've heard the term disnumerate used for number blindness, the arithmetical equivalent of word blindness (dyslexia), but you won't find it in the dictionary. It isn't a matter of poor spelling either; the word

---

1 Also known as Mary I, Queen of Scots. It was perhaps fortuitous for historians with dyscalculia that her great-great-granddaughter was Mary II of both Scotland and England, due to her first cousin once removed Mary Tudor being Mary I of England. There is no such luck with Edward VII (actually Edward I of Scotland) or Elizabeth II (actually Elizabeth I of Scotland). Charles will be III of both kingdoms if he chooses that as his regnal name. William will be William V of England but only William IV of Scotland if he rules in that name.

dysnumerate doesn't appear either. The correct term for number blindness is 'dyscalculia'.

ROBERT THE BRUCE WAS NOT KING OF SCOTLAND

AND EFTER KING ROBERT
YE BRVCE MARIIT YE
DVKE OF HVLLESTERIS DOCHTER

Actually, he wasn't totally Scottish either; his ancestry was Normo-Scottish. His father was known as Robert de Brus (please note Robert *of* Brus) and had lands, as did a lot of his noble contemporaries, on either side of the English–Scottish border. Our man seems to have been known as Robert Bruce, or just Bruce. The adding of 'the' as an honorific to make him Robert the Bruce or The Bruce took place after his death.

In addition he was not titled King of Scotland but King of Scots. This may come from a previously created distinction between the kingdom of Alba / Scotland (the Scots being incomers from Ireland) and the kingdom of the (aboriginal) Picts, although this seems to be the product of later medieval myth and some confusion over a change in nomenclature. The title *Rex Pictorum* (King of the Picts) became *Ri Alban* (King of Alba) under Donald II at the end of the ninth century, when annals were switched from Latin to the vernacular, by which time Alba in Gaelic referred to the kingdom of the Picts rather than to its older meaning, Britain as a whole.

The kingdom of the Picts just became known as the kingdom of Alba in Gaelic, later becoming known in English as Scotland, which are the terms retained in both languages to this day. So by the late eleventh century at the very latest Scottish kings were using the term *Rex Scotium*, King of Scots, to refer to themselves in Latin.

THE SHETLANDS AND THE ORKNEYS

There are no such places as the Shetlands or the Orkneys, and the locals will be quick to correct you if you get this wrong. It's Shetland and Orkney in the singular, or at a push the Shetland Isles/Islands and the Orkney Isles/Islands. The names come from the Old Norse Hjaltland (*Hjelt* being a hilt of a sword reflecting the shape of the archipelago) and *Orkn*, meaning a seal.

The Shetlanders and Orcadians regard themselves as belonging to their island homes first and Scotland second. If you ever hear one mention 'the mainland', they are referring to the biggest island in their respective groups, not Great Britain to the south.

PONTIUS PILATE'S BODYGUARD

Pontius Pilate's Bodyguard was the nickname of the Royal Scots, formed as the Royal Regiment of Foot in 1633 from the rump of a Scottish unit in the service of Sweden. Prior to becoming the 1st Regiment of Foot in the British army it fought for the French, until being recalled to England in 1661 by the newly crowned Charles II. It ended its days as an independent unit in 2006, when it was amalgamated with the King's Own Scottish Borderers to become the Royal Scots Borderers, First Battalion Royal Regiment of Scotland. The nickname is often mistakenly ascribed to a connection between the regiment being the oldest in the British army and the belief that the much-reviled hand-washer[1] was born in Scotland. We have a reference from the *New York Times* in 1899 that relates it is commonly believed that his father was Roman ambassador to the Caledonians and Pilate was born in Perthshire. If there any is truth in this story, the nickname doesn't come from it.

There are variations to the story, but it's the version that appears in *Brewer's Dictionary of Phrase and Fable* that most appeals to me. While

---

[1] Only Matthew's Gospel has him doing this, actually.

in French service in the seventeenth century, officers of Le Régiment de Douglas (named as it was after its then colonel) argued with officers of Le Régiment de Picardie (the oldest regiment in the French army) as to their units' respective antiquity. The French ridiculed the Scots' claims by saying if they were really that old, they must have guarded Christ's tomb for Pilate after the Crucifixion. The nickname stuck, but the Scots retorted that the French must have been guarding the tomb because if Scottish soldiers had been on duty they wouldn't have been asleep and Christ's body wouldn't have disappeared.

Contrary to popular belief, Pontius Pilatus wasn't actually governor of Judaea.[2] He was, according to Tacitus, more properly called an equestrian procurator. This might however also be a mistake as recent archaeological evidence suggests his official title at the time was prefect. As a final note, and perhaps surprisingly to Western Europeans, his wife, known to history as Claudia Procula, is revered as a saint throughout the Eastern Orthodox Church and also in the Ethiopian tradition of the Oriental Orthodox Church. The Oriental Orthodox Coptic and Ethiopian Tewahedo Churches (which although originally part of the Coptic became autocephalous in 1959) surprise us even more: they recognised Pontius Pilate himself as a saint in the sixth century. I have yet to research whether the Eritrean Orthodox Tewahedo Church, which itself became autocephalous on that country's political independence in 1993, also maintains this tradition.

---

2 Actually correctly spelt Iudaea, as the Roman's didn't have a j. They didn't have a w either, rarely used a k and used the letter v instead of a u. Modern Italians have gone further and use only twenty-one letters, there being no j, k, w, x or y.

SINGING MEATLOAF

—— ❧ ——

Meatloaf never had hits with 'Bat out of Hell', 'Dead Ringer for Love' or 'I'd Do Anything for Love'. That's because meatloaf is a dish made of ground meat formed into the shape of a loaf. Marvin Lee Aday took the stage name Meat Loaf (two words not one). He regularly referred to himself, and was referred to by his friends, as Meat, his chosen forename.

Another popular error is that he has been vegetarian for many years. He is largely but not totally vegetarian, a consequence of his policy: 'If it's got a face, I don't eat it.'

Oh, and the reason I refer to Meat Loaf in the past tense? He changed his name to Michael in 2001.

THE BAGEL WAS NOT NAMED TO HONOUR A POLISH KING

—— ❧ ——

It's Vienna, 1683. Yet again the Turkish sultan and his armies have overrun the valley of the Danube, this time reaching the gates of the great imperial city itself. The walls are on the point of being breached. The situation looks desperate not just for Vienna, but Western civilisation as a whole. On 12 September heavily armoured Polish hussars swoop down on the Ottoman lines and smash them. Jan III Sobieski, King of Poland and Grand Duke of Lithuania, at the head of 80,000 troops has saved the day. Joy in the city is unrestrained. Ordinary people kiss the feet, hands and clothes of their saviour, and the bakers of the city invent the bagel in his honour, the bread roll mirroring the stirrups of his brave cavalry.

It would be nice if this well-worn story was true, but it isn't. Actually Sobieski and his troops might even have brought the bagel to Vienna themselves, as it is thought to have originated in Krakow as a competitor to the *bublik*, a bigger, denser more chewy type of bread. It was already a staple of the Polish national diet in the sixteenth and early seventeenth centuries. Its name comes from the Yiddish *beygel*, in turn from the German *beugel*, a word for a bracelet, not *bugel*, the German word for a stirrup.

COFFEE IS NOT A BEAN . . .

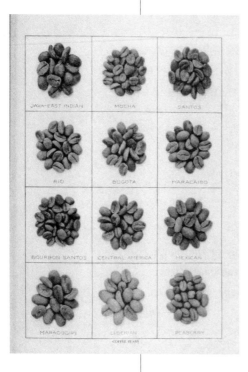

Continuing the breakfast theme, what better to go with your toasted bagel than a cup of the old java, made from the freshest coffee beans? But come to think of it, how can this delicious beverage be made from the same family of seeds that gives us baked beans, the kidney beans for a chilli con carne, or even Hannibal Lecter's favourite variety, fava beans?

It isn't. Coffee, like the bean, is a seed, but it is the pit inside the red or purple cherry-like fruit of the coffee plant. It is usually found in pairs but sometimes forms as a peaberry – a single pit. It is due to its resemblance to lots of members of the bean family that coffee is often called a bean.

. . . BUT A BLACK-EYED PEA IS!

This is getting confusing. Coffee is not a bean, but a black-eyed pea is? It seems that some things get a common name well before their true natures are revealed. I'll cover some more of these later; suffice to say confusion reigns when other similar beans, such as the *frijol ojo de cabra* (goat's eye bean) of northern Mexico, are sometimes mistaken for black-eyed peas and vice versa.

THERE ARE NO MANDARINS IN CHINA

—— 🙠🙡 ——

The idea goes that the mandarin is a type of orange that originated in China, and is named after the Mandarin region, which also lends its name to a senior official, a type of duck and the language of the area.

The problem is the locals wouldn't have the first idea what you were talking about. The word mandarin is not Chinese; it's a Western imposition that comes from the unrelated language of Sanskrit, and originated as a word for an official much further south. Europeans simply applied it to the civil service officials they encountered on their early visits to the Far East. The language these officials spoke was thus the language of the mandarins. The duck and the orange were also thus called, and there is some suggestion in the *OED* that the fruit got its name from the similarity of its colour to the robes worn by the Chinese officials.

THAT'S JUST NOT PIZZA

—— 🙠🙡 ——

There are two general and slightly contradictory misconceptions here. First the pizza doesn't come from Italy. Well, I'm afraid the pizza *is* Italian. OK then, if that's true, then the ubiquitous fare served up everywhere else in the modern world is the same as the pizza in Italy. This is also wrong. Pizza in Italy is thin bread that has been flavoured with oil and salt. That's it. Nothing else added: no toppings, no filled crusts, no deep pans.

Even the Roman *placenta*, sort of borrowed from the Greeks, was a bit fancier and usually included honey, cheese and bay leaves. So why do we have such a variety of products sitting in the freezer compartments of supermarkets up and down the land masquerading as pizza? These developed from a regional dish called *pizza alla napoletana*, which in Italy is seen as something quite different from plain old pizza. The Neapolitans have a wonderful gastronomic history, and one of them came up with the idea of adding tomatoes and anchovies or a few other things that might be to hand and, hey presto! Neapolitan pizza! The experiments continued. In

*Anyone now wishing
to claim their pizza
is genuinely* alla
napoletana *has to
run it past a special
commission.*

1889 the classic *pizza magherita* was created and named in honour of the then queen. The red tomatoes, the green basil and the white mozzarella supposedly represent the three colours of the Italian tricolour.

The modern pizza, especially its ubiquity and the proliferation of non-standard ingredients, has angered the Neapolitans so much they have taken action. The Italian farmers' association has supported the campaign by complaining that half of the 25,000 pizzerias up and down the country use the wrong ingredients, such as Polish cheese or Ukrainian flour. The campaign, which insists only items like San Marzano tomatoes and buffalo mozzarella can be used, has been so successful that in 2010 the EU granted a 'traditional speciality guarantee label'. Anyone now wishing to claim their pizza is genuinely *alla napoletana* has to run it past a special commission. That's food for thought. The very idea: having to test pizza all day. As they say in Italy, '*Che pizza!*' (What a bore!)

RIVIERA IS A FRENCH WORD

As the most famous and chicest bit of the Mediterranean coast is the French Riviera, we have named Torbay the English Riviera in an attempt to emulate its attractiveness.

In reality, *riviera* originated as the name of the Italian seaboard around Genoa, and was only applied to the wider Mediterranean coast from Marseilles in France to La Spezia in Italy when it became an area for fashionable winter resorts in the nineteenth century. At the time the area right up to Nice in the west was Italian. *Riviera* is simply coast in Italian.

VENETIANS DON'T SPEAK ITALIAN

Up and down Italy, the people of the various regions speak what are generally referred to as *dialètti*, which we would understand as meaning dialects. This would suggest that these are varieties of the Italian language. This is very misleading. Let's take Venice as an example.

The people of Venice speak Venetian, a language that grew naturally and quite separately out of the Late Latin spoken in the north-east of what is now Italy, and in fact predates the manufactured Italian language by hundreds of years. Italian was created to ease communication between people speaking the various regional *dialètti*. Because the great writers Dante, Petrarch and Boccaccio came from Tuscany, it was the vernacular there which formed its base. It is estimated that Italian only became the lingua franca for the country as late as the second half of the twentieth century.

Do not despair for Venetian. It has not suffered the same (hopefully temporary) fate as Manx and Cornish in these islands, and is still a robust source of identity for the citizens of the city and surrounding area. It is actually quite impenetrable to the majority of other Italians, to whom it is as different from their own language as Spanish or French. We can also celebrate its survival by speaking our own language, English. Are any of these words familiar? Artichoke, arsenal, ballot, casino, contraband, gazette, ghetto, gondola, lagoon, lido, lotto, marzipan, pantaloon, pistachio, quarantine, regatta, scampi (and its singular scampo) and sequin. All borrowed from Venetian. So let me end by saying *Ciao!* This is a contraction given to us by the ever-courteous Venetians from their phrase *vosto sciavo* – your humble servant.

IS '*VOLARE*' A TRADITIONAL ITALIAN SONG?

———— ❧❦ ————

Everyone join in . . .

> *Volare, oh oh*
> *E contare, oh oh oh oh*
> *Nel blu, dipinto di blu*
> *E ci dice di stare lassu . . .*

Well, even if we don't know the proper words we can all at least sing along to Dean Martin's version of this old Italian folk song.

Like 'When Irish Eyes Are Smiling', it's a bit of a fraud. It was actually written in the 1950s by Domenico Modugno and Franco Migliacci, the former bringing it to world attention by singing it at the 1958 Eurovision Song Contest. It came third.

THE EUROVISION THEME WAS WRITTEN FOR THE TV NETWORK

———— ✥ ————

Everything is branded these days, so everybody who needs a theme tune writes a theme tune, sings a theme tune, etc. So when we hear that familiar melody every year at the beginning of the Eurovision Song Contest, it's easy to let the thought pass through our minds: 'I wonder who wrote that for them?'

The man who wrote it actually didn't write it for them; he wrote it for God. Just as the EU decided to go into the past to find Schiller's 'Ode to Joy' in the setting of Beethoven's Ninth symphony for its anthem, so the founders of the Eurovision network turned to the prelude from Marc-Antoine Charpentier's seventeenth-century *Te Deum*, an early Christian hymn of praise.

'LA MARSEILLAISE' WAS SUNG DURING THE FRENCH REVOLUTION

———— ✥ ————

It all depends on your definition of French Revolution. If you regard the entire period from June 1789, when the Tennis Court Oath was taken, until the rise of Napoleon ten years later as the Revolution, then at a pinch I'll concede your point. But the song was written as late as 1792, the year France was declared a republic, so the Revolution was all but over and the country's fight for survival in that form had begun. And there's another good reason why it is difficult to class it as a revolutionary song: it isn't about the Revolution.

Its original title was '*Chant de guerre pour l'Armée du Rhin*' ('War Song of the Army of the Rhine'), and when you look at the lyrics you can immediately see that it is a marching song – a call to arms to repel the foreign armies invading the fatherland. It was written by Claude Joseph Rouget de Lisle at the behest of the mayor of Strasbourg, that eastern city being under threat at the time. It became popularly known as '*La Marseillaise*' in the summer of 1792, when soldiers from Marseilles marched

on the Tuileries Palace in the capital. It hasn't had an easy ride as the French national anthem, either. The ruling Convention accepted it as the French national anthem in a decree passed on Bastille Day 1795, but it was banned in turn by Napoleon I, Louis XVIII and Napoleon III. Only in 1879, ninety years after the revolution, was *'La Marseillaise'* restored as the country's national anthem, remaining so ever since.

Before I forget, I'll give you the best reason why I believe it cannot be classed as a revolutionary song. The very name of its composer, Claude Joseph Rouget de Lisle, gives a clue. Undoubtedly a patriot when France was threatened by foreigners, de Lisle was also a royalist who missed meeting Madame Guillotine by a whisker.

RED SQUARE WAS NAMED BY THE COMMUNISTS

As the colour of communism is red, we look back from our post-communist twenty-first-century viewpoint and assume the most famous square in Moscow was named for the glories of the 1917 Russian Revolution. The more inquisitive of us might ask, 'What was it called before 1917?'

The answer is it was called Red Square. Devised as Moscow's main market and ceremonial centre, it is believed that the square was originally called Pozhar (burnt-out place), but it has not been known by that name since the sixteenth century. The name doesn't come from the surrounding brickwork (sometimes this has been whitewashed anyway); it came about because the word *krasnaya* can mean either red or, in a more archaic sense, beautiful. In this latter meaning, it was applied to the square's main landmark St Basil's Cathedral, and by association the description came to be applied to the square itself. The old meaning of *krasnaya* slipped out of use, and since the seventeenth century, well before the tsars relinquished power, we have been left with Red Square.

KENNEDY DIDN'T SAY,
'I AM A DOUGHNUT'

———— ❦ ————

*The doughnut is called
a* Berliner *in various
parts of Germany,
but not actually in the
capital.*

The urban myth is that by not saying *'Ich bin Berliner'* but instead *'Ich bin ein Berliner'* JFK didn't say he was a citizen of the city in question, but a deep-fried food named after it. Not so, I'm afraid.

In German the indefinite article *ein* is omitted if speaking of your profession or residence, but included when speaking figuratively. Kennedy wasn't saying he was from Berlin, but stood alongside them, and in this sense *'Ich bin Berliner'* would have been grammatically incorrect. Anyway, the doughnut is called a *Berliner* in various parts of Germany, but not actually in the capital. So the audience wouldn't have associated what he said with the food anyway.

Rumours of Ronald Reagan making a similar faux pas in either Hamburg or Frankfurt are thus also discredited.

LATTE

———— ❦ ————

This word, as usually spoken, is one of the most annoying ever to be adopted into English. Café culture-vultures seem hell-bent on adding any number of rs in there, so LATTAY becomes LARRRTAY, usually with the word darling added for effect. I despair.

The *OED* tells us that it appeared as a stand-alone word in the USA as late as 1989. The real name for coffee made with more or less equal amounts of water and steamed milk is a caffe latte.

MODERN ARCHERS ARE FAR BETTER
THAN MEDIEVAL ONES

Oh yeah? You're telling me that a Native American, a nomad from the steppes or the Middle East or a bowman at Agincourt wouldn't stand much of a chance against a modern archer with all his technological paraphernalia? Actually, that's my point.

I'd love to see the winner of the gold medal at the Beijing Olympics go out onto the prairie and bring down a buffalo from the back of a horse, let alone without the benefit of a saddle. Likewise, could he or she manage what the ancient Parthians could do? The Parthian shot was executed on horseback at full gallop and without the aid of stirrups during a feigned retreat. It involving turning the body round to shoot at a pursuing enemy. Could they achieve the range and rate of the longbowman? In Edward III's day an archer could fire an arrow nearly a quarter of a mile, but didn't like to push his rate to more than six a minute in case it tired him out.

Case proven, I think.

IF YOU HIT SOMEONE IT'S ASSAULT

A ctually it isn't. Well, south of the Cheviots it isn't. In England and Wales assault and battery is not, as often thought, a tautologous phrase. Under English and Welsh law, if you attempt or even just threaten violence then you have committed an assault. If you make a violent physical contact then it's battery. This allows the law to say someone trying to rob a jewellery shop without actually physically harming anyone has committed an assault.

In Scottish law, assault is an 'attack upon the person of another', and there is no distinction between assault and battery. However, I don't recommend anyone with criminal intent to head north in the hope of getting away scot-free. 'Evil intent' is enough to occasion assault there, and even holding up a bank as a prank is still construed as assault.

'THE ASSYRIAN CAME DOWN LIKE THE WOLF ON THE FOLD'

D on't waste your time looking in the Bible for this phrase. It isn't biblical; it's from an 1815 poem called 'The Destruction of Sennacherib' by Byron, in the remarkably named *Hebrew Melodies*. It is only inspired by an event in the Bible, which occurs in the Second Book of Kings.

'A POOR THING BUT MINE OWN'

——— ❦ ———

This is my attempt to make amends for blaming Shakespeare for misguiding us over the owl's call. As with the Bible, he is often given the credit for phrases he didn't create, and this is one of them. The actual passage, spoken by Touchstone in *As You Like It*, is 'a poor virgin, / sir, an ill-favoured thing, sir, but mine own'.

THIRTY-NINE COMMANDMENTS?

——— ❦ ———

Ten commandments are enough, surely? It's hard enough to keep on the straight and narrow without having more than ten rules to live by. God obviously didn't think so because what we think of as the Decalogue actually appears more than once in the Bible.

The Ten Commandments is usually taken to refer to the passage in Exodus 20: 2–17. This passage is as good as repeated, but not exactly, in Deuteronomy 5: 6–21. Some scholars regard this set as the Ethical Decalogue and different from the set that appears in Exodus 34: 11–27. These are referred to as the Ritual Decalogue.

The matter is complicated further when you see that the alternative Ritual Decalogue in Exodus 34 is the only one to actually contain just ten imperative statements; the Ethical Dialogue in Exodus 20 has fourteen; the list in Deuteronomy 5 has fifteen. The Bible nevertheless counts each as ten.

Because of these variations in the number of imperatives, different Christian denominations have divided the statements into groups of ten in different ways, and different languages often also translate them differently. So be careful, ye sinners.

FORNICATION

—⁂—

The general belief is that fornication, that is consensual sexual intercourse between at least one unmarried person and another, is prohibited by the Bible. But actually it is more complicated than that. Yes, the Bible does proscribe sexual immorality, but something has definitely been lost in translation. In the New Testament, written for the most part in Greek, the word *porneia* has usually been translated incorrectly into English as fornication; its more accurate meaning is sexual immorality or even sexual perversion. It is this that is prohibited. *Porneia* was often used as a blanket term, and even lustful sexual thoughts were considered wrong under the laws outlined in Leviticus, particularly Chapter 18.

Definitions of fornication itself can vary. The *OED* has it as 'voluntary sexual intercourse between a man (in restricted use, an unmarried man) and an unmarried woman. In Scripture, extended to adultery.' The second definition takes it into the otherworldly by stating, 'in Scripture: the forsaking of God for idols; idolatry; also, spiritual fornication'. Wow, now there's a strange thought. The *OED* also says it's an architectural term for vaulting or arching. This leads us to the origins of the ruder usage of the word.

The actual original meaning of the word is a little amusing, if one is in a saucy mood. To reiterate, the New Testament was written in Greek. However, the translators of the work into English used the language of their time. Fornication as a word, and perhaps as an activity, derives from the Latin of ancient Rome. Their word *fornix* means an archway or vault, and was also used as a euphemism for a brothel. Prostitutes often solicited for clients in the vaults beneath Rome. Therefore, to get to the point, *fornicatio* meant to be 'done' in the archway, and thus originally referred to prostitution. The first recorded use of the noun in its modern meaning was in the early fourteenth century, and in the same way as the noun ski appeared a long time before the verb skiing, the verb fornicate actually didn't seemingly appear until 250 years later.

THE ROMANS INVENTED THE CRUCIFIX

By choosing this form of execution for Jesus, the Romans inadvertently changed a practical means of killing into a symbol for a world religion. We might associate the cross with the Romans as they did for the most famous person to die in this way, but they were very good at borrowing ideas from other cultures and effectively making them their own.

The belief that crucifixion had a ritualistic element – that it avoided the spilling of blood on the ground – is actually unfounded. It was almost never performed for ritual or symbolic reasons before the death of Jesus. It was employed for far more practical motives. Death by crucifixion is particularly slow, painful (hence excruciating), gruesome and humiliatingly public. It was perfectly devised to encourage potential criminals to think again.

It probably started with the Persians, and got to Rome via Greece, Carthage and Macedonia. Crucifixion methods varied considerably between these civilisations. (Is that the correct word in this context?) For example, as Romans guards couldn't leave the site of a crucifixion until the victim died, they were recorded as hastening the end by variously breaking the tibia and/or the fibula, stabbing into the heart with a spear, severely beating the victim's chest, or even building a fire at the foot of the cross to asphyxiate the victim with smoke.

Crucifixion was widespread, and was even introduced into Japan during that country's Age of War, contemporary with our Middle Ages. It is believed to have been suggested to the Japanese by the arrival of Christianity. Interestingly, despite contemporary Jewish historian Josephus and others writing of thousands being crucified by the Romans, there has been only one archaeological discovery of a crucified body from around the time of Jesus and the Roman occupation, in Jerusalem in 1968. However this is unsurprising. A crucified body was nearly always left to decay on the cross. It added to the deterrent value. The body would only have been preserved if the victim's family members took them down for burial.

Now, where have I heard that story before?

There has been only one archaeological discovery of a crucified body from around the time of Jesus and the Roman occupation, in Jerusalem in 1968.

EXPLAINED

JULIUS CAESAR'S DYING WORDS

—❦❧—

In the modern
vernacular, Caesar
was saying, 'Your turn
next', 'Go to hell', or
even, 'Up yours'.

'Et tu, Brute?' What better way to sum up the betrayal of one man by another. The man was a great orator, was he not, even though he was supposedly cursed with a high-pitched voice?

My apologies, but I seem to be back to Shakespeare bashing again. These are thought to be Caesar's dying words because the Bard uses them in the eponymous play. Actually, it is a strange insertion as the whole line, 'Et tu, brute? Then fall, Caesar!' is macaronic – it mixes languages – and on this occasion there is no pun or play on words.

Where did Shakespeare get the phrase from? It had already appeared in contemporary dramas in England: in Richard Eedes's 1582 work *Caesar Interfectus* and Shakespeare's own 1595 work *The True Tragedie of Richarde Duke of Yorke*, which is regarded as a source for *The Third Part of King Henry VI*. Shakespeare was following Suetonius, the first- and second-century historian, who reported that others unknown claimed Caesar said, '*Kai su, teknon?*' This Greek phrase translates into Latin as '*To quoque, Brute, fili mi?*' and into English as 'You too, my child?' Suetonius himself believed Caesar said nothing, echoing Plutarch, who says Caesar merely pulled his toga over his head on seeing Brutus.

If Caesar did exclaim, '*Kai su, teknon?*' it is generally accepted that this was less an expression of shock at his betrayal by Brutus, and more a curse. Caesar was using a Greek aphorism the Romans had adopted. The complete phrase possibly translates as 'You too, my son, will have a taste of power', and Caesar only needed to spit out the first few words to suggest to Brutus that he would also die violently. In the modern vernacular, he was saying, 'Your turn next', 'Go to hell', or even, 'Up yours'.

A PAINFUL ELBOW IS TENNIS ELBOW

—❦❧—

It is widely known that although pain in the elbow is commonly referred to as tennis elbow, the condition isn't exclusively suffered by Andre Agassi, Billy Jean King or others of that ilk, be they professional or amateur.

However, a surprise awaited me when I recently had to visit the doctor with a sharp pain. I joked that as I didn't play tennis, I didn't know how it had developed. She asked where the pain was, and I showed her, pointing to the inner part of the joint. 'Wrong sport,' she advised me, 'that's golfer's elbow.'

Both are forms of tendonitis, but golfer's elbow is medial epicondylitis – it affects the inner elbow and the flexor muscle. It's interesting to note that in North America the condition is sometimes referred to as pitcher's elbow because of its prevalence among baseball players. In contrast, tennis elbow is lateral epicondylitis, occurring in the outer elbow and affecting the extensor muscle. There is also a related condition, bursitis, which occurs at the rear of the elbow, but that is inflammation of the synovial sacs, whose purpose is to lessen friction in the joints.

So why isn't golfer's elbow as widely known as its counterpart condition? Most probably it's down to the fact it's only about one fifth as prevalent. But that's not to say more people play tennis than golf, because both conditions are commonly seen in people overusing their arm to do something else. In my own case, as I am left-handed and the pain was in my right elbow, it wasn't swinging a club that did it. How about a direct blow on the elbow? Alas, I remain undiagnosed. I do, however, have the following additional potential causes to pick from:

- arthritis
- rheumatism
- gout (a subject covered elsewhere in this book)
- a neck problem (via the nerves from the neck)

Rest is advised once the condition has set in. As to advice if you do not yet suffer from either? To avoid tennis elbow, don't open jars; and if you are prone to golfer's elbow, don't shake hands – and also avoid opening jars.

PLAYING AT ST ANDREW'S

Firstly, the town doesn't have an apostrophe in its name, but we're going to talk golf here. It is widely held that the home of the game of golf, host to the Open (and I make no apology for refusing to call it the *British*

The courses, including the Old Course, are public and managed by the St Andrews Links Trusts, a charity that directly owns and runs the seven golf courses around the town.

Open) on so many occasions, is the most exclusive course in the world, and the chances of playing there are only a pipe dream for those committed to the game across the world. I'm pleased to say I've a nice surprise for you. If you can get your travel and accommodation costs sorted, you won't have to spend additional thousands and wait for years for your chance to play the Old Course.

The Royal and Ancient Golf Club of St Andrews is now simply that – a golf club. It might have 2,400 members, and its clubhouse might be situated behind the first tee of the Old Course, but the club doesn't own the course. In fact, it doesn't own any of the courses in St Andrews. Despite being the original arbiter and rule maker for the game, members must share tee times with members of other local clubs, residents and visitors alike. The courses, including the Old Course, are public and managed by the St Andrews Links Trusts, a charity that directly owns and runs the seven golf courses around the town.

By the way, despite being Royal and Ancient, the club cannot lay claim to being the first and oldest club. That would be the Honourable Company of Edinburgh Golfers at Muirfield.

WAS GOLF INVENTED IN SCOTLAND?

Not wishing to rub salt into Scottish wounds after encouraging thousands of visitors to descend on St Andrews to claim their right to play what is a public course, I have another revelation. The game isn't Caledonian in origin.

The Romans played a game called *paganica*, using a bent stick to whack a leather ball filled with feathers. Then again, the Low Countries could be heard to resound to the sport of *kolven* being played, very similar to golf in all aspects apart from it being a winter game played on ice.

I'm not denying it has been played for a long time in Scotland, though. James II demanded 'fute-ball and golfe be utterly cryed down' in 1457. In contrast, his descendant James IV is recorded as a keen golfer. He might have benefited from playing eighteen holes instead of turning up at Flodden in 1513, where he died fighting in the front rank with his men.

MEDAL PLAY

There is no such thing in golf, though it is widely referred to. The rule book refers to only to stroke play.

OBE MEANS ORDER
OF THE BRITISH EMPIRE

To get an OBE is a great achievement. It's actually one better than an MBE but not as good as a CBE, but hey. To get a KBE or DBE would be out of this world, and getting a GBE would be stellar. On consideration, I think I'd settle for an Order of the British Empire, and not lose any sleep over the others.

Actually, OBE does not stand for Order of the British Empire, and the gongs I've mentioned are actually all different ranks of the Order of the British Empire. The Most Excellent Order of the British Empire, to give it its full title, is an order of chivalry established in 1917 by George V. The order has five classes in civil and military divisions:

- Knight Grand Cross (GBE) or Dame Grand Cross (GBE)
- Knight Commander (KBE) or Dame Commander (DBE)
- Commander (CBE)
- Officer (OBE)
- Member (MBE)

The highest two ranks give the recipient a knighthood or a damehood, and as you can see OBE stands for *Officer* of the Most Excellent Order of the British Empire.

THE VIKING BLOOD EAGLE

Those of a squeamish disposition skip this piece. Have you gone? Good, then those who remain prepare to be horrified. The blood eagle was a means of execution mentioned in the Norse sagas. The victim was laid face down, and then the ribs were cut adjacent to the spine and broken, so as to resemble bloody wings. To add to the effect, the lungs were pulled out, spread over the broken ribs and salted. The Northumbrian king Ælla, King Maelgualai of Munster and even the churchman Archbishop Ælfheah are all recorded as departing the planet in this way.

It seems a bit of a fuss just to kill somebody, does it not? They haven't found any bodies evidencing the practice, so it seems to be just like the convoluted ways to get rid of him that James Bond's enemies come up with. It's all very thrilling and good for the storyline, but doesn't really stack up. Despite the theories of Alfred Smyth about blood sacrifices to Odin, I think it is within the pages of sagas that the practice should remain.

PRIDE GOES BEFORE A FALL

———— ✥✥ ————

This is a pretty good way of saying don't get too convinced of your own importance as you'll get your comeuppance. It's not what it says in the Bible, though. The actual quote from Proverbs is 'Pride goeth before Destruction, and a haughty spirit before a fall.' On reflection, that sounds more serious.

MEETING YOUR WATERLOO

———— ✥✥ ————

Talking of a fall, how big was the one that Napoleon suffered at the hands of the British at the battle fought in and around the village of that name in Belgium? Wellington's victory was so decisive that it is now celebrated in a commonly used English phrase. It even inspired a Eurovision Song Contest winner in 1974. We don't talk of 'meeting your Trafalgar' or 'meeting your Agincourt', do we? Maybe we will if we deconstruct the myths that have grown up around the events of Sunday 18 June 1815.

To start with, it wasn't fought in or around Waterloo, but a mile to the south at least. There was another suggestion as to the name, but more of that later. We should also look at the order of battle. Wellington thought his army was weak, badly equipped and led by inexperienced officers, at least below him. He had about 67,000 men, of whom only 24,000 were British,

or just over a third. Six thousand were nominal Hanoverians from the King's German Legion (there were another 11,000 troops from Hanover); 17,000 were from the Low Countries; and there were 9,000 other Germans – 6,000 from Brunswick, and 3,000 from Nassau. A bit of an exaggeration then to claim this as a British army.

We also have to face the fact that Marshal Grouchy had failed to pin the Prussians down elsewhere for Napoleon, and it was their arrival on the field that really won the day. The allied and French armies were evenly matched in numbers with the French having around 69,000 at the battle. It seems clear the arrival of two and a half Prussian corps totalling 48,000 was, as the *Sun* would report it in the modern vernacular, 'what won it'.

After the scrap, the Prussian commander Blücher met Wellington at Napoleon's centre of operations, an inn called La Belle Alliance. In a remarkably lucid bit of thinking for the old soak, he suggested commemorating the European Seventh Coalition of Britain, Russia, Prussia, Austria, the Netherlands, Sweden, Spain, Portugal and Sardinia, along with a number of other states, by naming the battle after their meeting place. I don't know if Wellington was prone to swearing, but he seemingly made it clear that as he had chosen the field, he had commanded an army which had fought the French since 11.30 that morning and he had rested in Waterloo the night before, that was going to be the name. What was more, he was going to be especially damned if he was going to name his brilliant victory after the loser's command post. Blücher seems to have backed off, but nevertheless the Rondellplatz in Berlin was renamed Belle-Alliance-Platz soon after. The battle still bears this name in Germany, although the plaza is now the Mehringplatz. The French also, perhaps in an understandable fit of pique, refuse to use the name Waterloo. If Johnny Hallyday had won the Eurovision Song Contest in 1974, he would have sung 'Mont Saint Jean', not quite as catchy a title.

O' WESLEY – THE VICTOR OF WATERLOO

Wesley actually, but I make the joke to make the point.
Field Marshal the Duke of Wellington was born the Honourable Arthur Wesley, fourth son of Garret Wesley, 1st Earl of Mornington. He

didn't become Arthur Wellesley until somewhere around 1789. His brother Richard Wesley, who had become the second earl, for reasons of both re-establishing linkage with their medieval ancestors and quite possibly to put distance between his immediate family and some troublesome relatives, changed the spelling. The pronunciation of the name however, remained WESLEE. Also the English hero Wellington wasn't English. He was born in Dublin, or possibly at Athy in Kildare, and at the date of his birth in 1769 Ireland remained separate from the rest of Britain as the conquered kingdom of Ireland, over thirty years away from being made a part of the United Kingdom.

The English hero Wellington wasn't English. He was born in Dublin, or possibly at Athy in Kildare.

THE LAST BRITISH MONARCH IN BATTLE

I might be accused of semantic quibbling, but the following assertion has often received short shrift when used in my presence: 'The last British monarch to be involved in a battle was George II at Dettingen in 1743.' I'm not claiming he wasn't there, but even if the statement was changed to 'to lead his troops' I would still have a problem on two fronts. Firstly, George II was in his youth a military man, but the Earl of Stair was in overall command at Dettingen. In fact, there are reports the King's horse bolted, and he ended up sheltering under an oak tree for much of the time. So I tend to think it was his generals that did the actual leading. Secondly, I don't quite see him in the front line and potentially paying the ultimate price, as James IV of Scotland definitely did at the Battle of Flodden Field in 1513. So he might have been in the vicinity; his presence might have been a morale booster for the troops; but not in any sense of the word was he doing any real leading.

However, it is not the Stewart king to whom I give the accolade, but someone who some 400 years later saw active service under fire, and not as a soldier but as a sailor. Step forward George VI. No, I am not referring to the bombing of Buckingham Palace by Hitler's Luftwaffe; we are talking of much earlier in his life. Remember that Prince Albert, later the Duke of York, was not initially first in line to inherit the throne, so there was no compunction among the great and the good about him going into a combat zone. More recently his grandson Andrew (later also the Duke

of York) saw service in the 1982 Falklands War. Another royal younger brother, Prince Harry (probably a future Duke of York), has also been allowed to go into the line of fire in this century, in Afghanistan.

So when war broke out in 1914, Midshipman Prince Albert was immediately placed on active service. He didn't see battle before or after (mainly due to suffering a duodenal ulcer for the second half of the war), but he was at the Battle of Jutland in 1916. Not only was he there; he was mentioned in dispatches for his actions as a turret officer aboard HMS *Collingwood*. Recently released government documents reveal that he raised himself from his sickbed to take part, after an illness brought on by 'a surfeit of soused herrings'. Given the fate of one of his forefathers, Henry I, it was fortunate it wasn't lampreys.

As a coda, George VI is also to date the last British monarch to compete at Wimbledon, which he did in 1926.

THE MADNESS OF KING GEORGE (III)

I think we can all stop sniggering now at the idea that the title of Alan Bennett's drama was shortened when made into a film because American audiences would be confused as to how they had missed parts I and II.

A common belief about 'Farmer George' in these more enlightened times is that he wasn't really mad or insane but temporarily mentally ill due to the disease porphyria. Porphyria is a blood disorder, and modern investigations of records have tied the king's wine-red urine in with the condition. It is devastating, causing severe abdominal pain, cramps, seizures and epileptic fits, and is often diagnosed incorrectly even now as a mental disorder. However, this is not the whole picture. The strange thing about

King George III was his pattern of suffering, and the fact that he suffered at all. It is intriguing that it wasn't until he was in his fifties that he started to have his attacks, and men do not usually show any symptoms anyway.

The clue may have come to light in 2003 when, on analysis, hair found in an envelope marked 'Hair of His Late Majesty King George 3rd' was found to contain over 300 times the toxic level of arsenic. On its own, the arsenic that would have been present in the face cream and wig powder used by George III didn't explain the massive levels of the element. Further digging revealed the king received antimony several times a day in a common medication called James' Powders, and even when purified, antimony has significant traces of arsenic.

So there's the irony. It is most probable that the king's 'madness' was brought on by the very men who were trying to cure him and the medication they employed. The root of his problems was almost certainly arsenic poisoning.

NELSON'S LAST WORDS

Porphyria is devastating, causing severe abdominal pain, cramps, seizures and epileptic fits, and is often diagnosed incorrectly even now as a mental disorder.

Nelson actually said, 'Kismet, Hardy,' as he lay dying, did he not? He was asking about HMS *Kismet*, one of the ships at the battle. No, he didn't, because there was no ship at Trafalgar called *Kismet* on either side, and according to the *OED* the word didn't appear in English until 1849. So what are the alternatives?

I believe that Hardy accompanied Nelson below deck when he was shot, but returned to his post soon after. The possibility that Hardy was actually present for Nelson's last words is slim, as he was a ship's captain and needed in the battle, which was still raging. Sources report Nelson's last words to Hardy as 'God bless you, Hardy', spoken after Hardy had kissed him. However, 'Kiss me, Hardy' is equally likely. Kissing between men at the time didn't carry the same overtones as it does today, as can be seen from Johnson's definition of a kiss as a 'Salute given by joining lips'. Between officers, it was to honour the recipient, and we don't know if Hardy actually kissed him on the lips anyway.

Nelson's final words, related in three written accounts of those who were with him when he died, were 'Thank God I have done my duty.' He apparently repeated this until he was unable to talk. But one of those who reported this, Beatty the surgeon, wasn't present when Nelson became unable to speak. The ship's chaplain, Scott, and the purser, Burke, might have been with him throughout, but to my mind this is all a little dubious. A major hero was at the point of death, and a heroic quote would be brilliant for British morale. It also bears a striking resemblance to Nelson's flag signal before the battle, 'England expects that every man will do his duty.'

I support a more human theory. Nelson had just had his spine shot through. He was in immense pain, stuck in a hot, noisy area below decks for three hours before he died. Another reported refrain – 'Rub, rub . . . fan, fan . . . drink, drink' – although not suitably heroic, seems the most likely.

ON WHICH EYE IS NELSON'S EYEPATCH?

It's on neither, and if you don't believe me go to Trafalgar Square and take a look. I have even heard of London cabbies who think the statue has one. No tip for them. It hasn't got one because the man didn't wear one.

He did lose the use of his right eye, along with part of his right arm, but as the damage to his face was not disfiguring, he didn't bother to cover it up. Ironically, sailing in sunny climes as he often did, he frequently wore a *shade* over his good left eye to protect it.

TO THE BITTER END . . .

———— ❦ ————

The bitter taste of defeat has nothing to do with this phrase, which derives from the nautical term for the inboard end of a line or cable, especially the coiled bit. To go to the bitter end is to go to the furthest extremity possible, successfully or not.

HEIR TOMORROW, NOT HEIR TODAY

———— ❦ ————

I think only a very churlish legal brain would try to prove that the use of the term 'son and heir' in a will negates it. The argument for this is that in a will or even in a conversation the term – or 'daughter and heiress' – carries no legal meaning. In law, a person isn't referred to as the heir to any property until, through the death of its previous possessor, he or she becomes entitled to it.

THE ENGLISH CIVIL WAR – CIVIL BUT NOT ENGLISH

———— ❦ ————

In recent decades, the English Civil War has come to be seen as part of a bigger pan-European conflict, the Thirty Years War of 1618–48, itself the tail end of the religious wars that started in the sixteenth century. This is tough for the English to swallow, as the conflict has been seen as almost quaint instead of the bloody war it actually was, and definitely our war and nothing to do with Johnny Foreigner and his type beyond the Cliffs of Dover.

However we must go further: to call it the English Civil War is nonsense. 'Ah!' I hear you interject. 'You're making the point that there wasn't just one war during the 1640s and 50s, but three.' You would be quite correct with this assertion, but this is not the whole story. It is rather that the three English Civil Wars were not just satellite conflicts of the war

Sʳ THOMAS FAIRFAX
General van de Armee van de Parliament van Engellandt. Æ 1648.

raging on the continent, but also a component part of one taking place in these British Isles. And I don't mean by this that we must recognise the role played by the Scots on English soil, such as at the 1644 Siege of York and the subsequent battle of Marston Moor.

In my view, the whole conflict is probably best entitled the Wars of the Three Kingdoms, the reigning head of the then separate kingdoms of England, Scotland and Ireland actually being one man, Charles I. This rolling ball of a conflict actually started three years before the First English Civil War, lasted for eleven or twelve years, and comprised:

- The Scottish Bishops' Wars 1639 and 1640
- The Irish Rebellion 1641
- The running conflicts in Confederate Ireland 1642–9
- The First English Civil War 1642–6
- The Scottish Civil War 1644–5
- The Second English Civil War 1648–9
- The Cromwellian conquest of Ireland 1649–53
- The Third English Civil War 1650–1
- The royalist rising in Scotland 1651–4
- The Penruddock Uprising in south-west England 1655
- Booth's Uprising in the Welsh Borders 1659
- Venner's Uprising in London in 1661 following the restoration of the monarchy 1660

I think this puts the English part of the bigger conflict into its rightful perspective.

FRANCO WAS FIGHTING REVOLUTIONARIES

———— ✥ ✥ ————

The popular error, mainly due to Franco arranging for the re-establishment of the monarchy after his death, is that he was on the side of legitimate government and ultimately succeeded in beating back the tide of revolution, thus saving Spain.

The truth is very nearly the opposite. The Spanish Civil War, which devastated the country from July 1936 to April 1939, began with a coup by

a group of Spanish generals. Spain was already into its second republic
and the legitimate government was left-wing. The coup was supported
by the political right in general, monarchists known as Carlists, and the
fascist Falange. Following the coup, working-class uprisings spread across
the country, but in support of the legitimate government, and three years
of conflict were to follow. Although not the original coup leader, the
dictatorship that followed was led by General Franco.

THE ENGLISH GAVE TEA DRINKING
TO THE WORLD

Setting my sights a little lower by accepting that the stuff was grown
and imbibed in the Far East long before the British got there, and
putting aside the fact that surveys usually have the Irish drinking more
tea per head than we do, rather I will say that we introduced the wonder
beverage to the rest of the *Western* world. However, I'm afraid we must
thank the Portuguese for bringing the art of tea drinking to these shores.
Actually it was one very important Portuguese, the queen of Charles II,
Catherine of Braganza. That is not to claim that she brought the first tea
chest over individually, but she did make drinking the stuff fashionable,
and indeed an art.

Portuguese traders had imported tea for some time and its high
price and exoticism made it fashionable at the Portuguese court where
Catherine grew up. Tea was also popular among the elite in Holland by
the middle of the 1600s, again through trade with the east. At this stage
Britain lagged behind. Pepys only mentions drinking a 'cupp of tee' for
the first time in September 1660. Since he was a fashionable wealthy man
moving in the right circles, this suggests tea drinking in these islands was
rare. However, Charles II had been restored to the throne earlier that year,
and Catherine's father John IV of Portugal sent several ships full of luxury
goods, including a chest of tea, with her as part of her dowry.

The story goes that Catherine arrived in May 1662 and on her arrival
immediately asked for a cup of tea. A glass of ale was proffered instead.
This was not a good start as it seemed to make her feel ill. Following
marriage, Catherine, a deeply pious Catholic who had been schooled in

*Pepys only mentions
drinking a 'cupp of
tee' for the first time in
September 1660.*

a convent, initially found the English court not to her taste, but over time she imposed her will and became a trendsetter. She might have embraced English fashion, but she kept her liking for Portuguese food and drink. Starting with the court, the drinking of tea spread to the nobility and then the wealthier middle classes. Tea drinking as a fashion, and then as a way of life for the citizens of Britain, was imported rather than exported.

CORTEZ WAS THE FIRST TO EUROPEAN TO SEE THE PACIFIC

I was taught this at school as a fact, whereas it is actually a bit of poetic licence. It's from Keats, the offending poem being 'On First Looking into Chapman's Homer'.

> Or like stout Cortez when with his eagle eyes
> He star'd at the Pacific – and all his men
> Look'd at each other with a wild surmise –
> Silent, upon a peak in Darien.

The poem doesn't actually explicitly claim he was the first, but as the poem is about discovery that's the usual interpretation. This event was supposed to have taken place in 1519, but six years earlier the future governor of Panama, Vasco Nunez de Balboa, crossed the Darien isthmus to reach the Pacific.

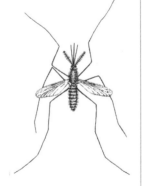

THE MOSQUITO COAST IS NAMED AFTER AN INSECT

The 1986 film starring Harrison Ford, which in turn was based on the 1982 novel by Paul Theroux, might suggest this. *The Mosquito Coast* is set in the jungle along the insect-infested Caribbean coast of Nicaragua and Honduras. In reality, the area is named after the main group of native tribes in the region, the Miskito Indians. They are still there, making up over 50 per cent of the 100,000-plus inhabitants.

AN AUTOGIRO IS NOT A TYPE OF HELICOPTER

———— ❧❦ ————

Not all aircraft with rotating blades are helicopters. The autogiro came first, being invented in Spain by Juan de la Cierva in the 1920s. The interesting thing about this craft is that once the thing is in flight the rotating blades are not driven by an engine. Because of this it has to go forward at all times to keep aloft just like a fixed-wing aircraft, and can't hover, fly backwards or sideways and can't perform vertical ascents or descents like a chopper. If you look closely at an autogiro it has wings and a propeller to provide lift, just like a conventional aircraft.

A BUTTERFLY FLUTTERS BY

———— ❧❦ ————

The butterfly has nothing to do with butter and is so called because in Tudor times the flutterby was rechristened by a simple inversion of its name. So the term is the result of a spooneristic play on words. Unfortunately, the first known written reference in English to a 'buttorflédoe' comes from 500 years earlier. The early Dutch word for a butterfly, *boterschijte*, actually suggests a more scatological origin, but let's not go there, as they say.

I can, however, give you an example of an inversion. The burnside was a style of facial hair affected by American Civil War General Ambrose Burnside and consisted of a moustache, whiskers and a clean-shaven chin. A short side whisker on its own was thus named after him by inverting the two syllables.

NICE!

Talking of inversions, some people these days don't like to be described as nice because they think it's a bit soppy even if meant as a compliment. If only they knew the origins of the word and its journey through the English language, they might actually punch anyone who describes them thus on the nose. The great majority of meanings this very flexible word can carry are anything but complimentary.

The word derives from the Latin *nescire*, meaning not to know, and *nescius*, meaning ignorant. By the time it was being used in medieval England it could mean both foolish and wanton. A number of different meanings developed and indeed existed alongside each other, including showy, ostentatious, fussy and difficult to please. It started to be used to mean refined and cultured around the end of the sixteenth century, and 200 years after this began to take on its modern connotations of respectability, virtue and decency. There are actually fourteen distinct meanings for the word as an adjective alone listed in the *OED*, with many subtle variations within those meanings.

Although it has become largely a positive word, in the majority of cases nice retains an underlying barb aimed at its subject.

There are actually fourteen distinct meanings for the word as an adjective alone listed in the OED, *with many subtle variations within those meanings.*

DIVAS V. PRIMA DONNAS

As used to describe women whose behaviour is high-handed or self-important – actually let's say it, unnecessarily difficult – these two words have become interchangeable. In my youth, a person of this ilk was more likely to be referred to as a prima donna, but in these days of text-speak and supposedly shorter attention spans, the more concise diva has taken over.

For me the difference in meaning was highlighted the other day by a TV pundit, who used the term prima donna as a compliment to highlight the musical skills of a famous female pop singer, but as far as I knew she had never been the leading lady in an opera company, nor was she an opera singer of great renown. He should have called her a diva, as this is a more general term for a distinguished female singer. If you look closely at the definitions, a prima donna is always a diva, but a diva is not always a prima donna.

MUSIC, BOTH CLASSICAL AND ROMANTIC?

It was while delving into the *Oxford English Dictionary* the other day that a common error in the classification of a very wide group of different styles of music into the catch-all term classical was highlighted. It is the 1885 quote used from one J C Fillmore (Could this be the same musicologist as Professor John Comfort Fillmore, the famed student of Native American music?) that cuts to the chase.

> 'Classic' is used in two senses. In the one it means, having permanent interest and value . . . In the second sense . . . music written in a particular style, aiming at the embodiment of a certain ideal, the chief element of which is beauty of form . . . In classical music, in this sense, form is first and emotional content subordinate; in romantic music content is first and form subordinate.

So there we have it. He suggests there is a difference between classical and romantic music, and so there is. Although we usually lump anything that is not popular and up-to-date (for that read mainly noisy and tuneless) into the classical bracket, musicologists generally use the following dates to categorise music.

* Medieval AD 500–1400
* Renaissance 1400–1600

- Baroque 1600–1750
- Classical 1750–1820
- Romantic 1820–1910
- Modern 1910+

So Beethoven can be regarded as a classical composer, while Tchaikovsky was a romantic.

'TRUMPET VOLUNTARY'

I grew up thinking this piece of English baroque music was by Henry Purcell because for many years it was wrongly attributed to him. We owe Jeremiah Clarke, organist at the Chapel Royal, a collective apology for not giving him the credit. From the 1870s until the 1940s the work was published, attributed to Purcell, in William Sparkes's *Short Pieces for the Organ, Book VII, No. 1.* This version was recorded in two different orchestral transcriptions by Sir Henry Wood, whose liking for a work he thought was by Purcell reinforced the incorrect attribution. Clarke's 'Trumpet Tune in D' was also attributed to Purcell, but we might have an excuse for getting this one wrong. It was from an 'opera-like' work entitled *The Island Princess,* a joint effort by Clarke and Daniel Purcell, who was Henry's younger brother, so the general confusion probably started with this.

I also thought, as its title suggests to the less musical of us, that the 'Trumpet Voluntary' was a work intended for the trumpet, and indeed I have seen many performances where a trumpet is employed. A fourth error was believing that the 'Trumpet Voluntary' was one work; I now know it is the title of a number of pieces from the baroque period. In the matter of instrumentation, I should have taken a clue from the fact Jeremiah Clarke was an organist: these pieces were intended for keyboards. As they were most commonly composed and played on an organ, it is the trumpet stop to which the title alludes. They were generally written with a slow introduction followed by a faster section, the right hand playing fanfares over a simple accompaniment from the left hand.

I am afraid to admit to a now-corrected fifth error. As I have said, 'Trumpet Voluntary' was a generic term for an organ piece utilising the

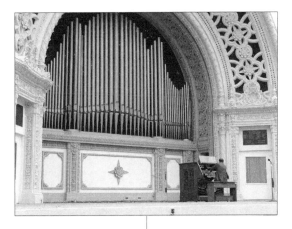

trumpet stop. The proper title of the once wrongly attributed piece by Clarke is 'Prince of Denmark's March'. The most notable occasion on which this was heard was the wedding of Charles and Diana in 1981.

A final point of interest is Clarke's sad demise. It was not a prescient insight into a nineteenth-century misattribution that affected him, but a 'violent and hopeless passion for a very beautiful lady of a rank superior to his own' which caused him to take his own life. In a tragi-comic chain of events, before shooting himself he considered hanging or drowning, and to decide tossed a coin – which landed in the mud on its side. Not despairing, he took his life by gunshot. According to some sources, it is possible that even though suicides were not generally allowed burial in consecrated ground, an exception was made for Clarke, and he was buried in the crypt of St Paul's Cathedral. Others say his fate was to be buried in the unconsecrated part of the cathedral yard.

PINK FLOYD ARE NOT FRIENDS OF DOROTHY

Pink Floyd's recent legal victory, which ensured their masterwork of 1973, *Dark Side of the Moon*, can only be downloaded in its entirety rather than track by track as desired by EMI reminded me of a generally but wrongly held belief about this album.

The theory goes that by watching the film *The Wizard of Oz* with the soundtrack turned down and simultaneously listening to *Dark Side of the Moon*, a disturbing amount of synchronicity can be detected. The theory is then extrapolated to suggest that this is not merely coincidence, and that the 1939 film was massively influential in the creation of the album some thirty-four years later. The fact is that however you try to create *The Dark Side of the Rainbow*, *The Wizard of Floyd* or *The Dark Side of Oz*, you should let Pink Floyd drummer Nick Mason have the final word, seeing as he was there when the album was made. Speaking to MTV in 1997, he categorically denied the connection: 'It's absolute nonsense. It has nothing to do with *The Wizard of Oz*. It was all based on *The Sound of Music*.'

Actually, my apologies, that's not the final word. Spare a thought for the musical duo of John Fiddler and Peter Hope-Evans, the second of whom brought the Jew's harp to prominence as a pop instrument. In 1972, a full year before Floyd's seminal work, they recorded their third album as Medicine Head . . . and unfortunately for (their) sales entitled it *Dark Side of the Moon*.

'YOU DO SOMETHING TO ME' AND 'THERE SHE GOES' – HEROINES NOT LOVERS

More pop and rock musical urban myths. 'You Do Something to Me' was a 1995 hit for Paul Weller, while 'There She Goes' has visited the charts three times, in 1989, 1990 and 1999 for lovable Scousers the LA's. Both these songs are widely believed to be about the effects of heroin. Looking at the lyrics, one can see where this idea came from. In both cases there has as yet been no confirmation from the writers that this is the case. If you want a song about drugs, may I suggest the 1977 release by Eric Clapton 'Cocaine', which was written by J J Cale and released on his album *Troubadour* a year before Clapton popularised the song.

FAR FROM THE MADDENING CROWD

Crowds are maddening, aren't they? All that noise and bustle, no wonder in Thomas Hardy's 1894 novel Bathsheba Everdene seeks peace and quiet far not just from the crowd but at times from her three suitors. Hardy took his title from that other hymn to rural life 'Elegy Written in a Country Churchyard, in which Thomas Gray wrote,

> Far from the madding crowd's ignoble strife
> Their sober wishes never learn'd to stray;
> Along the cool sequester'd vale of life
> They kept the noiseless tenor of their way.

Gray uses the word madding and so does Hardy. So I believe that we are mistaken in concluding that the two literary giants see the crowded urban life as merely annoying, but rather as frenzied or even something that can in a very real sense drive the individual to madness.

SAMUEL RICHARDSON AND PAMELA, J M BARRIE AND WENDY . . . AND PETER PAN

Samuel Richardson published the novel *Pamela: Or, Virtue Rewarded* in 1740 and invented a new girl's name. Likewise, in the 1904 play *Peter Pan, or The Boy Who Wouldn't Grow Up* J M Barrie gave the world Wendy as a girl's name, and introduced us to Peter Pan. In the first two cases, I would suggest popularised rather than invented; in the third, Peter had appeared earlier.

Richardson borrowed the name. Pamela is a poetic invented name for a 'sweet' girl, and is most probably based on a contraction of the Greek *pan-mela* (all honeyed). The name appeared for the first time in Sir Philip Sidney's late-sixteenth-century work *The Countess of Pembroke's Arcadia*. As

for Barrie's supposed invention, the name Wendy appears in the census records of the USA as far back as the first decade of the nineteenth century, a hundred years before Wendy Darling. Strangely, Wendy crops up as a boy's name in the English and Welsh census of 1881, but this may be a transposition or a downright mistake. Nineteenth-century census returns contain plenty of errors. The most probable origin of the name is a pet form of the Welsh Gwendolyn.

The genesis of Peter Pan is neither simple nor theatrical. In contrast to the widely help belief that the boy who wouldn't grow up was created by Barrie for a stage play, Peter Pan first appeared in a novel he wrote for adults called *The Little White Bird* in 1902, two years before he debuted as a character in the eponymous play. After the success of the play, part of this 1902 novel was extracted and adapted to become the 1906 novel *Peter Pan in Kensington Gardens*. The play was then adapted to become the 1911 novel *Peter and Wendy*, which went through two changes of name, as *Peter Pan and Wendy* and then just *Peter Pan*.

J K ROWLING AND HOGWARTS

Given their worldwide popularity, I don't really feel in a position to question the originality of the stories based around the character Harry Potter. Heaven knows I have read each and every one of the books to my three girls, and taken them with varying enjoyment to virtually all the films, though I was hugely amused by my sixteen-year-old's verdict on the film version of *Harry Potter and the Half-Blood Prince*: 'Too many hormones.'

I don't think Jo Murray, as I now believe she likes to be known, would deny that Harry Potter staple ingredients such as dorms, feasts, house cups and school bullies all previously appeared in, among other varied tales, the *Magnet* comics' and *Holiday* annuals' early-twentieth-century tales of Greyfriars and St Jim's. Bunter, the Famous Five of the Remove, the thick-headed Coker and Mr Quelch are all magical characters. Adding the wizardry bit, that was the genius. Calling the school Hogwarts was also very clever as it's a very recognisable name, but where did she conjure it from?

There are two possible sources for the name. In the 1986 film *Labyrinth*

Sarah accidentally calls another character called Hoggle, Hogwarts. A very plausible source, but I personally prefer another, as it has some remarkable connections with Rowling's school of wizardry and witchcraft. Although I originally believed I had spotted the connection – I am a fan of this potential source – it was actually discovered by Oxford classics professor Richard Jenkyns in 2000, so to him the spoils. In *How to Be Topp* reluctant schoolboy Nigel Molesworth, writing under the pen name Marcus Plautus Molesworthus, writes a cod Latin play in which he fantasises about sending the masters into fits of laughter. This play is called *Hogwarts*.

I should also mention that in Geoffrey Willans' stories the headmaster of a rival school to St Custard's, Porridge Court, is called Hoggwart. I would like to state here that the tousle-haired, round-bespectacled Molesworth and his friend Peason were far more anarchic and troublesome than Harry Potter and Ron Weasley ever are.

SPIKE MILLIGAN WROTE 'THE GOONS'

Let me be not so pedantic as to say it was actually *The Goon Show*, not 'The Goons'.[1] That's not the point I'm making here. The Goons themselves were Terence 'Spike' Milligan, Harry Secombe and Peter Sellers, and in the early days Michael Bentine. For those that know little about, but still enjoy episodes of *The Goon Show*, the accepted truth is that manic genius Milligan wrote every single one of 'em. We also know that the pressure of producing a new show virtually every week coupled with the mental illness that had plagued him since his experiences in the Second World War meant he spent time during the 1950s in mental asylums. But if there was so much pressure on Spike that he couldn't write and perform, and with a new show was needed every week, then why do we not see vast gaps in the lists of recording and broadcast dates? Also, as Harry Secombe had a parallel theatrical singing career and Sellers was breaking Hollywood,

1 The show was called *Crazy People* throughout its first series in 1951. This in part was due to the powers at the BBC not knowing the term goon, being borrowed as it was by Spike from characters in *Popeye*. There is even a suggestion that in early discussions the comedy commissioners thought Milligan had written something called *The Go On Show*, or more uncomfortably *The Coon Show*.

how did they manage to turn up and produce manic genius each and every week?

The answer is that they were helped. Milligan devised the show and was its main writer, but others wrote in collaboration with him and on occasions produced solo work. Eric Sykes is probably the best remembered of his co-writers today, but others included Larry Stephens, John Antrobus and Maurice Wiltshire. Other interlopers, this time on the performing side, included the original announcer Andrew Timothy, father of actor Christopher, who was replaced at the end of the third series by the more familiar Wallace Greenslade. Many played themselves, including newsreader John Snagge, *Kind Hearts and Coronets* star Dennis Price, actor A E Matthews and actor, writer and producer Bernard Miles. Jack Train reprised the character of Colonel Chinstrap from *ITMA*. Radio's 'Man in Black' Valentine Dyall played a raft of sinister characters, and when they needed someone more womanly than Milligan's Minnie Bannister, Charlotte Mitchell and Cecile Chevreau appeared. Dick Emery played Emery-type Seagoon in the absence of Neddy Seagoon (Harry Secombe), and replaced Spike a few times, as did Graham Stark. At different times *Carry On* regular Kenneth Connor stood in for both Secombe and Peter Sellers.

So less of an individually written series, more of an ensemble piece.

THE LORD OF THE RINGS IS A TRILOGY

As a fan of this story since I was a teenager, I find myself correcting this common error quite often. I am not as vitriolic as a close friend of mine (who has had pet cats called Bilbo, Frodo and Samwise, to give you an idea of his perspective), who is so disturbed by the additions and exclusions in the Peter Jackson trilogy of films he refuses to watch them ever again. I do not blame Jackson for playing with the story; he was making films, which is a very different art form to the novel.

I have not made an error in referring to the films as a trilogy, as that is what they are, but in the original printed version *The Fellowship of the Ring*, *The Two Towers* and *The Return of the King* are all volumes containing two books each.

Interestingly, the image of Tolkien as a gentle Oxford don meeting his fellow 'inklings' at the Eagle and Child actually sits at odds with the epic battles fought between him and his publishers. It seems that at times he really believed he was fighting a dark lord. As he was finishing off his tale in 1950 he found himself in dispute with his publisher, George Allen & Unwin, over two issues. He wanted *The Lord of the Rings* to be published in its entirety as one volume, and *The Silmarillion* (still far from being in a publishable state) to be released alongside it. Allen & Unwin, struggling with post-war paper shortages, wanted to hold off from publishing the more scholarly *Silmarillion*, and to stagger the release of *The Lord of the Rings* by producing it in three volumes. Miffed, Tolkein offered *The Lord of the Rings* to Collins, who told him it needed cutting. He refused and found himself cornered. He went back to Allen & Unwin and told them he'd accept publication in parts.

Allen & Unwin put *The Silmarillion* on the back burner (it was finally published in 1977, four years after Tolkein's death) and published the six books that make up *The Lord of the Rings* in three volumes. Book 1, *The Ring Sets Out*, and Book 2, *The Ring goes South*, went into *The Fellowship of the Ring*. The third book, *The Treason of Isengard*, and the fourth, *The Ring Goes East*, were to become *The Two Towers*. Finally the fifth and sixth, *The War of the Ring* and *The End of the Third Age*, appeared as *The Return of the King,* along with indices and appendices. Despite his major work finally appearing in print, Tolkien was not satisfied. The three volumes did not appear until July 1954, November 1954 and October 1955 respectively. Tolkien was also not much taken with *The Return of the King* as the title for the third volume: he thought it gave the plot away. He suggested *The War of the Ring*, but received short shrift from Allen & Unwin.

A coda to this epic battle of the publishing world is the title *The Lord of the Rings* itself. Most take it to refer to the ring of power destroyed towards the end by Frodo. As the main ring among the others it is sometimes seen as their lord, but the title refers to the dark lord who forged the rings of power in the first place, Sauron.

Tolkien was not much taken with The Return of the King *as the title for the third volume: he thought it gave the plot away.*

CLAY-CLANGER

Clayhanger, the series of novels by Arnold Bennett more properly called *The Clayhanger Family*, is also usually referred to as a trilogy. Actually, there are four novels: *Clayhanger* (1910), *Hilda Lessways* (1911), *These Twain* (1916) and *The Roll-Call* (1918). The confusion probably arises from the first three novels being published as a single volume called *The Clayhanger Family* in 1925.

Bennett had previous on this, as they say. He had released a novel about life in the Staffordshire Potteries called *Anne of the Five Towns* in 1902. The trouble is there are six. The town of Newcastle-under-Lyne, although in the vicinity, is usually excluded from any list of Potteries towns because it remained separate on the formation of Stoke-on-Trent in 1910. The six towns that amalgamated were Stoke itself, Burslem, Hanley, Tunstall, Longton and Fenton. In Bennett's work Knype is recognisable as Stoke, Bursley as Burslem, Hanbridge as Hanley, Turnhill as Tunstall and Longshaw as Longton. As to what the citizens of Fenton had done to Bennett to warrant their exclusion, I don't have the smoggiest idea.

'ALICE IN WONDERLAND'

ALICE IN WONDERLAND

LEWIS CARROLL

Having previously mentioned a friend's dislike for a particular film adaptation of a piece of literature, I would like to explain one of my own. I think there is a conspiracy among film producers to ensure the story of *Alice's Adventures in Wonderland*, which is the correct title of the book, isn't retold on the screen in a way that is faithful to Dodgson's original work. I find this disappointing as it is such a wonderful and self-contained story.

The attractiveness of Tweedledum and Tweedledee as characters seems to be the nub of the problem.[1] Even though they appear in print in

---

[1] Tweedledum and Tweedledee possibly come from an old English nursery rhyme, but the names had also previously been used to refer to Handel and fellow composer Bononcini, who were known for their disagreements.

in Dodgson's sequel, *Through the Looking Glass, and What Alice Found There*, they feature in Disney's 1951 *Alice in Wonderland* as well as Tim Burton's 2010 film of the same name. Other transpositions are used in these films (as well as in other productions). In both *Wonderland* films Alice talks to the plants and the insects, a vignette borrowed from *Through the Looking Glass*. The Queen of Hearts in Burton's film is actually the Red Queen, living in opposition to her sister the White Queen, both *Looking Glass* Characters. A poem from *Through the Looking Glass*, 'Jabberwocky', becomes a central plank of the story in the Burton *Wonderland*, with Alice becoming the slayer of the fabulous monster. On the other hand, the use of characters from the sequel in *Wonderland* films has led to a number of favourite characters being omitted, such as Father William, the Gryphon and the Mock Turtle, the Duchess and the Cook, and so on.

THE HUMAN LEAGUE

The Human League is widely thought to be the first band named after a computer game. However, this is effectively impossible.

The Human League ended up as a very successful pop band, with enough of a following to this day to ensure an audience whenever they choose to get back together and tour. Their most memorable line-up had Phil Oakey as lead singer, with the attractive Susanne (now having reverted to her original name of Susan Ann) and Joanne providing the female vocals that gave them their unique sound. But they had an incarnation before this, as an avant-garde electronic band, a band whose real successor was created by the men who actually invited Oakey into the band in the first place. This was first the British Electric Foundation, and then, when they chose to go for the mainstream with Glenn Gregory doing the singing (ironically the first choice over Phil Oakey as the vocalist for the original Human League), Heaven 17.

This was the late 1970s. Martyn Ware and Ian Craig Marsh had previously launched themselves as the Dead Daughters and the Future.

Frustrated with their progress, they approached Ware's old school friend hospital porter Phil Oakey, a man with a reputation for his strange dress sense in their home city of Sheffield.[1] He joined, but they needed a new name to go with their new image. It did not however come from a computer game, an unfounded assertion I have read time and time again.

In the late 70s, even Pac Man hadn't come out. We had Pong (1972) and Space Invaders (1977), but, try as I might, I don't remember the defending forces in Space Invaders being referred to as the Human League. In 1978 Martyn Ware came up with the name by gleaning it from a board game, a relatively sophisticated product released in 1974 called Starforce: Alpha Centuri. One of the protagonists in this sci-fi space war was the Human League. At no stage were computers involved. But happily for lovers of synthpop, we didn't have to wait until AD 2415, as we did in the game, until our version of the Human League emerged.

FITZ

I have often detected a certain pride in the possessors of this surname[2] and those whose surname is prefixed with Fitz-. They sense perhaps a certain rakishness in their genealogical origins, believing as they do that it indicates illegitimacy and the involvement of at least minor aristocracy in the more distant branches of their family tree. In Ireland, for example, the families collectively known as the Fitzes believed it indicated Anglo-Norman origins and were inclined to look down on those lesser mortals whose names began with a Mac- or an O'.

I feel a little reluctant to dispute such cherished beliefs, but it seems it is no more an indication of illegitimacy than the prefix Mc- in my own name. It simply means, say in the name Fitzherbert, that the original holder of the name was the son of Herbert. The modern French word for son is *fils*. As with a large number of French words imported with the Conqueror in 1066 and then adopted and adapted into English, fitz was an Anglo-French

---

1   In one interview in the *New Musical Express* Phil Oakey admitted he had discussed joining the band at the Leadmill, Sheffield's premier new music venue at the time, wearing a pair of tights as a shirt and a baked bean tin strapped to his head as a hat.
2   There are at least fifty households in the UK with the surname 'Fitz'.

spelling of the Old French *fiz*, pronounced FITS. The *Oxford English Dictionary* tells us this Anglo-French spelling derived from the pronunciation rule of Old French that a palatalised L converted a succeeding s into a TS. This was written as a z. Simple.

In addition, the prefix Fitz- was not, as you might think, only applied to paternal origins. Henry II of England was referred to in a history of 1470 as 'Henrye le Fytz Empryce', due to his mother having been married to the Holy Roman Emperor before taking up with his father, Geoffrey of Anjou. The expressions *beau fitz* (fair son) and *fiz a putain* (son of a whore) were also common.

There is a glimmer of hope I can offer those I perhaps harshly disinherited earlier in this piece. The reason Fitz- became synonymous with illegitimacy is perhaps its later use by royal princes for their illegitimate offspring. So all you Fitzroys out there, take heart.

MÉNAGE À TROIS

—————— ❧❧ ——————

Now often taken to describe a sexual act in which three people are involved, it actually refers to a living arrangement in which three people live together as partners – husbands and wives, or however they wish. The domestic arrangements in a ménage à trois do not have to include

sexual relations, but I'm not so naive as to think that this is usually the case. Using the phrase as adopted into English, three students or flatmates living together with absolutely no bed-hopping going on could be said to be in a ménage à trois, such as with the characters Robin, Chrissy and Jo in the 1970s sitcom *Man About the House*. Then again, the writers couldn't resist squeezing humour out of every occasion on which Robin found himself fancying his flatmates.

To reiterate the original meaning of the phrase, the translation from the French is household of three, thus relating to living, rather than sleeping, arrangements.

FRENCH FRIES ARE NOT FRENCH

Food is one of the areas in which the British and the Americans are truly two nations divided by a common language. Jelly and jello, biscuits and cookies, candy floss and cotton candy, crisps, chips and French fries: try ordering any of the above in the USA using the British term and see what you get, and I don't just mean a strange look.[1]

Although in these islands we now tend to use French fries to describe the thinner-cut style of deep-fried potato found in fast-food takeaways, by mostly otherwise using the term chips we avoid the etymological faux pas common among our transatlantic cousins. This is because French fries are actually Belgian.

I think the Americans missed a trick. Potatoes are originally from over there, are they not? They could have claimed them for their own. Then again, the term French to describe food prepared or cooked in a particular way does seem to have been used more broadly in the past; now it is almost exclusively applied to potatoes. When Thomas Jefferson referred to potatoes cooked in the 'French manner' in the early nineteenth century, he most likely meant they had been deep fried, as we find deep-fried onions

---

1   I am not referring here to the mildly amusing but temporary attempt to rename French fries, 'freedom fries' in the more conservative-minded states in the USA, following the lack of support from France for the US-led invasion of Iraq in 2003.

and chicken pieces being described in this way around a hundred years later. An alternative derivation, which actually appears in some dictionaries, is that during preparation vegetables that have been julienned (that is cut into slender strips as in carrots julienne) are said to have been frenched. This is also a term that can be applied to the trimming of excess fat from a piece of meat.

The move from French being used as a generic culinary term by chefs catering to the upper classes to the now ubiquitous use of French fries to denote sliced and deep-fried potatoes seems to have been the result of a large number of 'ordinary Joes' from America finding themselves in Flanders in the latter part of the First World War. Although they were sitting in Belgian mud, the language they heard around them was Wallonian French, and so the tasty fried potatoes they were eating and which they raved about on their return to their homeland were by derivation French fries.

I don't know if the Belgians felt slighted by this misnomer, but it is recorded that as long ago as the seventeenth century their predecessors, the poorer inhabitants of the Spanish Netherlands (that's roughly modern-day Belgium to you and me), were the first people to eat chips.

Vegetables that have been julienned (that is cut into slender strips as in carrots julienne) are said to have been frenched.

AMERICA'S SWEETHEART AND THE BRAZILIAN BOMBSHELL

At least all those 'ordinary joes' sitting in Flanders could dream of their very own Mary Pickford back home. She was America's Sweetheart even if the fries were French. The only problem was that she was born a Canadian subject of our very own Queen Victoria in Toronto in 1892.

Twenty-five years later, the World War Two GIs who were fans of Carmen Miranda were generally also under an misapprehension as well. The Brazilian Bombshell was actually born in Portugal.

WHICH RICHARD WAS
THE BEST KING OF ENGLAND?

We have three to choose from. A quick poll usually results in an order of preference that follows the regnal numbers. Richard I was the best, and borders on being a folk hero. His popularity is underlined by there being an equestrian statue of him outside the Palace of Westminster. Richard II lies in the middle ground of general indifference as the least known of the three, though his reputation is dependent as with so many of our historical figures on the quill of William Shakespeare. Also with a reputation heavily influenced by the Bard, Richard III has entered the common memory as a villainous cripple who always takes up at the rear in this particular popularity contest. Oh how wrong history can be.

I have to declare a personal interest here. I am a Ricardian, that is, I feel the posthumous reputation of Richard (III) of Gloucester deserves a makeover. Shakespeare especially did for his memory by popularising the image Thomas More had promoted; in the opposite way Walter Scott boosted that of Richard I in *Ivanhoe* and *The Talisman*. The historical evidence does not support these literary legends. In another more tongue-in-cheek literary work, *1066 and All That*, Sellar and Yeatman have John as one of the five bad kings mentioned in the book's subtitle. If they had been serious, they should have turned their gazes on his older brother. Richard I was a very bad king, possibly the worst England has had.

We know he was called Coeur de Lion even before he succeeded his father Henry II, due to his military qualities. This nickname came from France because that's where he spent most of his time, in his dukedom of Aquitaine; he had little if any regard at all for his lands across the English Channel.

'Hang on,' I hear you say. 'Before you assassinate his character, surely the fact he was in receipt of such a superb sobriquet while still alive reflects what a popular guy he was?' I don't think so. Military leaders at the time weren't admired because they were loved but because they were feared. His order to kill more than 2,500 Muslim prisoners in Palestine can be seen as murder. Scott's chivalrous 'Good King Richard' as portrayed in many a Robin Hood movie is about as historically accurate as the usual portrayal of the title character. While talking the talk about chivalry, Richard didn't

exactly walk the walk. Actually, what makes me smile in these Hollywood films is that King Richard generally makes his appearance at the end of the film to put the kingdom back to rights after mismanagement by the usurper John. Robin was extremely lucky to meet his king because in his ten-year reign Richard spent about six months in England. In fact, he was totally absent for the entire second half.

I do accept that he was cruel and ruthless because he had to be, but he seems to have liked a bit of excess. As he liked a scrap[1] and England at that time was too peaceful for him to find one, once he had finished in his French lands he had to look further afield. He liked to promote himself as a pious man, so what better than going on crusade to the Holy Land? When he needed to pay for this trip, he saw England as a cash cow to be milked dry. The booty resulting from the king turning a blind eye to a series of pogroms against the English Jews acted as another cash stream. While on the subject of his supposed piousness, I'd like to make the point that he also comes across as that strange combination, an avowedly religious man whose private life and public activities were less than in total keeping with his faith.

Although some modern historians regard him as gay, I actually go with Jean Flori's conclusion that he was probably bisexual. This historian has discovered that Richard's two public confessions and the penitence that followed both relate to male sodomy at a time when any form of homosexuality was regarded as a mortal sin. He also joined a rebellion against his father and married his wife while officially betrothed to somebody else. As it was a political marriage, he then didn't seem to think twice about treating her despicably. All things considered, about the only positive thing I can bring myself to say about him is he seems to have written some good poetry.

Let me conclude with the words of Victorian historian William Stubbs, Bishop of Oxford, who puts my thoughts on this man into far better words than I could ever manage.

> He was a bad king: his great exploits, his military skill, his
> splendour and extravagance, his poetical tastes, his adventurous
> spirit, do not serve to cloak his entire want of sympathy, or even

---

1   Wonderfully, if bizarrely, summed up by Virginia Mayo's character, Lady Edith, in the 1954 film *King Richard and the Crusaders*: 'War, war. That's all you think about, Dickie Plantagenet.'

*Richard I saw England
as nothing more than
cold and wet and is
said to have declared,
'I would have sold
London if I could find
a buyer.'*

consideration, for his people. He was no Englishman, but it does not follow that he gave to Normandy, Anjou, or Aquitaine the love or care that he denied to his kingdom. His ambition was that of a mere warrior: he would fight for anything whatever, but he would sell everything that was worth fighting for. The glory that he sought was that of victory rather than conquest.

Richard saw England as nothing more than cold and wet and is said to have declared, 'I would have sold London if I could find a buyer.' No Englishman indeed. To quote Stubbs again, 'a bad son, a bad husband, a selfish ruler, and a vicious man'.

Now what of Richard number two? Often portrayed as insane, it seems he did have some psychiatric problems, especially towards the end of his life, but for most of the time he behaved quite normally, if a little haughtily. In contrast to Richard I, his father the Black Prince and his grandfather Edward III, he wasn't a warmonger or a warrior. He tried to end the Hundred Years War, which seems to me quite commendable. He was also a great supporter of the arts and his court was relatively cultured.

If Shakespeare seems to blame Richard II's deposition by his cousin Henry IV and the Wars of the Roses on his 'misrule', the modern view is more balanced. It rejects putting the total blame on Richard, but does not exonerate him totally. His ideas of kingship weren't outlandish, but he just seemed to act in a manner that the established political animals at court couldn't stomach. Like many kings in many lands, he picked unpopular favourites and then tried a bit too hard to get his own back on those who questioned his judgement. He was also unlucky in having to deal with the aftermath of the Black Death, which had occurred a few decades before his reign.

The Peasant's Revolt of 1381 had its origins in conflict between landowners and peasants caused by the social and demographic upheavals that followed a third of the population dying, although it was Richard's poll tax that created the spark. My conclusion is that, while not being totally good, Richard was certainly not totally bad.

Now, turning to Richard III, how did he compare with his namesakes? Well, he and his wife Anne Neville endowed both King's College and Queens' College at Cambridge, and made extensive grants to the Church. He planned the establishment of a large chantry chapel in York Minster. His Council of the North worked to improve conditions in that part of the country and helped it to become less financially dependent on London. Sadly, however, despite his depiction by propaganda-driven Tudor writers as a deformed and evil-minded monster long being discredited, this is the image that still prevails.

To counter these common misconceptions, in the twentieth century the Richard III Society and the Society of Friends of King Richard III were both established. They draw their inspiration from a contemporary pre-Tudor proclamation made in the city of York in 1485 following his death: 'King Richard, late reigning mercifully over us, was . . . piteously slain and murdered, to the great heaviness of this city.' Now that doesn't sound to me as if he was unpopular. In addition, in an age when television allows justice to be seen to be done, he has been found unanimously not guilty of the murder or even complicity in the demise of his nephews, the Princes in the Tower. A mock trial presided over by three judges from the US Supreme Court cleared him of all charges.

Therefore, while not totally swallowing Peter Cook's kindly portrayal of him in TV's *The Black Adder*, Richard III should definitely be remembered on balance as a better king than Richard I, and probably better than Richard II. Indeed, it is pleasing that this particular tide appears to be turning without any help from me. Although not exactly outside the Houses of Parliament, we now have a statue to Richard III – in Leicester, where he stayed before the fateful Battle of Bosworth Field. Perhaps more telling is that in a BBC poll of 2002 to find the hundred greatest Britons, Richards I and II didn't appear, yet Richard III came eighty-second. Then again, Diana Princess of Wales came third, actor Michael Crawford seventeenth, and Paul McCartney and David Bowie nineteenth and twenty-ninth respectively. Oh, and Robbie Williams came seventy-seventh.

ARE THE CURRENT ROYAL FAMILY WINDSORS, MOUNTBATTENS OR MOUNTBATTEN-WINDSORS?

I promised that during the earlier discussion on Queen Victoria's true surname I'd take a similar look at our current royal family. This is going to be a little bit complicated, so bear with me. I am starting with the common misconception that when George V dropped the Germanic dynastic name inherited from his father, he also decided that any current or future member of the royal family was to be called Windsor, and that was that. Sadly for those of us that like neatness, orders-in-court usually seem to leave things a little more complex.

I mentioned earlier that the convention is that noblewomen do not become part of their husband's house on marriage, and the woman we know by the title Queen Victoria actually had the proper name Alexandrina Welf. So she did not adopt the personal surname of her husband, Prince Albert, which was Wettin. Their son, although christened *Albert* Edward after his father and grandfather and known as Bertie, took the title Edward VII in deference to his mother's wishes that he did not use Albert as his regnal name. As his house was that of his father, after nearly 200 years the ruling dynasty ceased to be the house of Hanover and was replaced by that of Saxe-Coburg and Gotha. His personal surname he also took from his father, so he was a Wettin. In turn, his son George V of Saxe-Coburg and Gotha also had the personal, if unloved and unused, surname Wettin.

Matters, however, became complicated for George four years after his accession, when the United Kingdom went to war with Germany. Anti-German sentiment was of course widespread, and it didn't seem a good idea for the royal family of the time to have a German name. H G Wells wrote of Britain's 'alien and uninspiring court'. The King's reply was succinct: 'I may be uninspiring, but I'll be damned if I'm alien.' However, he acted. By an order-in-council of 1917 he legally changed the name of the royal house from Saxe-Coburg and Gotha to Windsor.

This was a popular move but there seems to have been no recognition of, or reference to, the personal surname Wettin. So to me the question is, did George V's order-in-council include both the dynastic and personal surnames of the royal family? If it didn't, then he and his descendants Edward VIII, George VI and Elizabeth II were, and are still, all Wettins. If it was his intention that his personal surname be changed, then that became Windsor too. I rather think that he meant to get rid of all Germanic references, evidenced by him immediately giving his relatives with Germanic names and titles new British ones following his order-in-council. Thus, for example, Prince Louis of Battenberg became Louis Mountbatten, 1st Marquess of Milford Haven. There will be more to write about that side of the family and the further complications they've brought to the issue in a moment. The wording of the order seems to support the total swap to the new name. Windsor was to be the surname for all descendants of Queen Victoria then living in the United Kingdom. This seems pretty inclusive, but he added a qualification that would, only thirty years later, reignite the confusion. He excluded women who married into other families and their descendants.

In 1947 Elizabeth Windsor (or Wettin) of the house of Windsor married Philip Mountbatten. Although born a member of both the Greek and Danish royal houses he had by 1947 fought for the UK in the Second World War, become a British citizen, renounced his titles and adopted the surname of his maternal grandparents. So at the time of his marriage he was simply Lieutenant Philip Mountbatten RN. The marriage raised a question. Did Elizabeth, as first in line of succession to the throne, fall under the part of the 1917 order-in-council that made all descendants of Victoria (resident in the UK) into Windsors in perpetuity, or did she come under the exclusion by marrying into the Mountbattens? This matter was compounded the following year when Prince Charles was born. Was *he* a Windsor or was he a Mountbatten? When he comes to the throne, will he be of the house of Windsor or the house of Mountbatten? The questions remained until Elizabeth tried to sort the matter out by, like her grandfather before her, issuing an order-in-council. This she did in 1960.

'I believe the following to be the case. The dynastic name and the surname of the royal house will continue to be Windsor until the succession falls to a cadet branch of Prince Philip's male-line descendants not previously bearing princely styles. If this happens, the reigning branch will be named Mountbatten-Windsor, and its members will have that personal surname. As Charles, his sons and his siblings already have princely titles, if and when they come to the throne, they will continue the house of Windsor, and legally have the surname Windsor. After further reading around the ambiguous wording, I suggest the only people who will hold the surname under the order-in-council are any male-line great-grandchildren of the Queen not in direct line to the throne. That would be the children of any sons of the Duke of York and Earl of Wessex. This so far only applies to the children of James Windsor, Viscount Severn. It also seems that the surname would be given to any male-line great-grandchildren of the Queen if one of her granddaughters were to have a child while unwed. Also, following Charles becoming king, his male-line great-grandchildren not in direct line to the throne would also use the surname. The surname also applies to any descendants of the Queen and Prince Philip who do not hold the style of Royal Highness and the rank of Prince or Princess of the United Kingdom. Although not wishing it of course, it is interesting to speculate what would happen if a disaster wiped out those highest in the order of succession. King Peter or Queen Zara might retain the house of Windsor, or alternatively could issue their own order-in-council to establish the house of Mountbatten-Windsor, or even use their surname to establish the house of Phillips.

To return to the core of this discussion, the different question as to the personal surname of members of the royal family, Prince Philip is a Mountbatten, and the Queen and the majority of her direct descendants I believe to be Windsors. The Princess Royal has had the surnames Mountbatten, Windsor (post-1960), Phillips and Laurence. So why do the younger members of the royal family continue to waspishly confuse the issue? Is it in deference to their father and grandfather, the Duke of Edinburgh?

Despite during their naval service Princes Charles and Andrew both being referred to as Lieutenant Windsor or by their ducal titles, they have both made use of the surname Mountbatten-Windsor. Indeed, this was the name Andrew used to sign the wedding register in 1986, as did Princess Anne in 1973. For army service William and Henry have both called themselves Wales; Beatrice and Eugenie call themselves York; and Edward now calls himself Wessex. These are styles which they are perfectly entitled to use, but they too have made use of the Mountbatten-Windsor surname. So although it doesn't carry any legal standing, the younger members of the royal family follow a practice that is becoming common in the UK, and use both parents' names with a hyphen, seeing themselves as Mountbatten-Windsors.

Should we now go into the matter of the Mountbatten-Windsors being a cadet branch of the house of Schleswig-Holstein-Sonderburg-Glucksburg, or even the Schleswig-Holstein-Sonderburg-Glucksburgs being a branch of the house of Oldenburg? Perhaps not.

MRS IS NOT AN ABBREVIATION OF MISSUS

—❧❦—

This is all down to changing meanings. Mr is an abbreviation of Mister, but Mrs is an abbreviation of Mistress, and I think the majority of people would now regard a wife and a mistress as mutually exclusive. Missus is a phonetic representation of Mrs, not the original full word, so the latter cannot be regarded as an abbreviation of the former.

NETS ARE NOT COMPULSORY IN FOOTBALL

—❧❦—

Football fans are now so used to being thrilled by a thunderous shot 'hitting the back of the net', they don't often consider that under the laws of the game even FIFA's World Cup final could be played with unadorned goalposts. Law 1 states only that nets *may* be attached, and that is as long as they are properly supported and do not interfere with the goalkeeper. Jumpers for goalposts are not allowed however.

THE LETTERS ON RUSSIAN FOOTBALL SHIRTS

—❧❦—

Prior to 1991 and the fall of communism, Russian football shirts were emblazoned with the letters CCCP. Or so I thought at the time. I was wrong on two accounts.

Firstly, the shirts weren't Russian. Russia was just the biggest of the commonwealth of fifteen notionally autonomous republics in the Union of Soviet Socialist Republics, the USSR. This also contained the republics of Estonia, Ukraine, Georgia and Kazakhstan, among others. If there was one thing the Soviets were good at it was political correctness. The republics were actually the Estonian SSR (Soviet Socialist Republic), the Ukrainian SSR and so on, and athletes of these nations played for the USSR. Russia itself was more properly the Russian Soviet Federative Socialist Republic, or RSFSR for short. This contained a large number of ethnicities other than Russian within its borders.

The other matter on which I was wrong was presuming the Russians used the same alphabet as I did. In Western Europe we borrow our alphabet from Latin, but a lot of Slavic peoples (and some non-Slavic ones as well) use the Cyrillic alphabet, formalised mainly from Greek in the ninth century. In Cyrillic the symbols represent sounds. The sound we represent with an s becomes c in Russian, and the Western r sound is rendered as p. So the Soviet football shirts had the letters CCCP to represent SSSR, these letters standing for Soyuz Sovetskikh Sotsialisticheskikh Respublik. The actual real words in Cyrillic are Союз Советских Социалистических Республик.

RSFSR in full Cyrillic is Росси́йская Сове́тская Федерати́вная Социалисти́ческая Респу́блика, shortened to РСФСР. Maybe a little too much to get on a jersey all at once.

CZECH IS ACTUALLY POLISH

The Czechs' name for their own country is Česká republika.

A reform of Czech orthography (correct spelling) in the late Middle Ages meant the z in the name disappeared. We actually get our English spelling with the z via the language of their neighbours to the north-east, the Poles. There seems to be a surfeit of zs in Polish, because unlike the English version of Scrabble, which has one Z worth ten points, Polish has five worth one point each. However, as it is classed as a different letter, there is only one Z with a dot over it (Ż), worth five points, while Z with an acute accent over it (Ź) is apparently even rarer. The Polish game also has one of these, value nine points.

QVC

———— ❧ ————

I still come across both fans and detractors of TV shopping channels who think this is an initialism of Quality, Value, Choice. Joseph Segal's vision when he founded the corporation in the 1980s was Quality, Value, *Convenience*.

ACRONYMS

———— ❧ ————

Initialism is actually a much underused word, and we often use acronym when we really mean initialism. Radar is an acronym because we have taken the initial letters of a number of words and combined them to form a new word. FIFA is also an acronym, even though it has not as yet been transformed into a word in its own right. If we spell the letters out, as in TNT, BBC or QVC, it is more properly referred to as an initialism. We can also refer to initialisms as alphabetisms. Some alphabetisms, although pronounced letter by letter, are now spelt as words, deejay and emcee being examples.

THE YOGH AND SIR MENZIES CAMPBELL

———— ❧ ————

Yogh is not a new name for an abominable snowman, but the name of an ancient letter. My research into this particular item has answered a question that rattled around my brain whenever Sir Menzies Campbell made a TV appearance or was mentioned in the newspapers. Why does he always seemingly mispronounce his name MINGIS when there is a z in the middle? I now have to admit it was me who was misguided, not him.

It was a trip to Culzean Castle in Ayrshire that started me on my route to the answer. I was standing in the kitchens at that ancient pile discussing a wonderful piece of equipment known as a smoke jack with a very helpful guide by the name of Mr Mark Fletcher when my mobile phone rang. I advised the caller I was at a place I pronounced as KULLZEEAN Castle. After finishing my call, the young man corrected me. 'It's KULLAYN, not KULLZEEAN.' 'Why?' I enquired. 'I'm afraid I don't know,' he replied. 'Then I shall find out,' were my departing words.

I'm pleased to say Mark was on duty when I revisited the stately pile just recently. This is what I told him. This place name, like Menzies, was originally spelt with a yogh, a now-abandoned letter previously used in English and Scots. The letter was represented by a symbol similar to the number 3, which is also the copperplate-style representation of the letter z. The conquering Normans disliked the non-Latin character, and used a y or g instead. When printing arrived a few centuries later, although the less normanised Scots still retained the yogh in place and personal names, printers found it easier to use a z. The spelling was thus effectively changed, but as certain pronunciations had already been established, people just accepted (as in a lot of other different anomalies in English spelling) that it might be spelt one way but pronounced another. So along with MINGIS and KULLAYN we have other examples, one of which is the surname Dalziel, which is pronounced DEE-ELL. The *OED* lists capercailzie as an accepted alternative spelling of the name for that large member of the grouse family, the capercailye, indicating the original existence of a yogh in the word.[1]

In some cases however, the transformation has been total. Although originally pronounced MACKENYIE, the surname MacKenzie is now almost universally pronounced with a z. Ironically, it seems the other famous Menzies, the company John Menzies, is now commonly pronounced with a modern z as MENZEES even in Scotland. The company has a humorous limerick explaining the 'correct' pronunciation MINGIS on its website. Yes, I am referring to this company in the present tense. Another popular error is that this organisation became defunct when its high street retail operation was bought out in the late 1990s. I am pleased to say they are still going strong in the fields of distribution and aviation.

---

1 The common modern spelling capercaille only appears as an alternative rather than the main spelling in the *OED* online.

HARLEQUINS AND GRASSHOPPERS

We normally pluralise the names of these famous clubs, and I do not denigrate anyone who does. The correct names are however the Harlequin Football Club and Grasshopper Club Zürich (since 2005 more correctly the Neue Grasshopper Fußball AG), both in the singular.

There are some interesting other little-known facts as well. Harlequin FC actually started as the Hampstead Football Club, well away from its long-term home the Stoop in south-west London. When the Hampstead became the Harlequin, the malcontents went off and formed that other great club Wasps. Just to make the name thing a bit more complicated, the Super League rugby league club that grew out of the London Broncos in 2005 is the Harlequins Rugby League Club. So the singular and the plural are used at the same club!

Grasshopper too are a club involved in not just one sport, and put most English sporting clubs to shame. At the last count they had representative teams in Association Football, rowing, ice hockey, field hockey, unihockey, rugby union, handball, lawn tennis, court tennis, squash and curling. Phew!

THE LOWEST RANK
IN THE ARMY IS PRIVATE

It is in some units, but in some others you might be called something else. Equivalent titles for this rank are numerous. The Royal Engineers currently has sappers, the Royal Signals has signallers and the Royal Artillery has gunners. Foot Guards regiments have guardsmen of course. You're a fusilier in some regiments, a rifleman in others, a highlander in parts of the Royal Regiment of Scotland and a ranger in the Royal Irish Regiment and of course the Royal Irish Rangers. Even if you're a woman you're a craftsman in REME. Cavalry regiments in the Household Division and the Royal Armoured Corps have troopers, as does the SAS, and even the Honourable Artillery Company has them rather than gunners. The

Household Cavalry also still has trumpeters in the lowest rank. The Royal Marines (which are Royal Navy anyway) retain bandsmen, who are now called musicians in the army's bands. Returning to Highland units, they have musicians called pipers; the Rifles retain buglers; and infantry regiments have drummers. The Army Air Corps has airtroopers, but my favourite is in the Duke of Lancaster's regiment, where there are kingsmen.

While we're on the subject of rank, have you ever wondered why major is a superior rank to lieutenant, but a major general is subordinate to a lieutenant general? It's because in days of yore the three top positions in any army were, in descending seniority, captain general, lieutenant general and sergeant major general. A captain general is now just a general, and the sergeant bit has been lost as well, but the title lieutenant general has remained.

BASEBALL IS 'ALL AMERICAN'

Shall we upset those Americans who believe their national summer game is a purely home-grown pastime? I'm afraid this is like claiming American football (sorry any American readers, football) wasn't influenced by rugby –at least they are honest about it.

The claim that baseball was invented, perhaps spontaneously, by a gentleman by the name of Doubleday in New York State in 1839 actually originates with a committee or commission of 1908. They obviously hadn't read *Northanger Abbey*, because in its pages the heroine declares a preference for cricket and baseball over academic pursuits. Jane Austen wrote the book at the end of the eighteenth century, a good few years before the supposed invention of the game.

I am not claiming the game she referred to was exactly like modern baseball, but the similar game of rounders had been in existence long before it was described in print in 1828. So what I am claiming is that even if Austen was referring to a game more akin to modern rounders than modern baseball, the two games are actually more akin to each other than American football is now to rugby.

I suppose I would be unwelcome at the Baseball Hall of Fame, which has existed at Abner's Cooperstown, New York, since 1939.

WHEN IS AN ISLAND
NOT AN ISLAND?

—❧❧—

While we are in New York State, should we take a trip to Coney Island? Most of us think of the place as synonymous with a day at the beach, a cotton candy on the boardwalk and a ride on a Ferris wheel. We even get a trip out on a ferry from the workaday bustle of the city. A perfect day out. However, although once clearly thought of as an island – when a creek separated it from Long Island – we can forget the ferry trip. Since the filling in of the creek during the building of a major road in the twentieth century, it is now a hammerhead-shaped peninsula.

Other anomalies akin to this occur much closer to home, along the coast of the British Isles. The Isle of Thanet, home to the Kent resorts of Margate, Broadstairs and Ramsgate, was at one time separated from the mainland by the Wantsum Channel. This once-mighty waterway to the sea has been reduced by infilling to nothing more than a drainage ditch, and now it feeds the River Stour. A similar fate has not befallen the Isle of Sheppey, a bit further along the coast of Kent. It is still separate, accessible from the mainland by a bridge carrying the A249. Then again, Sheppey was once one of three islands. Due to silting, the once-separate Isles of Elmley and Harty are now joined to it.

In contrast, the Isle of Purbeck in Dorset cannot claim to have ever been an island. It is actually a large peninsula in Dorset lying between Poole Harbour and the English Channel. We might also question the status of the Isle of Portland near Weymouth, just to the west. The eighteen-mile-long Chesil Beach attaches it to the mainland, and as this is a permanent feature which remains uncovered at high tide, surely we should not refer to Portland as an island?

I would also like to refer to the questions that arise over two inland islands of England. Seemingly once a true island in the River Thames, the Isle of Dogs in the East End of London is now separated from the rest of the city by West India Docks. The only access is via roads over the eastern and western entrances to the docks. As these are not a natural feature, I come down on the side of those who argue that as the area is now cut off by a man-made structure, it is no longer a true island. If it were, the

The Isle of Purbeck in Dorset cannot claim to have ever been an island. It is actually a large peninsula in Dorset lying between Poole Harbour and the English Channel.

233

construction of the Corinth and Potidea Canals in Greece would have made the Peloponnese and Kassandra Peninsulas into islands. This is not regarded as the case by the locals.

The other English inland island is our old friend from the beginning of this book, the Isle of Ely. This area, now truly attached to the surrounding countryside, was once so inaccessible because of marshes and fens it was indeed an island. Hereward the Wake used it as a base to fight for Saxon interests in the years following the Norman Conquest because it was so difficult to get to. Nowadays, more like the Isle of Dogs than the Isle of Thanet, it is the hand of man (mainly in the form of Dutch Engineers) rather than nature that has ensured its island status remains in name only.

Let's finish this discussion with an example of an island that is often wrongly thought of as two. I refer to the *island*, not the *islands*, of Lewis and Harris. Call it what you will – Harris and Lewis, Lewis with Harris, or any other combination – it does not have a common name that refers to the whole of the island in either English or Scots Gaelic. Sometimes the Scots Gaelic an t-Eilean Fada (the Long Island) is applied, but this is more correctly a reference to the Outer Hebrides as a whole. Although one island, Lewis to the north is generally flat while Harris is topographically very different, being quite mountainous. This difference was recognised many years ago, as before the counties of Scotland were reorganised in the 1970s Harris was part of Inverness-shire, (sometimes spelt with three s's in a row as Invernessshire) while the northern part of the island belonged to Ross and Cromarty.

The Isle of Ely, now truly attached to the surrounding countryside, was once so inaccessible because of marshes and fens that it was indeed an island.

RABBITING ABOUT CONEY ISLAND, CONEYTHORPE AND CONEY STREET

While on the subject of Coney Island, I am reminded that explaining popular errors can be injurious to one's health. Let me explain. Coney Island's modern name almost definitely comes from early Dutch settlers in the area calling the place Conye Eylandt – in English, Rabbit Island. The Dutch word for rabbit is very similar to an old and now rarely used term for a rabbit in Britain, coney.[1] The connection looks obvious. Those who know this old word often presume that any place with coney within its name has an association with rabbits.[2]

I found myself a few years ago enjoying a pint of beer in a pub run by one of my old school friends, and a mighty good pub it is too. I was chatting to one of the regulars, a clever and sharp-minded individual. We were talking about this and that when the conversation turned to place names. He recounted that he had once lived in the village of Coneythorpe, a name which obviously reflected the large number of rabbits to be found in the area. Even though I remembered from a previous conversation that this man, who still looked reasonably fit, had been a champion boxer in his youth, I swallowed and quietly corrected him.

We were in the centre of what was once a Viking kingdom, I explained, well within the Danelaw of northern and eastern England. One of the main shopping streets of the city we were in is called Coney Street. I suggested that it was not in keeping with how things usually pan out that an important street would be named after rabbits. Rather, the name more probably came from the Viking *conig* (Anglo-Saxon *cyninges*) for king – so, King's Street. Similarly, Coneythorpe most probably derived from the earlier Conig's Thorpe (King's Farm), originally the location of a settlement that belonged directly to or sent its produce to the King.

I was fixed with a boxer's stare. 'Really?' he said. There was a moment's silence. I now feel the need to thank my old friend, the landlord, for arriving at our table to show me some photographs from his latest charity effort, thus changing the subject. Thank you, Jim.

---

1   J R R Tolkien, whose Hobbits use the Old English vernacular, has Sam Gamgee use the word in *The Lord of the Rings*.

2   The most important place generally taken to be named after rabbits is Spain. Although other theories exist, it is most probable that the Carthaginians, who ruled there before the Romans won the Punic Wars (Barcelona is named for Hannibal's family name Barca, pronounced BARKA), named the land from their word *tsepan*, meaning rabbit. A popular error is that the Latin name for Spain, Hispania, means Land of the Rabbit. The Latin name actually derives from that of the previous Carthaginian occupiers (*tsepan* leading to Hispania). The Latin word for (the burrowing) rabbit is *cuniculus*, which can also denote a channel, mine, excavation, secret device or underground burrow, hole or tunnel.

'I LOVE ROCK AND ROLL'

A lot of us do, but the existence of websites that allow individuals to admit their long-held but mistaken takes on lyrics shows that, as in many walks of life, sometimes our love can transcend our understanding. Another good friend of mine believed the lyrics of Sting's song about Quentin Crisp, 'Englishman in New York', contained the revelation in the chorus that he was an evil alien, rather than the actual 'I'm a legal alien.' It still brings a smile to my lips.

A further lyrical mistake that still amuses me is the one made by one-time Radio 1 DJ Gary Davies in relation to the 1980 Peter Gabriel hit 'Games Without Frontiers'. Those of us old enough to remember know that this was the English name of a major pan-European knockabout competition on television which was first broadcast in 1965. Communities from West Germany (in those days), Italy, Holland, Belgium, Switzerland, France and the UK competed in silly games in an arena accompanied by an almost continuous apoplectic stream of laughter from main presenter Stuart Hall.[1]

It is believed that the idea of the competition originated with that well-known humorist Charles de Gaulle. Even if it didn't, the show did start in France, where it was called *Jeux sans Frontières* (*Games Without Frontiers*). Peter Gabriel's witty satirical song about the childishness of international relations paid obvious tribute to the TV show, as it had Kate Bush as backing vocalist singing '*Jeux sans Frontières*' during breaks in his lyrics.[2] So with a basic understanding of French and pre-knowledge of the TV show, Kate Bush's contributions were clear enough, but Gary Davies obviously had something else on his mind. After playing the song he enthusiastically but incorrectly echoed the words of the chanteuse as, 'She's so funky, yeah!'

I heard another variation on this sort of misinterpretation by a DJ recently which highlights how, as in the case of the Panama hat, strong

1 These seven countries appeared in the competition's heyday. In the period running up to the show's end in 1990 teams from places as far apart as Malta, Liechtenstein and even Tunisia got involved.

2 He also included the name for the UK domestic pre-qualifying competition *It's a Knockout* in the lyrics.

associations developed later can obscure the origins of something. In 2002 Britney Spears released 'I Love Rock and Roll', a very brash loud piece in the best traditions of the genre which it name-checks. I heard the song on the radio as I was driving down the motorway. When it finished, the DJ (Why are they always so enthusiastic?) shared with us that the song had been penned by that queen of rock and roll and ex-member of the Runaways girl group of the 1970s Joan Jett.[3] I'm glad to say she's still going strong, and if you were to meet her backstage after a gig today, she might tell you the true story.

The song was written and originally recorded and performed by a 1970s band called the Arrows, an Anglo-American trio that had their own British TV show contemporary to, and sharing a stable with, the Bay City Rollers series *Shang-a-Lang*. (Oh, happy days.) Joan was apparently touring in the UK with the Runaways in 1976 when she saw the Arrows perform the song on their eponymous show. Much taken with it, she recorded a version three years later with Steve Jones and Paul Cook of the Sex Pistols. It was her second recording with her band the Blackhearts in 1981 that took the song into the rock stratosphere, topping the Billboard Hot 100 chart in America for seven weeks the following year. So the song is now for ever associated with Ms Jett.

A similar long-term association is that of the striking anti-Falklands-War song 'Shipbuilding' with Robert Wyatt, who had a minor hit with the song in 1983. Elvis Costello's recording of the song was played in part during a broadcast of BBC Radio 4's *Today* programme in 2007 during a piece marking the twenty-fifth anniversary of the conflict. This was credited as his version of the 'Robert Wyatt song'. Unable to stop myself, I immediately rattled off an email to the show advising them that as Elvis Costello had written the song (he actually co-wrote the song, providing the lyrics for a tune Clive Langer had originally intended for Wyatt – hence his involvement) they should really have said, 'the Elvis Costello song made famous by Robert Wyatt'. To the producer's credit, as the nine o'clock pips approached, I was charmed to hear John Humphrys hurriedly if somewhat begrudgingly read a note he had been passed, correcting the misplaced authorship.

3   Born Joan Marie Larkin, I believe.

THE WINDY CITY

W hile accepting the rebuilding of Chicago after the Great Fire of 1871 led to the creation of a grid pattern of streets, forming wind tunnels fed by the breezes off Lake Michigan, Chicago is not noticeably windier than any other high-rise American city. So where did the nickname come from? Its first use in a derogatory sense is often erroneously attributed to one Charles Dana, editor of New York newspaper the *Sun*. He was a great supporter of New York's campaign to host the World's Columbian Exposition in the 1890s, a 400th-anniversary celebration of the arrival of Christopher Columbus in America, and was probably as miffed as other leading lights on the US eastern seaboard that the upstart city of Chicago won. However, there is no real evidence of him damning the opposition as the Windy City until the Chicago newspapers accused him of it four decades later.

The first known reference to Chicago as the Windy City actually predates both Dana and the rebuilding, and occurred in a local newspaper in the 1850s. Whether the original reference was meteorological or otherwise,

THE GREAT UNION STOCK YARDS OF CHICAGO.

the term seems to have been popularised over the following twenty years by the press in the city's great rival in the Midwest, Cincinnati – and their use of the nickname had nothing to do with the weather. Chicago and Cincinnati were rivals in both commerce and sport. Cincinnati used the term to emphasise the 'bluster' of the braggarts that lived in its neighbour to the north-west.

THE US CONSTITUTION IS NOT THE BILL OF RIGHTS

The Bill of Rights is the short title of an act passed by the English parliament[1] in 1689 more properly called An Act Declaring the Rights and Liberties of the Subject and Settling the Succession of the Crown. It is often now thought that any nation's constitution is also a bill of rights. Well, it's up to any country to call anything that belongs to them by whatever name they choose, but in the case of the USA it is wrong to refer to its constitution as the Bill of Rights.

This is the collective term for the first ten amendments to the US Constitution, put before the First United States Congress by James Madison as a means of lessening the conflict between Federalists and anti-Federalists, a conflict that was threatening the ratification of the original document itself. Within its text are memorable phrases that to this day cause debate, including the confirmation of 'the right of the people to

[1] Scotland having its own separate parliament until it voted itself out of existence during the Act of Union in 1707. The popular error here is that the United Kingdom came into existence when James I, already King of Scots, also became the King of England in 1603. Although the crowns were unified, England and Scotland were separate kingdoms until over a hundred years later.

keep and bear arms' (often rendered as just 'the right to bear arms') and the forbidding of 'cruel and unusual punishment'.

THE WORLD SERIES

The presumption was that as baseball wasn't played in many locations around the globe, American teams were naturally going to be the best and so were world champions by default.

There was a time when the soccer-loving nations on this side of the ocean found it comical and perhaps arrogant that the sport of baseball had an annual championship called the World Series. How could they, when only American teams competed for it, even if a few Canadians were thrown in for good measure? 'Try the FIFA World Cup,' was the usual mantra. 'Now that is a true world championship.' Received wisdom is now that the Americans weren't being as arrogant as we once thought. It is called the World Series because it was originally created as a climax to the season by the *World*, a now-defunct New York newspaper owned at the time (1903) by Joseph Pulitzer,[1] the posthumous benefactor of the eponymous prizes.

Well, let's go back to square one. It seems the title could be arrogant after all, and we were right in the first place. The presumption was that as baseball wasn't played in many locations around the globe, American teams were naturally going to be the best and so were world champions by default. The newspaper thought to have lent its name to the Fall Classic was actually called *New York World* and was not involved – never during its existence did it claim to have any connection with post-season baseball. A founding father of yellow journalism, Pulitzer made sure his paper lost no opportunity to promote itself. If it had been involved with the annual play-offs in any way, the story would have run virtually all year round. Copies of the paper from the time make no mention of a connection.

The term World Series in fact predates the championship now recognised by governing body Major League Baseball as the first, the one that took place in 1903. The nineteenth-century post-season play-offs between the winners of the American Association (as it was then) and the National League were billed as the Championship of the World and the World Championship Series. Over time, this was shortened to

---

1   Pronounced PULLITZER, not, as many believe, PEWLITZER.

World's Series. *Spalding's Base Ball Guide* in 1887 refers to the previous year's 'postseason series' between National League champions Chicago and St Louis, champions of the American Association, as the 'World's Championship'. It seems that as both leagues called their winners Baseball Champions of the United States a grander title was needed to describe the showdown between them.

This was perhaps a bit of puff from Spalding, a major sports goods company. It had a financial interest in exporting the game to other countries. In 1890 the guide stated that the 'baseball championship of the United States necessarily includes that of the entire world, though the time will come when Australia will step in as a rival, and after that country will come Great Britain; but all that is for the future'. As we know, this has never happened. Baseball is popular in the Far East, in Latin America and even Italy, but despite this the World Series remains fixed solidly in the USA and Canada.

The 1904 *Reach Guide* called the post-season series between the Boston Americans (now the Red Sox) and the Pittsburgh Pirates a 'World's Championship Series'. In 1912 this guide referred to the 'World's Series' as well as the 'World's Championship Series'. It switched to the term World Series in 1931. The previously mentioned *Spalding Guide* used World's Series until 1916, switching to World Series in the 1917 edition. The modern bible, *The Sporting News Guide*, used World's Series from its first publication in 1942 until 1963; the following year it also adopted the now generally accepted World Series.

MINIATURE PAINTINGS

Miniature paintings are so called because they are small. Well, they can be, but they don't have to be. The origin of our word is in the Italian *miniatura*, originally a reference to the art of illuminating manuscripts of any size. It derived from a Latin word, *miniatus*, the past participle of *miniare*, meaning to colour with red lead, a colour seen in the margin of many an old book.

NOT VERY 'ORIGINAL' SIN

———&✤&———

I f you think the doctrine of original sin has anything to do with sex, as some do, then you're wrong; Adam and Eve didn't commit the *original* original sin by producing Cain, Abel and Seth and their other unnamed children. Instead, its alternative name, as used extensively in the Orthodox Church, ancestral sin, gives us a clue as to the true nature of the doctrine. To put it succinctly, it is a Christian theory that humans are by default in a state of sin resulting from the Fall of Man.[1] The Fall is a post-biblical term for what occurred when Adam and Eve ate fruit from the Tree of Knowledge when God had told them not to, and moved from innocent obedience into guilty disobedience. So *the* original sin was disobedience to God.[2]

Ideas on what constitutes disobedience are broad, and, if you will excuse the attempt at a pun, cover a multitude of sins. It can be seen as something as minor as having a weak nature with a tendency towards sin, through to all humans automatically being disobedient sinners by merely being members of the species. At the latter end of the spectrum that is clearly guilt by association. Generally though, however assertively or passively an individual Church applies the doctrine, there seems to be one area of general agreement: the only way we can be saved from original sin (any sin in fact) is through the grace of God. To put this into modern parlance, you can build up heavenly brownie points as much as you want, but in the end keep everything crossed because it matters not a jot. You may avoid committing sins all your life, but you're already in a state of sin anyway. Now if that seems unfair, you belong to a Church that applies a severe interpretation of the doctrine, and you are considering the alternatives, then read on. You may have options.

1   By the way, I hope all you non-Christians and non-religious types find the misunderstandings that often arise around religious doctrine interesting. Whether you like it or not, these affect all our lives even if as an individual one doesn't believe in a God.

2   It strikes me that the post-biblical interpretation of God's actions after he discovered Adam and Eve's disobedience actually sit atop a philosophical question. How could they have committed a sin as at that time they were totally ignorant of what good and evil were? Interesting, but for another time. I think I'll return to the pages of Milton's *Paradise Lost* and see what he made of it.

Not only are there variations in application, the doctrine doesn't even exist in some Churches. I mentioned earlier the term is based on the post-biblical idea of the Fall of Man, and for many Christians if it's not in the Bible then it isn't the word of God. The doctrine is also absent from the two other Abrahamic faiths, Judaism and Islam, so you might want to consider these if the idea of original sin is too much to bear. The dharmic Hindu religion doesn't have it either, so there's another refuge for you.

A moment though, please. Before you decide to make drastic changes to your religious practices, if you have any in the first place, let me rein things in a little. Some see original sin as the cause of the actual sins that we commit in our lives, which does make original and actual sin difficult to distinguish. However, the major Churches seem to have a more relaxed attitude. The major Western Church, Roman Catholicism, sees original sin as a general condition of sinfulness – that is the absence of holiness and perfect love – which we are born into. This is distinct from any sin you may commit in your allotted span, now increasingly more than the 'three score years and ten' of the Psalms. This lets us off having to bear the direct guilt of Adam for committing the sin in the first place. Original sin is not our fault, but we do have to live with it.

Similarly, the Eastern Orthodox Churches offer us the idea that humans bear no guilt for the sin of Adam; we inherit the aforementioned ancestral sin like our hair and eye colouration. We all participate in original sin because we're all descended from Adam, but it is seen as a distortion of the nature of man. It's what separates us from God, because original sin is ultimately physical and spiritual death.

All in all then, as with most things in life, you 'pays yer money and you takes yer choice'.

> *The Eastern Orthodox Churches offer us the idea that humans bear no guilt for the sin of Adam; we inherit the aforementioned ancestral sin like our hair and eye colouration.*

THE IMMACULATE MISCONCEPTION

A quick few lines on another popular error related to the above concerning an idea held by a lot of non-religious people, and in fact some religious ones as well. I refer to the notion that the Immaculate Conception refers to Christ being born to a virgin by God's spirit. This is an error. It seems there is a general belief that the word immaculate must have something to do with God. Just as clothes can be spotless, stainless and free from flaws – and thus immaculate – the spiritually immaculate is merely something without moral blemish, pure and stainless.

The idea of the Immaculate Conception is rather that Mary the mother of Jesus was free from original sin at the moment she was conceived in her mother's womb. The importance of this comes to the fore when, as discussed in the previous piece, it is appreciated that original sin is inherited. Jesus was not only God on earth, he was God made flesh as well. As a man, as a descendant of Adam, he was quite capable of inheriting original sin. But the chain is broken by declaring that, although as a human Mary was capable of committing sin, if she didn't have original sin she couldn't pass it to her son. This is a very neat method of dealing with the problems that some interpretions of the teachings of St Paul had created. The idea didn't become Catholic dogma until Pope Pius IX said it was in the 1850s, but like most things founded on faith rather than fact, arguments had been going on for at least seven centuries before that.

FIRST FRUITS

-⁂-

Please believe me when I say I am not on a mission to bash the 1995 film *Braveheart*. I know I have mentioned it previously as a work that mixes fiction with fact, but that is not necessarily a bad thing in the cinema. It is an entertaining film and I still enjoy watching the action whenever I come across it while indulging in that most annoying of modern male habits to women, channel-hopping on the TV. I will make reference to Mel Gibson's work in due time.

I start here with my youthful misunderstanding of what the phrase first fruits actually means. It really means the offering of the first products of the harvest to whatever god or gods are thought capable of being upset at their help during the growing season being ignored. Hebrews, Greeks and Romans did it, and the Christian Churches carry it on with the tradition of the harvest festival. Modern Churches now only celebrate symbolically, with there generally being no insistence on a tithe (or tenth) of the crop going to the local priest, nor the items at the harvest festival service actually being the first items out of the field or off the trees. The idea persists in non-European traditions as well. I have seen a friend from the Indian subcontinent, after taking the cork out of a bottle of wine at a picnic, pour the first drop of the contents on the ground rather than into a glass with the words 'To the gods.' In addition, since 1966 the African-American Holiday of Kwanzaa has brought the first fruits celebrations of ancient African harvest festivals into the modern age.

My misunderstanding was that although I saw the connection with the actual meaning, I believed it was a prosaic way of saying that in feudal societies the local lord had the right to sleep with a bride on her wedding night in place of her new husband. It seemed to my mind, however cynically we may now look at the degenerate meat-eating wine-drinking lord in comparison to the hard-working mainly vegetarian small-beer-swilling ploughman, there was a belief that his rank brought fecundity.

This right was called in Latin *jus primae noctis* (law of the first night), or in French *droit de seigneur* (the lord's right). I referred to *Braveheart* earlier because in one scene a wedding is gate-crashed by the local lord and his thugs, and he declares from horseback he's insisting on his right of '*prima nocta*' – or that's what it sounded like to me. However, there is no sound evidence that such a right, if it existed in the first place, was prevalent in feudal Europe, and even less that it was enforced if it did. There are some suspect references to it, such as in a decree supposedly of the Seneschal of Guyenne in the fourteenth century, and Hector Boece's fifteenth-century claim that Evenus III of Scotland set it in law. The problem here is that Evenus III didn't actually exist.[1]

There is evidence from other parts of the world of the existence of customs allowing leaders to claim defloration rights, going back as far as the Mesopotamian *Epic of Gilgamesh* from 4,000 years ago. Kurdish chieftains are said to have held on to the right in the same area until the last century. Latin American and African history also provide some evidence of the practice.

It could be the case that as *droit de seigneur* and *jus primae noctis* have become almost synonymous, the problem of modern interpretation lies here. *Droit de seigneur* did exist in feudal European society, but it originally referred to a raft of rights a lord held over his vassals relating to hunting,

---

1   In the seventeenth century Claude Jordan named the real King of Scots Malcolm I as the culprit, but he was actually pre-feudal.

taxation, farming and other activities. It seems our smutty modern minds, with the help through the centuries of such literary luminaries as Aphra Benn, Voltaire, Beaumarchais and Orwell, have lumped sexual rapacity in with material gain.[2]

SPANISH FLY

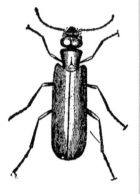

Talking of rapacity, the subject of aphrodisiacs comes to mind. We now live in the age of Viagra (more properly known by its non-proprietary name of sildenafil citrate), in which medical solutions are available to bypass dysfunction where sexual desire already exists. But what of those things that down the centuries have been supposedly able to get the ship's sails or engine working in the first place rather than improving seaworthiness?

The list is quite comical and at the same time borders on the tragic. Oysters and truffles of course are long-term favourites. Sadly for the awe-inspiring animals themselves, rhino horn and tiger whiskers are apparently much desired by uninspired elderly Oriental gentlemen. According to my research, boiled eggs, peppers and curry apparently have an effect that is actually quite different from the empirical evidence I have gathered over the years.

Within a much larger list than that which I have outlined above, Spanish fly seems to hold a special place in the minds of those who seek a solution to their lack of sexual ardour. Its name is whispered and its journey from source to boudoir is undertaken under many counters and via plain brown-paper bags. And why? Because people do not understand what it is or what it does. Whoever marketed the stuff in the first place should have received an award of some sort for creativity. Firstly it is not made from flies, but the wing sheaths of beetles – but I suppose Spanish beetle doesn't sound

2   The concept of *droit de seigneur* has been used to comic effect in a number of works. Twain refers to it in *A Connecticut Yankee in King Arthur's Court* (also entitled in some early volumes *A Yankee at the Court of King Arthur*), but for a truly marvellous plot device we should turn to Terry Pratchett, in whose *Wyrd Sisters* the right is mistakenly thought to refer to a big hairy dog that needs regular exercising. I leave the rest to your imagination.

as appetising. Secondly, even in very small doses, it causes vomiting (with blood in it), diarrhoea (likewise with blood), excruciating pain (especially in the genito-urinary system) and depression. It can also induce menstruation in women. If it is applied to the skin, it causes blistering. It *can* produce an erection, but so can a major blow to the nervous system around the base of the spine.

I think I'll stick to a candlelit supper, soft music and romantic repartee; the supper having oysters and truffles on the menu, of course.

THE NAZIS INVENTED THE SWASTIKA

This modern idea stems from the sheer scope of the hijack that the Nationalsozialistische Deutsche Arbeiterpartei (National Socialist German Workers' Party) perpetrated on this ancient symbol.[1] The majority of people in Western societies wouldn't even have been aware of it in pre-Nazi times; nor would we now if it wasn't associated with the horrors of the Third Reich. For example, many editions of the books of Rudyard Kipling from the late-nineteenth and early-twentieth centuries feature what looks like a swastika as a decorative element on their covers. Kipling (1865–1936), a British patriot, cannot in any way be associated with the Nazis. Even taking into account Kipling's jingoistic support for the British empire, the Nobel Prize winner's choice (or rather his publisher's choice) of what looks like a swastika cannot be used as evidence of any sympathy for fascism, which of course largely postdated his life anyway. The symbol was probably drawn from ancient Greek artefacts, although it could possibly have reached his consciousness via British colonial India. Indeed, it could have come from a whole host of places, as what we call the swastika has many different names and meanings in many different

1   Members of the Nazi Party usually identified themselves as National Socialists, and rarely used the term Nazi, a parallel to *Sozi*, which denoted a member of the Social Democratic Party of Germany. When Hitler won power in 1933, the currency of Nazi declined in Germany, although Austrian opponents still used it as an insult. Churchill later also used the term as an insult, but with his own idiosyncratic pronunciation NARZEE rather than the Germanic NATZEE.

The swastika is also often seen as a symbol of the sun-wheel, originating in the worship of the sun starting in the Bronze Age.

cultures. Our simplistic use of one term, and our association of the design purely with one political party[2] does not do justice to the history of this ancient symbol.

There is some evidence of the symbol being used as long ago as the Neolithic period. It seemed to occur almost spontaneously in basket-weaving societies that developed decorative elements, and is also often seen as a symbol of the sun-wheel, originating in the worship of the sun starting in the Bronze Age. This is just a sample: I could list a whole series of theories on the symbol's almost ubiquitous appearance across the globe. To borrow a phrase from literature, it seems that, whatever the source and geographical location, it just 'growed like Topsy'.

In ancient Greece the symbol was a *tetragammadion*, four (*tetra*) gammas (the third letter of the Greek alphabet) joined at the base. It could also be seen as a simplified *tetraskelion*, four legs joined together.[3] Perhaps because it had religious significance, the symbol is common in ancient Greek architecture. The shortened form of *tetragammadion*, gammadion, was more common than swastika in English dictionaries until the last quarter of the nineteenth century, when greater contact with Eastern religions led to a change. The Japanese call the symbol *manji* or *kanji* and the Chinese refer to it as *wan*. It represents positive things such as peace, strength or intelligence, and can be used facing in either a clockwise or anticlockwise direction.[4]

In the New World it was common among Native American peoples. An irony relevant here is the story of the United States 45th Infantry Division. This unit was formed around the nucleus of the Oklahoma State Militia in the 1920s. Oklahoma was called the Indian Territory until being granted statehood in 1907. To acknowledge the large number of Native Americans

2 Although I describe the Nazis as a political party for the sake of simplicity, they were rather a quasi-religious cult with political ambitions.

3 The three-legged heraldic symbol of the Isle of Man is called a triskelion.

4 I have also heard it said that the ancient swastika was always left-facing (anticlockwise) and always a symbol of goodness. Holders of this view go on to outline how Hitler made the conscious decision to reverse this, making it a symbol for evil. There is absolutely no basis for this. In fact, the material used to make the ensigns flown on German ships in the Second World War was thin enough to be see-through, so although on one side the swastika was the usual Nazi right-facing (clockwise) version, viewed from the other side the swastika was left-facing.

in the division, it was decided that its symbol would be drawn from their culture, and the swastika was chosen. But within twenty years the Nazis in Europe had made it their own, so, just prior to war breaking out across the Atlantic in 1939, the unit became the Thunderbird Division.

Returning to the symbol's frequent appearance in Indo-European culture, ethnic groups as diverse as Aryans, Persians and Hittites in the Middle East and Indian subcontinent, Caucasians, Scythians and Sarmatians in the mountains and Steppes of Russia, and Balts, Celts, Slavs, Sami and Finns in Europe have used it since the Iron Age. The design was formalised in medieval heraldry as a hooked version of the Christian cross, and known as the cross cramponned – in German the *Hakenkreuz* (crooked or hooked cross).

This brings us to the question of why Hitler chose the symbol to represent his political party. An older name in Germanic languages for the swastika is the *fylfot*, a term thought to have developed from another meaning four- or many-footed. One theory is that as a boy Hitler would have seen the *fylfot* in heraldic or architectural contexts. However, modern heraldic texts almost always show the *fylfot* sitting flat on one of its outer arms, which are truncated. Hitler's version has it at forty-five degrees,

The swastika is still
widely used today in
the Dharmic religions of
Hinduism, Buddhism
and Jainism.

with the inner and outer arms of equal length. But as it was already a well-established symbol in both Germanic and Christian culture, and as he revered both these things, surely Hitler just tweaked the design a bit? The answer is absolutely not. In *Mein Kampf* and other writings and speeches Hitler stated that he saw the swastika as the symbol of the Aryan victory in India. As this historical event had already been 'nordicised' to suit his ideas of Teutonic superiority, he saw the swastika as a natural design to adopt. Only, as usual, he wasn't being original. Hitler didn't come up with the idea of the racially pure Aryan race, nor did he come up with the idea that the swastika should be its symbol. This connection can be found in the writings of the nineteenth-century orientalist Emile Burnouf, and German nationalists had already used the swastika extensively before Hitler commandeered it. So rather than inventing it, he borrowed it, and then not even first-hand.

I mentioned above that the swastika is often held to have represented the sun-wheel, and there is a theory that the word derived from the Sanskrit for this motif, but Alexander Cunningham, the father of archaeology in India, rejected this. He believed that as *su* was a word for good and *asti* meant to be, so *svasti* meant well-being. The suffix *-ka* accentuated the meaning, so *svastika* translates into English as 'associated with well-being' – a symbol acting as a good-luck charm. It is a common given name in Bangladesh. During the nineteenth century Western academics mainly agreed on the term *sauwastika* (or *sauvastika* or even the misspelling *suavastika*) for the left-facing (anticlockwise) symbol. This orientation had origins in the pre-Buddhist animistic religions of Asia, where left-facing symbols seem to have been favoured. The *yungdrung*, as it is known in the Bön religion, and *gurung yantra*, as it is known in Gurung Dharma, were taken as evidence of differences in the meaning and auspiciousness of the symbol. However, this seems to have been a manufactured controversy by academics with a point to prove.

So what of the modern use of the symbol? Unaffected by the associations that plague it in the West, the swastika is still widely used today in the Dharmic religions of Hinduism, Buddhism and Jainism. In 2001 a coin featuring the symbol was issued by India to commemorate a major Jain anniversary. More amusingly, I hope Westerners using tourist maps in Japan, South Korea or Taiwan aren't shocked by the number of swastikas that appear on them. They denote the location of a temple.

In Europe it remains banned in Germany as well as a number of other countries. One interesting exception is Finland. A traditional swastika-like symbol in Finnish folklore is the *Tursaansydän*. This was later simplified into the simple symbol as used by the Nazis. Finnish air force planes bore swastika roundels until the end of the Second World War. There is a certain irony in this as their one-time German allies used swastikas on the tailplanes of their aircraft but retained the Germanic cross on the wings – thus the Finns flew with the swastika as their main identification mark whereas the Third Reich didn't. Although the Finns later changed their roundels, the flag of their air force still bears a swastika at its centre, and Boy Scouts there still sometimes use the traditional *Tursaansydän*.

CONCENTRATION CAMPS

One thing strongly associated with Hitler that we cannot blame him for is the invention of the concentration camp. The term first came into English to describe the camps set up by the British in South Africa at the start of the last century to confine Afrikaner non-combatants during the Second Boer War. The aim was to deprive the Boer commandos of food and shelter, but to the abiding shame of the UK at least 30,000 locals, mainly children, died of sickness and hunger through massive administrative incompetence and lack of basic care.

It is important to distinguish between concentration camps – which we would now call internment camps – and extermination camps. We can blame Hitler for the latter.

GREW LIKE TOPSY

UNCLE TOM AND TOPSY.

In the piece above on the swastika I used a phrase taken from Harriet Beecher Stowe's anti-slavery novel *Uncle Tom's Cabin*.[1] One of the characters is a young black girl called Topsy. At one point in the book she is asked if she knows who made her. She replies, demonstrating her ignorance of God and human reproduction, 'I s'pect I growed. Don't think nobody never made me.' 'Grew like Topsy' entered the English language first as a phrase to describe unplanned growth, later increasingly coming to mean exceptional or exponential growth.

If we actually look at what she says – all credit to a work colleague who pointed out this misinterpretation to me – we reach another conclusion. What Topsy is actually saying is that as she has no idea how she originated, she thinks she must have just spontaneously come into existence. Although at a stretch her words could be taken to apply to an unplanned pregnancy, they have nothing to do with speed or scale.

THE LAW OF AVERAGES

I pay tribute to the comedian Mark Steel for explaining the wrong-headedness of the usual use of this phrase, which he did on one of his radio shows.

Averages occur in statistics, but there are no laws governing them, never mind an overarching Newtonian-like universal principle. When a person refers to the law of averages he or she is trying to infer some conclusion from a bad use of statistics. The phrase is mostly used to justify wishful thinking. The scientific principle that variables that occur in a

---

1 Subtitled *Life Among the Lowly.*

random pattern will probably show a balancing out in their frequency of occurrence over a very (very!) large sample does exist, but there is no rule to say this will always occur in a fixed pattern. Referring to the law of averages typically assumes a balance should occur in the short term. As Mr Steel put it, if the law of averages existed, the balls used in National Lottery draws would not only have to be anthropomorphically ascribed memories, but would also possess a sense of fair play and good manners, allowing other balls to go first down the chute if it was their turn.

CROSS-COUNTY ARRESTS

——— &⁊⁊& ———

Near the beginning of this book I mentioned I would look into the matter of police forces making arrests outside their areas. There is a general belief that, for example, if I step across the border from Warwickshire into Gloucestershire after committing a crime in Stratford-upon-Avon, the police based in the former cannot collar me. I think we have again, as with most things in the legal sector, been over-influenced by the American film industry. We've all seen chases in American films. If the criminal (or usually the unjustly accused) just gets to the county or state line he will be safe.

In the UK, although many people think this is so, we do not have police forces based specifically on traditional counties. This might have been the general practice in the Middle Ages, when constables were part of the the shire reeve's (sheriff's) armoury, but does not apply these days. What if instead of Gloucestershire I headed for the Thames Valley? There is no county of this name, but there is a police force, which covers the traditional counties of Oxfordshire, Buckinghamshire and Berkshire. However, this neat three-county amalgamation should not lead you to assume that county forces have simply joined together to create bigger ones based on the same county structure. Policing has always been a fractious issue and remains very complicated.

Take for example the case of the town of Dewsbury in the West Riding of Yorkshire. Following the growth of the town due to industrialisation, in 1862 it was incorporated as a municipal borough, and the town fathers created their own police force for the borough. Other county boroughs in the West Riding did the same on incorporation, so a patchwork of forces grew up in the region. Most, including Dewsbury's, were amalgamated – along with the West Riding Constabulary, which had looked after everything not in a county borough – into the new West Yorkshire Constabulary in 1968. I say most because for a short time Leeds, Bradford and some other conurbations retained their own police. This changed on the creation of the new, supposedly more manageable counties of North, South and West Yorkshire (along with the abominations that were Humberside and Cleveland) in 1974, when the West Yorkshire Constabulary disappeared and there was effectively a general return to the one-county-one-force principle. Dewsbury was now looked after by the West Yorkshire Police, which comprised the bulk of the previous West Yorkshire Constabulary and the Leeds and Bradford forces. Most of the rest of the West Yorkshire Constabulary joined Sheffield and Rotherham in the new South Yorkshire Police, while various geographically peripheral bits were snaffled along with parts of the West Riding itself by the North Yorkshire, Humberside, Cumbria and, God forbid, Lancashire, forces.

On the whole, what we currently have in the UK are territorial forces looking after set geographical areas. This organisation has more to do with accountability and governance than what individual coppers are allowed to do at the sharp end. A territorial force has at its head a chief constable[1] appointed by a police authority. His or her officers have no restrictions on their powers of arrest outside their territory within the UK. Why should theirs be limited when every citizen has 'every-person powers', commonly called citizen's arrest? However, separate legal systems grew up before the kingdoms of Scotland and Ireland (now just the six counties of Northern Ireland) were lumped in with England and Wales, so there are exceptions.

It is the national borders of the separate components of the United Kingdom that place limitations on powers of arrest, not regional or county lines. The vast majority of officers attested in England and Wales have full powers of arrest in England and Wales (and their territorial waters), with the same principle applying to those attested in Scotland and those attested in Northern Ireland. Officers of a territorial force in one of these countries do have certain powers of arrest in the others, but this has

---

1 Every policeman is actually a constable in law irrespective of rank. Prison officers also have the powers of a constable.

required specifically worded clauses and articles in legislation to ensure that they can do their job everywhere within the borders of the United Kingdom. For example, when forces provide mutual support to each other (one force lends officers to another), the lent officers automatically assume the powers of members of the host force. Specific pieces of legislation, such as the 2000 Terrorism Act, give police officers the power to search or arrest regardless of where they are.

Some police constables are not members of a territorial force at all. The most well known are probably the officers of the British Transport Police (which does not operate in Northern Ireland), the Ministry of Defence Police and the Civil Nuclear Constabulary (formerly known as the United Kingdom Atomic Energy Authority Constablary). Their powers are usually exercised on land owned or used in matters relating to their work, but again legislation means that they can provide mutual aid to other forces. The other significant difference is they are true UK-wide forces. SOCA (the Serious Organised Crime Agency) is also UK-wide. Despite what is suggested in its name, the Scottish Drug Enforcement Agency isn't considered a geographically based force either.

The final pieces in the UK policing jigsaw to add to the non-geographical forces and England's thirty-nine (including the City of London and the Metropolitan Police), Wales's four, Scotland's eight, and Northern Ireland's single territorial force are those that exist to police specific places such as ports, parks, docks, harbours and roads.[2,3] The UK Police Service website tells us that the Port of Dover has its own force, as does the Port of Liverpool. The former came into being following an act of 1847 that also created separate forces for the docks in Belfast,[4] Larne,

When forces provide mutual support to each other, the lent officers automatically assume the powers of members of the host force.

2   There are also a significant number of non-legally constituted units run under the auspices of chief constables in England and Wales, staffed by officers seconded from territorial forces and providing a nationwide intelligence base. The National Wildlife Crime Unit is such a body. The West Midlands, West Mercia and Staffordshire have a joint motorway force, the Central Motorway Policing Group. Merseyside, Lancashire and Cheshire cooperate in the same way in north-west England.

3   Although Scotland is classed separately, the UK Police Service website puts the Police Service of Northern Ireland in its North-West Region, along with Cumbria, Lancashire, Merseyside, Greater Manchester and Cheshire.

4   This includes George Best Belfast City Airport. Belfast International Airport has its own constabulary.

Bristol,[5] Felixstowe, Portland and Falmouth. Dover and Falmouth have since also had legislation specific to themselves. Liverpool's constables come under an act specific to their location, as do the Port of Tilbury Police[6] and Tees and Hartlepool Port Authority Harbour Police.[7]

Some parks and forests have their own forces. The policing of the royal parks of England and Wales was taken over by the Met in 2004, but some of the staff of Historic Scotland have powers in Holyrood Park, Edinburgh. The Royal Botanic Gardens maintain their own constabulary at Kew, as does the City of London in Epping Forest, where an act of 1878 created the wonderfully named Epping Forest Keepers. A number of London boroughs have constables that enforce by-laws in their parks and open spaces. Hampstead Heath, for example, has a full-time constabulary, but defers to the Metropolitan Police for major crimes and incidents.

There are a few constabularies that do not fall into any of the categories above. Be careful not to commit a crime within four miles of Cambridge University, as its constabulary can arrest you. York Minster is thought to be the only church apart from St Peter's in Rome – which has the Swiss Guard – to have its own police force. The nine current constables are the successors to those created police officers in 1829, following the first of the two serious fires the building has suffered. They are not however attested and have to rely on every-person powers. The Mersey Tunnels have their own force of attested constables, as once did the markets of Birmingham. There is now again in Birmingham a force calling itself the Market Police, but they are not attested beyond applying the by-laws of the markets. I have discussed with some attested constables the right of non-attested constables to call themselves police. It is suggested by most who know or care about such details that by-law constables are not really

5   This also covers Avonmouth, Royal Portbury and the Bristol Channel islands of Flat Holme, Steep Holme and Denny Island.

6   This differs from other port police in that, as a successor force to the Port of London Authority Police, it has jurisdiction throughout England and Wales when chasing up a crime committed in the Port of Tilbury. It is also the oldest police force in England, being in existence since at least the Napoleonic Wars.

7   Port authority police forces generally have powers on the land owned by the port company and up to one mile from it. The Tees and Hartlepool constables have authority up to two miles from the port area.

police despite retaining the historical name. This in itself is thought to be unlawful (wearing a uniform with the word police on it could be seen as attempted deception, for example) but not criminal. This is a distinction I hope to investigate at some time in the future. While I remember, in contrast to Birmingham, Smithfield Market has continuously maintained its own constabulary employed by the Corporation of London.

The rule of thumb in the UK seems to be that police constables are fully attested in their country of origin and carry a warrant card. This includes special constables – reserves as they are known in Northern Ireland. Non-police constables fall into two groups, those attested to apply the by-laws of specific locations, and those who aren't attested at all but retain the title of constable for historical reasons. Both these latter groups – sometimes for historical reason but not lawfully, also call themselves police. Non-police constables don't carry a warrant card. I am sure however that somewhere there is an anomaly that someone reading this book will have spotted. Law in the UK is like that, isn't it?

Interestingly, three foreign police forces have some powers in the United Kingdom. The police of visiting military forces, such as those at American airbases, are one. Following the building of the Channel Tunnel, the French *Police aux Frontières* has jurisdiction at St Pancras station in London, Ashford station in Kent and on Eurostar trains; the British Transport Police has reciprocal rights at Paris's Gard du Nord. The *Police aux Frontières* also has a presence at Dover, and the Kent Police has officers at the French end of the Chunnel. Finally, the Irish Garda and the Radiological Protection Unit of Ireland have the right to inspect the Sellafield nuclear facility in Cumbria.

That's quite a list, I think you will agree, and I haven't discussed the four police forces of the army, Royal Navy, RAF and Royal Marines. Nor have I looked into the uniformed but non-warranted police community support officers introduced in 2002.[8] I have also ignored non-constabulary law enforcement bodies such the Health and Safety Executive, the fisheries agencies and the UK Border Agency. And what about the beadles of the Burlington Arcade? Perhaps another time.

Following the building of the Channel Tunnel, the French Police aux Frontières has jurisdiction at St Pancras station in London, Ashford station in Kent and on Eurostar trains.

8   Not in Northern Ireland due to budget shortfalls.

DOUBLE NEGATIVE

———❧❦———

Earlier, we referred to Topsy's verdict from *Uncle Tom's Cabin*: 'I s'pect I growed. Don't think nobody never made me.' This contains a double negative, and it is generally believed that if you use one, then you effectively reverse what you are trying to say. So 'nobody never made me' really means 'somebody did make me'. Well, I don't agree with that, no siree, not no how.

Prior to the Age of Enlightenment and its focus on the mechanical and mathematical, Geoffrey Chaucer wrote of the knight in *The Canterbury Tales*, 'He nevere yet no vileyne ne sayde In al his lyf unto no maner wight.' That is, to you and me, 'He never said nothing bad in all his life to nobody.' Chaucer knew what he meant, and it wasn't that the knight was always going round saying nasty things to people. Multiple negation was common in both Old and Middle English. It was only when wise heads decided the rules of algebra also applied to grammar that this practice started dying out. Such is logic.

PREROGATIVE, PEJORATIVE
AND SCHEDULE

———❧❦———

Three of the most commonly mispronounced words in the UK. I often hear, 'That's my perogative.' Well the word ultimately derives from the Latin *praerogativa* so the first syllable is pre, not per. As to the second word, its common mispronunciation is almost the reverse of the first. I learnt from a radio tribute to Kenneth Williams that he was mortified to be corrected on his pronunciation of pejorative at a dinner party. He had been saying it as if it were spelt perjorative (with an extra r).

As to schedule, this is becoming more than a transatlantic issue. I have no problem with the Americans pronouncing turbot as TURBO, Iraq as EYERACK, Caribbean as CARIBBYAN or schedule as SKEDULE. I do however find it annoying that so many people making announcements on public transport in Britain follow the Americans on schedule. Sadly, I recently even heard a BBC newsreader pronounce it thus. That truly is the thin end of the wedge.

HE'S NOT *THE* MESSIAH . . .

This is not a popular error arising from Terry Jones's line while playing the title character's mother in *Life of Brian*. It relates rather to the very popular and oft-performed oratorio by George Frideric Handel commonly called *The Messiah*. It is just *Messiah*.

POURING OIL ON TROUBLED WATERS

This phrase is now used metaphorically to denote doing or saying something to lessen a difficult or troublesome situation between people or within the mind of an individual. However, what of its origins? Do we, in these environmentally aware times, actually believe that doing this, as suggested by the Bible, will have a calming effect on a stormy sea? Wrong, I'm afraid, on a few accounts.

Firstly it is not a biblical phrase; it is rather from the classics, with Pliny the Elder and Plutarch both noting the soothing results of pouring oil onto rough (troubled) water: they seem to suggest the oil forms an emulsifying layer. To see if this ancient idea (probably discovered by the Greeks and borrowed by the Romans as with so many other things) worked, Benjamin Franklin conducted an experiment on a pond in Clapham. He found that if he poured on the oil from the leeward side it was just blown back to shore, but when he tried from the windward side, the area around where he applied the oil was actually pacified. That said, the negative outcomes for the wildlife must surely have exceeded the benefit of having a calm area on the surface of the pond. What's more Franklin highlighted a key factor.

Troubled waters are the result of friction as the wind acts on the surface of a wide expanse of water. The faster the wind in relation to the speed of the waves, the more intense they will become. No matter how much oil you use, if a high wind keeps blowing the sea remains rough. It is only when the oil reduces the friction enough to negate this effect that calming occurs. High winds are likely to break up the surface of an oil slick, so the calming effect of pouring oil on troubled waters is limited to low wind speeds. So I don't give much credence to what the Romans said.

Interestingly and moving on to a religious context, in the Venerable Bede's reference in his *Historia Ecclesiastica Gentis Anglorum* to Bishop Aidan giving seafarers oil for casting onto the sea, the oil in question was not a vast amount of the hydrocarbon-based stuff. This stuff was holy, and its target was the wind rather than the water.

By the way, the usual phrase these days refers to waters in the plural, rather than water. There is a popular error that the title song of Simon and Garfunkel's marvellous 1970 album is called 'Bridge over Troubled Waters'. A quick look at the sleeve will tell you that they draw on the older version of the phrase: it is 'Bridge over Troubled Water'.

LOUGH NEAGH

L ough Neagh is the largest lake in the British Isles. Over 40 per cent of land in the six counties of Northern Ireland drains into it. It is not as is often believed a basin in its own right, like the Caspian Sea; it is more like the Great Lakes of North America, having an outlet to the sea via the River Bann. There is a Coney Island in Lough Neagh, the only one currently inhabited out of eight in the lake.

THE LARGEST FRESHWATER LAKE IN THE WORLD

Many people believe this to be the Caspian and think it's a bit of a misnomer to call it a sea.[1] It covers the biggest area and has the biggest volume, so case proven. Not so, I say. The water in the Caspian Sea is brackish.[2] So with a surface area of nearly 32,000 square miles Lake Superior is the largest named body of freshwater on the planet. Only there are a couple of problems with this idea as well.

Superior's neighbours Huron and Michigan are actually two branches of a single lake.[3] It's just that the people who named it got it wrong. This lake covers over 45,000 square miles, so is nearly 50 per cent bigger than the perhaps-misnamed Superior. The second problem with Superior taking the crown is that surface area doesn't take into account how much water there is in the thing. We should really look at volume in determining the largest. We have already disregarded the Caspian Sea because it is brackish. The actual winner of the accolade is Lake Baikal in Russia, which has a volume of over 23,000 cubic miles. Second place goes to Lake Tanganyika in Africa. Lake Superior can take some solace, if lakes are capable of such a thing, in the fact it beats Michigan-Huron in the volume stakes, being third to its rival's fourth. Still waters must run a bit more deeply there.

Lake Superior's neighbours Huron and Michigan are actually two branches of a single lake.

1   It is a misnomer, but not because it is a lake. The Caspian Sea is large enough to be classified geologically and hydrologically as an ocean.

2   Brackish is used to describe bodies of water that are neither freshwater or seawater. Brackish water has higher salinity than freshwater, but is less salty than seawater. Estuaries, where freshwater rivers meet the sea, are more or less brackish, as are mangroves. The Baltic and Black Seas are also classed as brackish.

3   Lakes are separated from each other by rivers and streams. The two arms of Lake Michigan-Huron are joined by the 120-foot-deep Mackinac Strait, which is five miles wide in places. Some lakes aren't even as long as this channel is wide. As it is also at the same elevation as the two branches it joins, it is part of the same lake.

INDIA INK

The French have the drop on English-speakers here. They call India ink *encre de chine*. Quite right, seeing as it is actually from China.

COURT HOUSE, ON GRANT'S HILL, PITTSBURG, PENN.

PITTSBURG

Pittsburg in California, Kansas, Kentucky, New Hampshire, Oklahoma and Texas, yes – but not in Pennsylvania. There it is Pittsburgh with an h on the end. The most probable reason for this non-Germanic spelling is that the man who named the settlement after British prime minister William Pitt the Elder was General John Forbes. He was a Scot and was perhaps emulating the spelling of his nation's capital, Edinburgh.[1] If this

---

1 Despite an attempt to 'scoticise' the etymology, it seems pretty clear that Edinburgh's name derives from the seventh-century Anglo-Saxon king Edwin, and meant Edwin's borough or Edwin's fort. While not denying that the eminently defendable rock that Edinburgh Castle now sits on was previously occupied by Celts, it seems a tad ironic that Scotland's capital is named after an 'Anglishman', a Bernician king who ruled everything north of the Humber to the east of the Pennines including Scotland up to the Firth of Forth.

is correct, then perhaps the original pronunciation was something akin to PITTSBORO. Then again, I've been asked directions to SCARBORO on the North Sea coast of England by visiting Americans. As Chris Moyles once said on radio, 'It's SCARBRAH!'

THE RAT PACK

———— 8⌗⅗ ————

In my introduction to this book I promised to come back to the subject of Frank Sinatra, and I believe my words were 'to explain a different generally held misconception.' Well, here it is.

One term from entertainment history sums up a particular period of Hollywood excess, boyish tomfoolery and purely masculine bravado. It is the name of one particularly glamorous gang of alpha-male 'players' – the 'Rat Pack'. If you are not an admirer of the output of mid-sixties Las Vegas style glitz and kitsch then perhaps happily for you, or if you are then unhappily, history has got it wrong in a number of ways.

Frank Sinatra was never the initiating force or the leader of a purely masculine five-strong group of celebrity revellers called the Rat Pack. As far as he and his *Ocean's Eleven* co-stars were concerned, he was the 'Chairman of the Board' of a group of calling itself 'The Clan' or 'The Summit'.[1] It was merely that a celebrity-hungry populous, led on by the press's knack of attaching snappy labels to groups in the public eye, bought into this name for the three singer/actors Sinatra, Dean Martin, and Sammy Davis Jr., the Kennedy clan adjunct Peter Lawford and the comedian Joey Bishop. It was a misnomer borrowed from a few years before, and we have to look into the previous decade to find the true Rat Pack.

It can't be denied that back in the fifties a younger Frank Sinatra had been a member of the original gang, even holding the title of Pack Master. However, it was the man who rather modestly called himself 'Rat in charge of Public Relations' who kicked the whole thing off. His name was Humphrey DeForest Bogart. He was a man who liked a drink and a party. In Sinatra's conduct of his inherited leadership of the sixties grouping

1 Sammy Davis Jr. is reported as saying the name the Summit came from Sinatra wanting to parody a major international political summit of world leaders in Paris, by calling as many stars and other VIPs to his own 'Summit' in Las Vegas.

we can see strong indications of a wish to continue Bogart's prestigious legacy and reputation for possessing a devil may care attitude to life. I feel the philosophy of the originator of the Rat Pack is best expressed in the reported last line of Bogart's life, delivered on his deathbed in 1957 to his wife Lauren Bacall, 'I should never have switched from Whiskey to Martinis.'

It is Bacall who is credited in one version at least of coming up with the iconic name and kicking off the idea of putting an organisation around the party atmosphere. It came in an early morning comment spat out at her husband and his already well established (and at that moment well-lubricated) gang of cronies returning from a busy night's carousing in Las Vegas. It was something along the line of 'You look like a goddamn rat pack.'

The name stuck, the idea developed and Bacall became the pack's Den Mother. Other titles handed out, as well as Sinatra's Pack Master, were Cage Master to Judy Garland's third husband Sid Luft, Recording Secretary and Treasurer to talent agent Irving 'Swifty' Lazar, and Historian to author Nathanial Benchley (father of *Jaws* author Peter). The titles of other members, composer Jimmy Van Heusen and film luminaries Spencer Tracy, George Cukor, Cary Grant, Rex Harrison and David Niven are unknown to me.

We now think of the Rat Pack as exclusively male, but in addition to Bacall there were other female members; Tracy's long term partner Katherine Hepburn was definitely 'in', and Judy Garland was made the group's first Vice President.

Also of note, although the idea was that a rat pack was a fierce and mutually defensive group, actors Errol Flynn, Mickey Rooney and Cesar Romero, as well as singer Nat King Cole were all accepted as visiting members.

Not only was the Rat Pack in existence prior to Sinatra's leadership, the tradition of female members actually carried on into the post-Bogart era. Hollywood glamour-pusses Marilyn Monroe, Angie Dickinson, Juliet Prowse and Shirley MacLaine all revelled in the title of 'Rat Pack Mascots' (so named as a sop to media coverage of the 'Summit'), and in being as much members of the gang as the boys.

The idea of guest or visiting members also continued with the temporary inclusion during the filming of *Ocean's Eleven* of the actor

Norman Fell. Retrospectively, it might perhaps seem a mite bizarre to British readers without an inside knowledge of Fell's capacity to enjoy himself, that he was temporarily adopted into the glamorous Summit. This is because it is amusing to note Fell was later to star as the landlord Mr Roper' in *Three's Company*, the American version of the seventies UK sitcom *Man About the House*. It seems to me that never could such a character, as played by Brian Murphy in the original, be so far from the whirl of money, sex and bright neon lights that we now associate with Las Vegas.